MAKING THE MONEY LAST:

FINANCIAL CLARITY FOR THE SURVIVING SPOUSE

By

Jarratt G. Bennett, CFP, ChFC, CLU

KENDALL/HUNT PUBLISHING COMPANY
4050 Westmark Drive   P.O. Box 1840   Dubuque, Iowa 52004-1840

Copyright © 1995 by Kendall/Hunt Publishing Company

ISBN 0-7872-0962-7

Printed in the United States of America
10 9 8 7 6 5 4 3 2 1

Disclaimer

The information in this book has been carefully written and edited, and the services referred to are believed to be reliable. However, the accuracy is not guaranteed. The purpose is to help widowed persons develop their own financial plans, using concise, easy-to-follow formats.

The author and publisher are not engaged in rendering legal or accounting advice, and will not be held liable for any actions based on this publication. As always, competent legal, accounting and financial planning assistance is recommended.

ACKNOWLEDGMENTS

I am fortunate to be in a business I love. Over the past twenty-nine years I have learned much from my clients and hope they have profited from my relationship with them. This book is dedicated to those I have had the privilege to serve.

It takes more than one person to make a book a reality. Without the individuals listed below this book would not exist.

Thanks to Gregory P. Seal, CFP; Lewis J. Walker, CFP; Douglas G. Hesse, CFP; Lee D. Pennington, CFP; and David G. Hoffman, Attorney at Law, for their support, insights, and technical reviews. To Jeffrey P. Davidson goes a special thanks for bringing order and professional writing skill throughout the development of the manuscript.

Especially, my thanks go to my Executive Assistant, Sarah B. Murphy, who labored, unrelentingly, during the whole process and turned the manuscript into a polished, professional format.

And finally, thanks to my wife, whose patience, encouragement, and support helped give me the strength to bring the book to publication.

FOREWORD

As a long-time financial advisor, Jerry Bennett has doggedly pursued academic and professional training and certifications. He is a Certified Financial Planner (CFP)*, a Chartered Life Underwriter (CLU), and Chartered Financial Counselor (ChFC). He obtains 30 or more credit hours of continuing education every year.

Education is important to the learning process. But the vicissitudes of daily living are what "seasons" an advisor and counselor. And the experience that hits close to home is usually among the most powerful, painful, and impressionable of life's lessons.

Jerry has been counseling widowed persons since 1966. However, it wasn't until six years ago, when a 46-year-old friend and neighbor died—suddenly—on his own kitchen floor—that Jerry truly realized the in-depth needs of loved ones left behind.

There had been no warning, no previous illness. For his seemingly healthy neighbor, who everyone later agreed was "too young to go like that," his heart attack that day was his first and last. He and Jerry had discussed financial matters but they had never looked closely at what would be needed in the aftermath of his death.

"His wife was suddenly widowed," Jerry recalled, "with two grown children and young twin boys who were still living at home. She faced raising those boys alone, providing their living expenses and their eventual college educations, as well as her own support. Fortunately, her husband had a life insurance policy, issued years before his death. Still, there were a number of problems to resolve."

"There were critical issues the widow had to face: immediate cash flow, continuing income over a long period of time, building a reserve for the twins' college education, and, eventually planning for her own retirement."

"In addition to all of this, she was concerned about investing her money." Experience has taught Jerry that when widowed people have a substantial amount of money with which to work, they always worry about making a mistake with it.

Making The Money Last is not just about money; it's also about having quick access to answers about money problems. It's a book for people who have been widowed, whether the loss was recent or not.

Many books provide general consumer financial information, while others have been written about the grieving and recovery process. Yet, there is no definitive source book that deals with the multitude of financial questions faced by widowed persons, either about initial money decisions or long-term financial planning.

The few books that have attempted to approach this subject suffer from two major flaws: 1) they require readers to review most or all of the book to answer specific financial questions, and 2) while their authors may be experienced personal counselors, they have little background in financial planning, strategies, and procedures.

Thankfully, *Making the Money Last* covers the full range of financial concerns that widowed people have to face—everything from immediate money needs through the survivor's retirement and estate plan. Jerry has avoided technical terms, references to confusing regulations, and psycho-babble, and has kept language reader-friendly. Moreover, the book has been organized so that you don't have to read everything to get specific information.

While part of an integrated whole, each section can stand alone. If you have a particular problem, you can find potential solutions by reading just the section dealing with that issue. What you need to know has been streamlined to the essence; you can get information easily and act on it immediately.

Once you get started, you will find yourself taking sound, giant steps forward. I encourage you to make notes, photocopy pages, use the helpful forms, and even call Jerry. After all, nothing less than your financial health is at stake.

I commend Jerry Bennett for the dedication and diligence required to produce this most useful work and I commend you, the reader, for seeking guidance from one of the top financial planners in America.

Lewis J. Walker, CFP
Past President
The Institute of Certified Financial Planners

* CFP and Certified Financial Planner are federally registered service marks of the Certified Financial Planners Board of Standards.

INTRODUCTION

This book is not about death or dying, grief or bereavement. It is about money—your money—and your stewardship of the assets left by your deceased spouse.

We start from the premise that the funeral is over, that you've begun to realize the large number of tasks facing you, and that you've started some tentative planning. You're now at the point of paying bills, keeping daily financial activities on track, worrying about estate settlement and wondering how to make your money last. It is possible to take charge of your financial life. While you may not feel much like doing it while you're in mourning, there are decisions that must be made.

Many bereavement counselors suggest that organizing and restructuring the family finances is therapeutic and aids in the grieving process. Melba Colgrove, Ph.D., and Peter McWilliams, authors of *How to Survive the Loss of a Love*, note that when an emotional injury takes place, the body begins a process as natural as the healing of a physical wound.

Let the process happen; trust that nature will do the healing and the pain will ease. When it does, you will be stronger, happier, more sensitive and aware. A similar process will work for you as you come to grips with your financial future.

The widowed person faces one of life's greatest challenges. He or she must somehow make sense out of the death of a mate, while handling a huge array of financial problems, making mind-boggling adjustments, and building a new life.

Some 80 to 90 percent of women—who can expect to live a minimum of six years longer than their mates—will have sole charge of their finances at some time in their lives. Too often, women are obliged to assume this responsibility upon the death of a spouse. The choices made during such a stressful period are likely to be crucial to the widow's financial future, and that of her family.

As such, I've structured *Making the Money Last* so that you can quickly find the answers you need without being overwhelmed with information. It is a step-by-step procedure, so you can read what you need to know and leave the rest for another time.

Jarratt G. Bennett
Fairfax, Virginia
January, 1995

Of all emotions that are tense and strong,

And utmost knowledge, I have lived for these;

Live deep, and let the lesser things live long,

The everlasting hills, the lakes, the trees,

Who'd give their thousand years to sing this song

Of life, and man's high sensibilities,

Which I, into the face of death, can sing.

O death! Thou poor and disappointed thing,

Strike where thou wilst. Strike breast or brow;

For I have lived! And thou canst rob me now

Only of some long life that ne'er has been.

The life that I lived, so rich and keen,

Is mine. I hold it firm beneath thy blow,

And, dying, take it with me where I go.

—Rupert Brooke

TABLE OF CONTENTS

Page

Part I: Immediate Concerns

Chapter 1: The Financial Aspects of Widowhood   3
Chapter 2: First Things First: Immediate Concerns   7
Chapter 3: Claiming Everything That's Yours—Private Sources   27
Chapter 4: Claiming Everything That's Yours from
Government Sources   45
Chapter 5: Getting Organized—Bringing Order to Your
Financial House   61
Chapter 6: Settling Your Spouse's Estate   75

Part II: A Look at the Big Picture

Chapter 7: Retirement Planning—Making the Money Last   95
Chapter 8: The Surviving Spouse's Guide to Taxes   115
Chapter 9: Insurance—Understanding the Great Mystery   129

Part III: Ensuing Concerns

Chapter 10: Money, Children and You   151
Chapter 11: You and Your Home   163
Chapter 12: Funding College Education   185
Chapter 13: Long Term Care   201

Part IV: Prosperous Transitions

Chapter 14: Giving—How, When, Who and How Much   215
Chapter 15: Passing Along Your Wealth—Estate Planning   227
Chapter 16: The Financial Aspects of Remarriage   243
Chapter 17: Choosing Professional Advisors   253
Chapter 18: Frauds and Scams: Protecting Yourself   267
Chapter 19: Putting it All Together—You and Your New
Financial World   273

Index   285
Telephone Number Resource Directory   293
Bibliography   295
Epilogue   297

PART I:

IMMEDIATE CONCERNS

CHAPTER 1

THE FINANCIAL ASPECTS OF WIDOWHOOD

It was bad. Nothing in Nancy's life had ever ached as much and, now, on top of the unrelenting anguish and bone-deep sadness, she needed to deal with financial problems. Where would she find the answers?

Jim was dead—gone and buried. God, how the loss hurt. Nancy watched the ceiling begin to take on the colors of sunrise. Another day to face; could she get through it? What would she do for income over the next few weeks? How would her son continue college? What about Jim's pension and 401(k)? Would she have enough money ever to retire? What about probate, estate settlement, finding an attorney, investments? The endless questions raced through her mind.

Every year hundreds of thousands of husbands and wives lose their spouses. It is the most stressful event of their lives. For most it is also a nerve-wracking financial ordeal. Only a very few are fortunate enough to have highly-competent advisors on whom they can rely to share in financial decision-making.

Most widowed persons are not so lucky. They have neither the training nor the temperament to handle the assets left in their care, and they fear making a financial mistake. Their fear is not without substance: most widows and widowers suffer a substantial loss in asset value in the first two years.

TYPICAL WIDOWS: YOU ARE NOT ALONE

Death does not respect age or social status. There are widowed people in every conceivable life situation, at every age and in every financial bracket.

Consider Bob and Sarah who were married in 1950. They met in college, married when both were in their mid-twenties and were together

3

almost 43 years. Bob worked for several companies during his lifetime. They bought their first house for $42,000 and, twelve years ago, purchased their dream house for $195,000. Their home is worth approximately $300,000 today.

Now Sarah, who has two children and five grandchildren, is alone at age 62. Bob had handled most of the money in the family and although it's been a couple of years since his passing, Sarah is still apprehensive about making financial decisions.

Elaine is a young widow with two small children. When Russell was killed in a car crash, Elaine's world was shattered. After four months, she is beginning to come to grips with the financial aspects of widowhood.

Mary Jo, 51, is a middle-years widow. One of her sons attends a top Ivy League school, and the other will start college soon—if Mary Jo can afford it.

Don, Mary Jo's picture-of-health husband, collapsed on the ski slopes of the Pocono Mountains and died two days later. Don was a highly-paid corporate executive, who loved people and giving parties, and he had many company benefits and large insurance policies.

Sarah, Elaine, and Mary Jo share some common concerns, yet each has to approach her problems from different stages of life. They each have to handle immediate concerns, get financially organized, file claims, make investment decisions and, finally, consider strategies to solve the dilemmas unique to their individual situations.

THE BIG TWENTY

In working with widowed persons from all walks of life, there are some twenty financial issues that routinely come up after the loss of a spouse. Here's a roster of *The Big Twenty* concerns that you will likely face:

1. Do I have enough money for immediate needs?

2. Will there be enough money to last, even if I need long-term health care at some point?

3. Will the rising cost of living adversely affect me?

4. Will I have enough for retirement years?

5. What about medical insurance coverage?

6. How should I invest life insurance proceeds?

7. What should I do with 401(k), IRA and company pension funds?

8. Should I sell our home in favor of a smaller, less expensive home?

9. Should I use the one-time $125,000 capital gains tax exclusion now?

10. Will I have to file quarterly estimates for income taxes?

11. Can I afford to help my children or grandchildren with college expenses?

12. Should my will be changed?

13. Should I have a living will?

14. Will I have enough income to live on without working?

15. (If there are young children) how will I finance day care if I return to work?

16. Have claims been filed for everything that's coming to me?

17. When can I expect the Social Security check to arrive?

18. Should I and how do I choose a financial advisor?

19. What should I do right now?

20. What should I do first?

Taking Charge

The decision to take responsibility for your financial life requires making intelligent, ongoing financial decisions by:

- collecting the information you will need;

- assembling and organizing this information; and

- using the information to make correct or corrective decisions.

You will no doubt feel a strong temptation to continue deferring all but the most immediate judgments. If you surrender to the desire to postpone taking control, things will coast along as the years drift past. Eventually, you'll reach a point of no return and the opportunity to make those vital, long-term decisions will be lost forever.

This book is organized to begin with what you must do first, and take you gradually into the future of your financial life. Let's begin the journey.

FIRST THINGS FIRST: IMMEDIATE CONCERNS

As a newly-widowed individual, you will immediately be faced with a profusion of financial details. Your need to pay attention to these urgent matters coincides with a time of great emotional upheaval, such that you may think, "Decisions, decisions, decisions. Why must I deal with them now?"

You might feel uninformed and ill-prepared to deal with these issues in the aftermath of your mate's death. Nevertheless, it's important to set your emotions aside and face up to your finances.

If you're lucky, you and your spouse discussed finances before his or her death. In that case, you will find this chapter easier to go through. If you did not have such a discussion with your spouse, press forward; this chapter will help you deal with what needs to be done now, and in the weeks ahead.

"DO'S" AND "DON'TS" DURING MOURNING

Put off making long-term money decisions until you're able to face them unemotionally. You may think that you're functioning adequately, but most newly-widowed individuals behave erratically, even though they may not realize it. That's normal after suffering a major loss.

There will also be a tendency to want to take some action. While taking action may be therapeutic, taking action in some areas can be a major mistake. Don't take any action that you can't reverse later one. Do you have someone you know and trust to help you organize your papers and help you with your initial decisions? To the extent it's possible, you'll want to take certain actions while avoiding others, during the early part of the mourning period. At this stage you need time to let reality seep in and allow the healing process to begin. When you start to feel the ground more firmly under your feet, you'll be in a better position to make other decisions that will serve you well over the long term.

1. **DO** keep your money in a safe place—for example, money market accounts, certificates of deposit for three or six-month terms and passbook savings accounts. Accounts in any one bank are insured only up to $100,000, so put your money in more than one institution if you go above the $100,000 limit.

2. **DO** protect yourself from financial problems resulting from illness or accident by making sure you're covered by medical and, if you are employed, disability insurance.

3. **DO** be careful of impulse spending, especially on large-ticket items. You may later regret money spent recklessly now.

4. **DO** recognize that you are in mourning and that, right now, you are especially vulnerable to pressures. Hold back; be cautious with your funds.

AND:

1. **DON'T** make any major money decisions now that can be deferred to a later time.

2. **DON'T** remodel your house or buy a new car.

3. **DON'T** buy life insurance.

4. **DON'T** invest with well-meaning friends or relatives.

5. **DON'T** put your funds where you can't get at them quickly and at little or no cost.

6. **DON'T** borrow money, or lend it.

7. **DON'T** make major money decisions "for the good of the kids," unless that decision is good for you also. Give it a little time.

8. **DON'T** give away money, even to friends or relatives, until you've had time to determine how far your money will take you.

Over the next several months, and in the years to come, it may be appropriate to do some or all of the items listed above. However, "right now" is too soon after your loss. You need time to learn more about your financial status and to define the financial course you wish to steer.

WHAT TO DO RIGHT AWAY

When the funeral is over and all the relatives have gone back to their own lives, you may find yourself alone. This is a good time to face the financial details that require prompt attention.

The items in the "Dos and Don'ts" section above may seem to contradict some of those listed below, but the circumstances of your life might require that you do some things during the mourning period that cannot be avoided. The two lists are intended to make you aware of what's important, so that you can act in accordance with the time pressures of your own situation.

Some of the terms in the following checklist will be familiar and some will be new to you. The inclusion of strange-sounding terms is not intended to create anxiety, but to ensure thoroughness. In fact, some of the words will help you deal with various agencies so that you can determine exactly what your assets are. Don't be concerned if you don't understand every one of them right now; their meaning will become clear as we proceed.

Set up an area to work specifically on your financial affairs. You may want to have a desk and file cabinet with file folders for each important topic in your financial life. See the Chapter on Getting Organized on page 61 for suggested file topics. If you already have many of the files in various locations throughout your home, it will be helpful if you can put them all in one central location. Eventually some files will no longer be needed while others will become permanent files and serve you for the rest of your lifetime.

Keep notes and make lists; doing so will help you to handle the shock and grief that are part of the grieving process. When people give you information they will think you understand, and they will expect you to remember what was said. However, you will be unlikely to remember the details of the vast amount of information you will receive. The forms at the end of this chapter are meant to help you with this task.

"Right-away" Activities

Setting-up:

1. *Child Care*. If you have small children, arrange child care so you can concentrate on the logistics of what you need to do.

2. *Accurate Records*. Record all the money you spend on funeral and other costs associated with your spouse's death. These figures may be needed for income tax returns and may entitle your spouse's estate to income tax deductions.

3. *Phone Log*. Maintain a written log of everyone you talk to on the phone concerning business, legal and financial matters. Include in the log a summary of important facts, and answers to any questions you may ask. Various forms are provided at the end of this chapter.

4. *Incoming Mail*. Set up a system to collect and sort incoming mail into important categories—i.e., bills, life insurance matters and health insurance forms.

5. *Outgoing Mail*. Keep photocopies of everything you mail or deliver to someone else, and develop an appropriate filing system.

6. *Checking and Savings Accounts*. Examine all accounts and make a list of the totals in each. Doing so will help you determine whether you have enough available cash for the short-term. Then complete the Cash Resources form on page 11 to determine what else is forthcoming.

7. *Immediate Cash Requirements*. Now, to get a clear short term picture of whether the money will last, complete the Immediate Cash Requirements Form on page 12.

Immediate Cash Resources

0–30 Days

Name/Source   Amount Available

Checking Accounts:
1. _____ $ _____
2. _____ _____
3. _____ _____
       Total $ _____

Money Market Funds:
1. _____ $ _____
2. _____ _____
3. _____ _____
       Total $ _____

Savings Accounts:
1. _____ $ _____
2. _____ _____
3. _____ _____
       Total $ _____

Certificates of Deposit:
1. _____ $ _____
2. _____ _____
3. _____ _____
4. _____ _____
5. _____ _____
       Total $ _____

Investment Income:
1. Dividends_____ $ _____
2. Interest _____ _____
       Total $ _____

From Your Spouse's Employer:
1. Wages Due $ _____
2. Vacation Pay _____
3. Sick Leave Pay _____
4. Misc. Accrued Pay _____
5. Disability Pymnts. _____
       Total $ _____

From Your Employer:
1. Wages $ _____
2. Bonuses _____
       Total $ _____

Total Immediate Cash
(0–30 Days) _____ $ _____

Expected Within 30–90 Days

Name/Source   Amount

Life Insurance Proceeds:
1. _____ $ _____
2. _____ _____
3. _____ _____
4. _____ _____
       Total $ _____

Retirement Survivor Benefits:
1. 401(k) or Thrift
    Savings Plan $ _____
2. Pension/Profit
    Sharing Plan _____
3. IRA Account(s) _____
4. Social Security/Govt.
    Benefits _____
5. Previous Employer
    Pension Plan _____
       Total $ _____

Cash Values of *Your* Life Insurance
Policy(ies) Available as Loan or Withdrawal:
1. _____ $ _____
2. _____ _____
       Total $ _____

Spouse's Medical Payment
Reimbursements:
1. Medicare $ _____
2. Private Med. Ins. _____
       Total $ _____

Miscellaneous:
1. _____ $ _____
2. _____ _____
3. _____ _____
       Total $ _____

Total Cash (30–90 Days) $ _____

Total Cash (0–30 Days) $ _____
Total Cash (30–90 Days)   _____

Grand Total Cash
(0–90 Days) $ _____

CHAPTER 2

Immediate Cash Requirements

Item	Due Date	Amount Due
Household Operation (1 month estimate)	_____	$ _____
Funeral Expenses:		
1. _____	_____	$ _____
2. _____	_____	_____
3. _____	_____	_____
4. _____	_____	_____
5. _____	_____	_____
6. _____	_____	_____
Totals		$ _____
Outstanding Bills Now Due:		
1. _____	_____	$ _____
2. _____	_____	_____
3. _____	_____	_____
4. _____	_____	_____
5. _____	_____	_____
6. _____	_____	_____
7. _____	_____	_____
8. _____	_____	_____
Totals		$ _____
Total Expenses		$ _____

By comparing what cash is on hand and forthcoming, with your immediate expenses, you know where you stand and don't have to guess.

Your Spouse's Records:

8. *Checkbooks*. Make sure all checkbooks balance. Bounced checks will only add to your burdens.

9. *Your Spouse's Will*. Find your spouse's will and any trusts. Call your attorney and arrange a meeting to discuss these items. If you don't have an attorney, see Chapter 17, Choosing Professional Advisors.

10. *Your Spouse's Papers.* Go through your spouse's desk and files. Look for important papers, especially, unpaid bills.

11. *Outstanding Debts.* Make a list of all outstanding bills, debts and installment payments. If you anticipate a delay in meeting obligations, especially if you are waiting for life insurance proceeds to handle bills, call the creditors, explain the circumstances, and ask for an extension.

12. *Your Spouse's Employer.* If your spouse was employed, notify the company and request a list of benefits. For example, insurance, vested retirement benefits, 401(k), stock option plans, stock purchase plans, deferred compensation, supplemental insurance, medical benefits, vacation pay, sick leave pay, and any disability benefits due to illness before death. These items may seem complex to you at this point, but you needn't be concerned. Just obtain the list of benefits that you have coming to you; you will understand them in due course.

IMPORTANT
If you were covered by your deceased spouse's medical plan, you should immediately check with the employer to see if you and your family will automatically be covered. If not, apply for continuation of coverage under Federal COBRA conditions within 60 days. Under COBRA you pay the premiums.

Insurance-Related Matters:

13. *Life Insurance.* Contact the insurance companies that issued policies on the life of your spouse. Once you've received the proper instructions, submit the death claim forms along with certified death certificates. (See Chapter 9). Benefits may take up to six weeks to receive. In addition, if your spouse was killed on the job or while travelling on company business you will probably be entitled to worker's compensation survivor benefits. Contact your spouse's employer to process worker's compensation claims.

14. *Accidental Death Benefits.* If death was accidental, look for accidental death and dismemberment policies. If death was due to a car crash, check with your insurance agent about the death benefits and medical coverage provisions of your spouse's automobile insurance. Also, if your spouse belonged to an auto-

mobile club, check to see if accidental death benefits were included as part of membership.

15. *Credit and Mortgage Life Insurance.* Determine whether your spouse maintained mortgage life insurance, and credit life insurance on each installment contract and credit card. Such coverage will pay off, respectively, the balance of the mortgage on your home or the entire installment contract and credit card debt.

16. *Insurance and Taxes.* Check to ensure that your health, homeowners and automobile insurance policies, income taxes and property taxes are all up-to-date and paid.

Bank-Related Matters:

17. *Safe Deposit Box.* If your safe deposit box is jointly owned and you have the key, open it and review the contents. Make a list of anything that requires your immediate attention. Put aside items for your children and others, and plan to deal with them later. In some states, even safe deposit boxes that are jointly held are sealed after the death of one of the owners. In that case, consult your attorney about getting a court's permission to get access to the box.

18. *Certificates of Deposit.* Determine whether there are any certificates of deposit that are ready to mature. You may not want them to roll over for another investment period if you need the cash to pay bills. However, if a jointly-owned certificate of deposit has recently rolled over, your bank may allow you take the funds without penalty because one of the owners has died.

19. *IRAs.* Determine whether your spouse owned one or more IRA accounts, and where the money is located.

Government Benefits:

20. *Social Security Benefits.* You must apply to receive any Social Security funds to which you're entitled; the money will not be sent to you automatically. Set up an appointment with your local Social Security Office to apply for death and survivors' benefits.

   You will need to bring with you a certified copy of the death certificate, proof of marriage, and the Social Security numbers of your spouse and yourself. When you call to set up an appointment, ask if you will also need your children's birth certificates and Social Security numbers, and W-2 forms of the most recent tax year for both you and your spouse.

21. *Veterans Administration*. If your spouse served in the armed forces, contact the Veterans Administration. There may be burial or survivor's benefits to which you're entitled. Some funeral directors may be able to supply the necessary forms.

Membership Organizations:

22. *American Legion Membership*. If your spouse belonged to the American Legion, contact the local branch. The War Orphans and Widows Educational Assistance Act may provide benefits for a child who is 18–25 years old, for 36 months of schooling.

23. *Other Membership Organizations*. Notify any organizations of which your spouse was a member and inquire whether you are entitled to any benefits or income as a survivor. Membership organizations might include credit unions, trade unions, fraternal orders, college alumni groups and military service organizations.

Notifying Others:

24. *Death Certificates*. If you haven't done so already, order certified death certificates. The number of certificates you need depends on the number of claims you have—anywhere between ten and twenty copies, as a general rule. Examples for which you may need death certificates include life insurance policies (one for each policy); Social Security benefits; veterans survivor's benefits; retirement or pension plan survivor benefits; financial accounts at banks, savings and loan institutions and brokerage firms; safe deposit boxes; property insurance proceeds; automobile registration; health insurance policy proceeds; credit card companies; real estate title transfers; and stock and bond title transfers.

    The funeral director can order as many certified copies as you need. If you need additional copies at a future date, ask the funeral provider for assistance, or order them yourself from your state vital statistics or health agency.

25. *Foreign Death Certificates*. If your spouse died abroad, immediately notify the nearest U.S. diplomatic or consular mission. The staff will assist you with the logistics of trans-

porting the decedent's remains to the point of burial. A local funeral director will then prepare the body for shipment to, and burial in, the place you select.

The death certificate will be issued by the authorities of the country where your spouse died. Based upon the information in the death certificate, the U.S. diplomatic mission or consular office will prepare a report of death of an American citizen. The original of the report is sent to the U.S. Department of State, Office of Special Consular Services, for permanent filing.

26. *Filing Forms.* Check with your attorney, accountant or financial planner about filing the following documents: federal estate tax returns, inheritance tax report, federal individual income tax returns, state tax returns, and state tax returns for other states where property is owned.

27. *Beneficiary Changes.* If your spouse was the beneficiary of your insurance policies, annuities, IRAs and other retirement plans, request beneficiary change forms to protect your heirs.

28. *Financial Institutions.* Notify all financial institutions, stock brokerage firms, insurance carriers and investment companies of your spouse's death. Request that account registrations be changed as appropriate.

29. *Labor Unions.* If your spouse was a member of any labor union contact the union to determine if any death benefits are available.

30. *Attorney.* Contact your attorney to set up a time to review the will and/or living trust. If there is no will, talk to an attorney for instructions on estate settlement issues regarding *intestate* (dying without a will).

31. *Insurance Agent.* Call both your life and automobile insurance agents to set up claims procedures for your spouses policies.

32. *Accountant/CPA/Tax Preparer.* If you and your spouse used a tax preparer contact that person. Eventually you will need to meet to determine your overall tax picture and how it may change in the future.

33. *Bank.* Reposition accounts you held in joint with your spouse into your name. Open your own checking account if you don't have one. If your spouse was receiving direct deposit checks have the bank return them to the sender (e.g., Social Security). Open your own safety deposit box. Find out if your spouse had any benefits, such as credit life insurance, to pay off loans.

Other Considerations:

34. *Funeral Home Disputes*. If you have a problem regarding your funeral home bill, first discuss it with the funeral director. If you still have a problem, contact your state licensing board, the Conference of Funeral Service Examining Boards, 520 East Van Trees Street, P.O. Box 497, Washington, Indiana 47501 (812-254-9887), or THANNCAP, 11121 West Oklahoma Avenue, Milwaukee, Wisconsin 53227 (414-541-7925).

35. *Your Will*. Review your own will and discuss with your attorney any changes you wish to make.

36. *Outside Pressure*. For now, disregard unsolicited advice and pressure from others, especially about financial matters. Resolve not to make any major decisions now, particularly about business ventures with friends or relatives.

IMMEDIATE DEMANDS FOR CASH

In the first few days there are likely to be many demands for cash—usually, about $2,500 is needed within the first five to ten days, and more shortly thereafter. If savings and checking funds are insufficient, more money must be found or an arrangement worked out with creditors.

In the event you need emergency cash before insurance claims are paid, you can try to negotiate a cash advance from the insurance company, against the full amount of life insurance benefits due you. However, this may slow down the process of issuing the total face amount of the policies.

Do not ignore debt. If your creditors dun you for payment of bills—funeral home, hospitals, physicians, nursing homes—and you cannot pay them all at once, call each creditor, explain the situation, and offer to set up a payment schedule. Your attorney, accountant or financial advisor can do this for you if you can't face it yourself.

Hilda was coping with the loss of her husband, the reaction of his elderly parents and pressure from her boss. She just didn't want any more problems, so she placed all her bills in a large cardboard box. She meant to go through them, but she never found time and couldn't deal with it. Fortunately, her oldest son realized the situation and stepped in before there were serious problems. Debts won't go away and creditors can be nasty if they feel you may not pay.

When you receive money from insurance companies or your spouse's estate you may wonder what to do with it. There will probably be many suggestions from friends and relatives about how you should invest the money.

Unless you need the funds to pay immediate bills, or there is an emergency, don't do anything. Set up a money market fund at your local bank (FDIC insured, of course), and wait until you feel less overwhelmed or confused. You need a game plan to invest the money. When you're ready, find an objective financial advisor who understands your position and situation. Then, make whatever investment decisions you deem appropriate.

SECONDARY CONCERNS

Housing—You may feel pressure to make a decision about "what to do with the house." Well-meaning friends and relatives may insist you'd be better off in a place without so many memories, you may feel guilty living alone in a large house, or your children may think a smaller home requiring less upkeep would be an improvement for you. You may even hear from real estate agents with offers for your property that seem generous, considering what you paid for the house years ago.

> Joan's sister suggested several times that Joan sell the family house and live in a small condominium, and Joan's grown children were anxious to know if she was moving. Actually, Joan was content to remain in her home for the foreseeable future. She was comfortable there and wanted time to consider all the aspects of moving.

Joan was wise to wait. Moving is one decision that can be deferred until you're sure it's what you want. Remember also that the house you shared with your spouse has important psychological meaning for you. If you and your mate were happy there, remaining in your home may be instrumental in helping you work through your grief. Thus, unless the house is the only source of money, do nothing with it now. If housing is a pressing item for you turn to Chapter 11, You and Your Home.

Credit—Now that you're alone, you may be wondering about the status of your bank cards such as VISA, MasterCard, American Express,

Diners Club, as well as your retail store and gasoline credit cards. If the cards were in both names or you used your spouse's card, you're probably concerned about using them.

There are no specific rules about how your credit will be affected by the death of your spouse. When you contact creditors to inquire whether there is credit life insurance, some of them will permit you to retain their credit card, but may lower the dollar limit that can be charged. Others may cancel the card.

In any event, it is to your advantage to apply for credit in your own name. Some widowed people never notify credit card company's of their spouse's death. They go on using the same credit cards and paying the bills as they did prior to their mate's death. There are two problems with this approach. The first is that any credit life insurance will remain uncollected. The second is that the good credit rating continues to accrue to your deceased spouse, and not to you.

Other Secondary Concerns:

Here are several general topics that will need to be addressed eventually:

Bank

Real Estate Taxes

College Financial Aid

Health Club

Magazines

Utilities

Credit Cards (expired)

State Department of Motor Vehicles

Stockbroker/Financial Planner

Real Estate Title

Mortgage Holder

CHECKLIST OF IMPORTANT DOCUMENTS TO LOCATE

_____ Wills

_____ Trusts

_____ Life Insurance Policies

_____ Retirement Plans:

     _____ 401(k)

     _____ IRA's

     _____ Self-Employment Plans

     _____ Pension

     _____ Profit-Sharing

     _____ ESOP

_____ Business Agreement, Book and Records

_____ Uniform Donor Card

_____ Final Instructions Letter

_____ Birth Certificate

_____ Military Discharge papers of your spouse

_____ Marriage License

_____ Prenuptial Agreement

_____ Divorce Papers

_____ Birth Certificate and Adoption Papers for your children

_____ Deeds

_____ Title to burial plot

_____ Vehicle registrations to all vehicles

_____ Bank accounts

_____ Securities statements and certificates

_____ Last two years tax returns and related information

_____ Loan documents (including all mortgage information)

_____ Other insurance policies (auto, homeowners, flood, travel and accident, health).

_____ Credit Card information (See list at end of this chapter)

_____ Membership club information, auto clubs, etc.

_____ Citizenship papers

_____ Property appraisals

_____ Social Security cards

TELEPHONE LOG

Date	Name of Person	Company	Summary of Discussion

CHAPTER 2

Important People and Organizations

Date	Item	Contact Person/ Organization	Phone Number	Action Required or Completed

Information Needed To Apply for Benefits:
Personal and Social Data Required
Information About Your Spouse

Name: _____

Date/Place of Birth: _____

Marriage History:

Name(s) of Spouse(s)	Dates of Marriage(s)	Name(s) of Children	Children's Birth Date(s)
_____	_____	_____	_____
_____	_____	_____	_____
_____	_____	_____	_____
_____	_____	_____	_____

Soc. Sec. # _____   Military ID # _____

Branch of Service: _____

Dates of Service: _____

Discharge Date: _____

Employment History:

Name of Organization	Address	Employment Dates
_____	_____	_____
_____	_____	_____
_____	_____	_____
_____	_____	_____
_____	_____	_____

College/Alumni Groups: _____
_____

Fraternal/Membership Organizations: _____
_____

Extended Family History:

List parents, grandparents, siblings, grandchildren. If none are living, your attorney may require identification of other relatives, depending on the terms of the will.

Name	Relationship	Address	Date of Birth/Death
_____	_____	_____	_____
_____	_____	_____	_____
_____	_____	_____	_____

Information Needed To Apply for Benefits:
Personal and Social Data Required
Information About You

Name: _____ Soc. Sec. #_____

Date/Place of Birth: _____

Marriage History:

Name(s) of Spouse(s)	Dates of Marriage(s)	Name(s) of Children	Children's Birth Date(s)
_____	_____	_____	_____
_____	_____	_____	_____
_____	_____	_____	_____
_____	_____	_____	_____

Employment History:

Name of Organization	Address	Employment Dates
_____	_____	_____
_____	_____	_____
_____	_____	_____
_____	_____	_____
_____	_____	_____

Extended Family History:

List parents, grandparents, siblings, grandchildren. If none are living, your attorney may require identification of other relatives, depending on the terms of the will.

Name	Relationship	Address	Date of Birth/Death
_____	_____	_____	_____
_____	_____	_____	_____
_____	_____	_____	_____
_____	_____	_____	_____
_____	_____	_____	_____
_____	_____	_____	_____
_____	_____	_____	_____
_____	_____	_____	_____

Credit Card Master List

Credit Card Name	Account Number	Outstanding Balance	Interest Rate	Phone Number	Remarks
		$	%		
		$	%		
		$	%		
		$	%		
		$	%		
		$	%		
		$	%		
		$	%		
		$	%		
		$	%		
		$	%		
		$	%		
		$	%		
		$	%		

CHAPTER 2

CLAIMING EVERYTHING THAT'S YOURS—PRIVATE SOURCES

Almost all widowed persons are eligible for some type of death and/ or survivor benefits through insurance policies, pensions and profit sharing plans, self-employment plans, IRAs, and other benefit programs. This chapter will show you how to file for benefits correctly and in a timely fashion, and offer a way to track your claims.

The first rule is to photocopy and file every piece of paper—each letter, form, policy and any other documents—you give or mail to anyone. Keeping complete and accurate records makes good sense no matter what kind of business you're conducting.

> ### IMPORTANT
>
> Do not think of your claims as seeking "welfare," but as receiving benefits to which you're entitled. The best approach is to assume you qualify for everything, and apply if there is even a remote chance you are eligible. Remember that these programs were paid for by your deceased spouse, provided by his employer or are available through the government. View them as your legal and just entitlements, not as welfare.

LIFE INSURANCE

One of the first money concerns of many newly-widowed persons is how to get the proceeds of life insurance. Life insurance claims are not paid automatically following a death; you have to file the forms to get the benefits. A Master Claim Tracking Form is provided at the end of this chapter to help you keep track of your various policies.

1. *Locate the Policies.* If you followed the procedures outlined in Chapter 2, you've most likely found them already. If so, move on to step 2. If

not, look for the policies among your spouse's important papers. If you can't locate them, look through your spouse's checkbook register to find the name of the insurance companies to which payments were sent.

If you are unable to find the actual policy, call the insurance company and ask for a lost policy form. Most insurance companies have "800" numbers and "800-information" may be able to provide the number. If not, contact the local office of the insurance carrier for information.

If you are unsure whether or not your spouse actually owned a particular policy and you are unable to find the policy or even remember which agent he/she purchased the policy through, go through cancelled checks to see what company payments were made to.

If all else fails send a self-addressed stamped envelope to:

Policy Search
American Council of Life Insurance
1001 Pennsylvania Avenue, NW
Washington, DC 20004
and they will have its members do a free search for you.

Sometimes insurance forms can be confusing. When you're looking for a life insurance policy, the key word on the insurance papers is the word "Life." There are several kinds of life insurance under which your spouse may have been covered:

    A. *Personally, individually-owned policies* issued by regular life insurance carriers.

    B. *Group life policies issued through the deceased's employer.* Often there will be a certificate of coverage, rather than a policy. If you don't find it among your mate's papers, ask your spouse's employer.

    C. *Travel accident policies*, which often are issued by major gasoline credit card companies, and sometimes by banks and automobile club associations. Accidental Death policies fall under this heading.

    D. *Credit life policies* typically pay off the outstanding balance owed on an installment debt.

    E. *Mortgage life insurance* will pay off your mortgage, leaving your house "free and clear." Your mortgage lender will know if your spouse had this type of policy.

    F. *Group coverage offered through associations.* There are many professional, business, religious and other types of associations in the United States, and your spouse may have belonged to several. Examples are the Professional Engineers Society of America, the National Association of Female Executives, and B'nai B'rith. The Yellow Pages has an extensive listing of types of associations.

When you determine the name of the insurance carrier providing association coverage under which your spouse was insured, call the company directly. Most life insurance companies have a toll-free "800" number, which you can find by calling "800 Information" at 1-800-555-1212. When you call the company, ask for the life insurance claims department.

G. *Group coverage offered through fraternal orders.* If your spouse was a member of an organization such as the Elks, Lions, Moose, Kiwanis, Masons or Woodmen, you should check with them about their benefits.

H. *Cancer care policies* under which your spouse was covered may include death benefits.

I. *Guaranteed issue policies* cover individuals with health problems. This coverage offers reduced benefits in the early years, paying only ten or twenty percent of the face amount if death occurs in the first year or two. The percent increases for each year the insured remains alive, until the coverage reaches one-hundred percent of face value.

J. *Survivorship life or "second-to-die" policies* insure both spouses, but pay the proceeds only when the surviving spouse dies. If you are covered by such a policy, notify your insurance agent; some survivorship policies offer options to the survivor upon the death of the first insured.

K. *Automobile Insurance.* If your spouse was killed as a result of an auto collision, contact your automobile insurance carrier to see if any death benefits were included in the policy.

L. *Worker's Compensation.* Contact your spouses' employer if his/her death was work related.

A form is included on page 42, to help you stay organized.

2. *Contact the Insurance Company.* Check to be sure that no premiums were paid on life insurance policies after the date of your spouse's death. If, in the confusion of the moment, premiums were paid, ask for reimbursement.

Then, write letters to the insurance company using the sample letter on page 30. Include with the claim letter the policy number, the actual policy and a certified copy of the death certificate. Some companies also like to have a copy of the obituary notice.

Many companies will permit you to start the claims procedure with a phone call in advance of formal filing. This process helps to expedite things once the company receives the claim forms. If you cannot find the policy, call the insurance company or your agent and ask for a "Lost Policy Form." Once it arrives, follow the claims procedure above, substituting the Lost Policy Form for the policy.

Where there is more than one primary beneficiary under a specific policy, each beneficiary needs to file a claim form. Insurance companies will provide additional claim forms at no charge.

The face amount of the policy accrues interest from the date of death until the date the check is cut to you. Thus, if you're owed $100,000 and the insurance company pays twenty days following the date of death, you should receive twenty days' worth of interest.

Note that if your spouse named a trust as beneficiary, then the trustee will be the person to complete the claims information, sign the forms, and submit all the documents to the insurance company.

Sample Insurance Company Claim Letter

_____(Date)_____

ABC Life Insurance Co.
Claims Department
Street Address
City, State, Zip Code

Re: _____ Policy No. _____

Dear Claims Department:

My (husband/wife), (John/Jane) Doe, died on ___(Date)___. His/Her Social Security Number is_____. I wish to file a claim for the life insurance benefits from the above-referenced policy.

I am enclosing the (policy/lost policy form) and a certified copy of the death certificate. Please provide me with a detailed account of how you determine payment, as well as the various settlement options available. I (am/am not) subject to backup withholding. My Social Security number is (_____/ provided on the enclosed IRS Form W-9).

I appreciate your prompt attention to this matter.

Sincerely,

Your Name

Provide your Social Security number on Internal Revenue Service form W-9 (Request for Taxpayer Identification Number and Certification), a copy of which appears on page 32.

The W-9 form provides information the insurance company needs to notify the Internal Revenue Service of the interest paid to you; while the face amount of the life insurance is not subject to federal taxes, the interest paid is taxable. Any IRS office can provide a W-9 form, although a facsimile will do, or the insurance company may have a form of its own. *The important point is to make sure the insurance company has your Social Security number*.

Most insurance carriers do not require that you notarize claim forms. However, photocopies of death certificates are not acceptable. Certified (raised seal) copies are required.

Carefully read the beneficiary provisions of your spouse's life insurance policies. If the primary beneficiary on the policy—the first person named to receive the proceeds—is deceased, a certified copy of that primary beneficiary's death certificate will be required. For example, suppose your spouse had a $10,000 policy and named your mother as primary beneficiary and your daughter as contingent beneficiary—the person to receive the proceeds if the primary beneficiary has died. The proceeds will not be released to your daughter, the contingent beneficiary, until the insurance company has proof that the primary beneficiary is deceased.

Sometimes after a death the cash on hand is so limited that all or part of the proceeds from your spouse's life insurance must be assigned to a funeral home to cover funeral expenses. The funeral home can supply an Assignment Form, which must be signed by funeral home officials and by all those who are named in the policy. For example, there may be several beneficiaries who are named to receive equal shares of the policy proceeds; each of them has to sign the Assignment Form.

3. *Contestable Periods*. Most life insurance policies reserve to the company the right to challenge claims filed for deaths that occur within one or two years after the policy was issued, and/or in the event the death was a suicide. Unless the policy states that no benefits will be paid in the case of suicide, survivors of a suicide may be eligible for full death benefits as long as the policy was in force longer than one or two years. However, any accidental death benefits that are part of the policy will not be paid, because suicide is not considered an accident.

Once you've submitted claim forms, the insurance company will conduct its own investigation to determine if there's any reason not to pay the claim. Aside from suicide, the primary reason not to pay a claim would be, for example, that your spouse had cancer when the policy was issued, knew about it, and didn't inform the insurance company. If

Form **W-9** (Rev. March 1994) Department of the Treasury Internal Revenue Service	**Request for Taxpayer** **Identification Number and Certification**	**Give form to the** **requester. Do NOT** **send to the IRS.**

Please print or type

Name (If joint names, list first and circle the name of the person or entity whose number you enter in Part I below. **See instructions on page 2** if your name has changed.)

Business name (Sole proprietors see instructions on page 2.)

Please check appropriate box: ☐ Individual/Sole proprietor ☐ Corporation ☐ Partnership ☐ Other ▶ ....

Address (number, street, and apt. or suite no.)

Requester's name and address (optional)

City, state, and ZIP code

Part I	**Taxpayer Identification Number (TIN)**	List account number(s) here (optional)

Enter your TIN in the appropriate box. For individuals, this is your social security number (SSN). For sole proprietors, see the instructions on page 2. For other entities, it is your employer identification number (EIN). If you do not have a number, see **How To Get a TIN** below.

Note: *If the account is in more than one name, see the chart on page 2 for guidelines on whose number to enter.*

Social security number

OR

Employer identification number

Part II For Payees Exempt From Backup Withholding (See **Part II** instructions on page 2)

▶

Part III	**Certification**

Under penalties of perjury, I certify that:

1. The number shown on this form is my correct taxpayer identification number (or I am waiting for a number to be issued to me), **and**

2. I am not subject to backup withholding because: **(a)** I am exempt from backup withholding, or **(b)** I have not been notified by the Internal Revenue Service that I am subject to backup withholding as a result of a failure to report all interest or dividends, or **(c)** the IRS has notified me that I am no longer subject to backup withholding.

Certification Instructions.—You must cross out item **2** above if you have been notified by the IRS that you are currently subject to backup withholding because of underreporting interest or dividends on your tax return. For real estate transactions, item **2** does not apply. For mortgage interest paid, the acquisition or abandonment of secured property, cancellation of debt, contributions to an individual retirement arrangement (IRA), and generally payments other than interest and dividends, you are not required to sign the Certification, but you must provide your correct TIN. (Also see **Part III instructions** on page 2.)

Sign Here | Signature ▶ | Date ▶

Section references are to the Internal Revenue Code.

Purpose of Form.—A person who is required to file an information return with the IRS must get your correct TIN to report income paid to you, real estate transactions, mortgage interest you paid, the acquisition or abandonment of secured property, cancellation of debt, or contributions you made to an IRA. Use Form W-9 to give your correct TIN to the requester (the person requesting your TIN) and, when applicable, (1) to certify the TIN you are giving is correct (or you are waiting for a number to be issued), (2) to certify you are not subject to backup withholding, or (3) to claim exemption from backup withholding if you are an exempt payee. Giving your correct TIN and making the appropriate certifications will prevent certain payments from being subject to backup withholding.

Note: *If a requester gives you a form other than a W-9 to request your TIN, you must use the requester's form if it is substantially similar to this Form W-9.*

What Is Backup Withholding?—Persons making certain payments to you must withhold and pay to the IRS 31% of such

payments under certain conditions. This is called "backup withholding." Payments that could be subject to backup withholding include interest, dividends, broker and barter exchange transactions, rents, royalties, nonemployee pay, and certain payments from fishing boat operators. Real estate transactions are not subject to backup withholding.

If you give the requester your correct TIN, make the proper certifications, and report all your taxable interest and dividends on your tax return, your payments will not be subject to backup withholding. Payments you receive will be subject to backup withholding if:

1. You do not furnish your TIN to the requester, or

2. The IRS tells the requester that you furnished an incorrect TIN, or

3. The IRS tells you that you are subject to backup withholding because you did not report all your interest and dividends on your tax return (for reportable interest and dividends only), or

4. You do not certify to the requester that you are not subject to backup withholding under 3 above (for reportable

interest and dividend accounts opened after 1983 only), or

5. You do not certify your TIN. See the Part III instructions for exceptions.

Certain payees and payments are exempt from backup withholding and information reporting. See the Part II instructions and the separate **Instructions for the Requester of Form W-9.**

How To Get a TIN.—If you do not have a TIN, apply for one immediately. To apply, get **Form SS-5,** Application for a Social Security Number Card (for individuals), from your local office of the Social Security Administration, or **Form SS-4,** Application for Employer Identification Number (for businesses and all other entities), from your local IRS office.

If you do not have a TIN, write "Applied For" in the space for the TIN in Part I, sign and date the form, and give it to the requester. Generally, you will then have 60 days to get a TIN and give it to the requester. If the requester does not receive your TIN within 60 days, backup withholding, if applicable, will begin and continue until you furnish your TIN.

Cat. No. 10231X

23

Form **W-9** (Rev. 3-94)

your spouse had cancer and did not know about it when the policy was issued, you may still be able to collect on the claim. The same procedures for filing a claim apply whether the policy is contestable or not.

4. *What To Expect*. Most life insurance claims take five to ten working days from the date the death notification reaches the department, until the initial claims handling is complete. During this time the claims department orders all applications from the company's files, sets up and reviews a claims file, checks for incontestability, prepares a letter to you and mails it.

Normally you will be assigned a claim number and given the phone number of a claims examiner, who handles your claim personally. In the event of a financial emergency, some companies will advance up to $10,000 to a beneficiary before completing the claims requirements. If you need to apply for emergency funds, you must state the amount needed; the beneficiary's name, address, date of birth and Social Security number; and the nature of the emergency. You will not be able to apply for emergency funds if your coverage is contestable.

Once you've sent all the documentation to the insurance company's claims department, you can expect a check to be approved and mailed within five to seven working days. However, if your claim is contested, it will take two to three months before the claims investigation is complete. Check with the insurance carrier every two weeks to determine the progress of a contested claim.

5. *Form of Payment*. Many companies automatically set up an interest-bearing checking account in your name, and mail you a checkbook drawn on that account for the life insurance proceeds. This method is superior to lump sum payments because it gives you options not otherwise immediately available.

For instance, you can close the account by writing a check for the entire amount and placing the funds elsewhere; because the funds are earning interest every day, the insurance company often provides a toll-free number so you can find out the exact amount to the penny. Alternatively, you can leave the funds in the account established by the insurance company, writing periodic checks for smaller amounts while the balance continues to earn interest, or leave the entire amount at interest until you decide what to do with the funds.

At some point in the claims process you will be asked to choose whether you want the life insurance proceeds in a lump sum or in an annuity. Here's what they're talking about:

1. *Lump Sums*. You receive the entire death benefit payment in full. In other words, if your spouse was insured for $100,000,

you get $100,000, and you and the insurance company have no further dealings regarding that policy. This is the most popular payout and one that makes the most sense for most individuals.

2. *Annuity Options*:

a) *Non-Refund Life Annuity*—You would receive payments, usually monthly, during your lifetime. All payments cease when you die. Use this option only in the extreme case that you're a rather young widow, have no dependents, and want to be assured of regular, monthly payments for the rest of your life. However, nearly all widowed persons—who usually have dependents and cannot predict how long they're going to live— would be better advised to take the lump sum payment.

b) *Period Certain Only Annuity*—In this case you would receive payments for the specified period—5, 10, 15 or 20 years —whether you live or die, but there are no payments after that specified time period.

c) *Life Annuity with Guaranteed, Time-Specified Payments*— You, or your estate, would receive guaranteed payments for a specific period of time—5, 10, 15 or 20 years—whether you live or die. If you live longer than the guaranteed period of time, *payments continue* for the rest of your life. This is particularly beneficial if you need a lifetime, guaranteed income. The payments in this case would be slightly lower than the payments listed in number 2, since they are allocated for a longer period of time.

d) *Installment Refund*—You would receive a periodic payment for life. If there are any unused funds left in the policy at your death, they go to a person or persons previously designated by you. The payments here would be lower than the previous options, which permits some funds to remain for beneficiaries at your death.

Although there are others, the annuity options summarized above are the most popular. Once you've selected an annuity option, regardless of how your financial situation may change in the future, you're stuck with it. Therefore, it makes sense for most readers to choose the lump sum payment, because they can put those funds into other types of financial vehicles, and maintain their flexibility in the years to come.

Life insurance proceeds paid to a named beneficiary because of the death of a spouse are not taxable income for federal or state tax purposes. If the proceeds of a life insurance policy are taken in installment payments the non-taxable portion of each installment equals the total amount payable at death divided by the number of installments to be paid. Anything paid to you over this amount in each installment would be considered taxable income.

> **NOTE:** Your insurance proceeds check may arrive through your insurance agent, who may have some suggestions as to investments. Do not make any decisions at this time that you can't change in the near future. Ask that any recommendations be put in writing so you will have time to carefully consider them, once you are in a better frame of mind to make investment decisions. At the same time, you should ask for an update on your own insurance policies, especially in regard to naming a new beneficiary, if your spouse was the named beneficiary on your policies.

ANNUITY CLAIMS

Annuity claims are handled in the same way life insurance claims are processed. The annuity company or your spouse's employer can help you determine if your spouse was receiving periodic payments from an annuity. Depending on the provisions of the plan, you may be entitled to benefits in the form of continued payments or a lump sum. If you have an annuity claim, you need to be aware of the most popular types of annuities.

1. *Single Premium Deferred Annuity.* A lump sum annuity with an interest rate that is guaranteed for a specific period of time. Once the time period is completed, a new rate is guaranteed for a new term. The principal is also guaranteed by the insurance carrier.

2. *Tax Sheltered Annuities (TSAs).* Often available through school systems to county or municipal employees, periodic contributions to TSAs are made, usually by employees, to a fixed yield or to a variable yield fund.

3. *Variable Annuities.* An annuity offering many different investments, ranging from money market to speculative growth stocks or even real estate. Contributions may be made monthly or in a lump sum. The principal or the value of the annuity, whichever is greater, is guaranteed to the named beneficiaries upon the death of the annuity holder.

Whether you are dealing with your spouse's annuity or life insurance, you may find the policy language difficult to follow. Feel free to call the company that issued the policy, and ask for an explanation. Staff members will go through the language line-by-line, and lay out the options available to you.

NOTE: Insurance company employees have no interest in keeping you from funds you're entitled to receive, but be forewarned: because they may not understand your particular situation, the information you get will be general.

This is why it makes good sense to have advisors—financial, insurance, banking and others—on your side in advance. More about professional advisors is discussed in Chapter 17.

YOUR SPOUSES' EMPLOYER: STARTING THE CLAIMS PROCESS

Contact the personnel department of your deceased spouses' employer. Do this whether your spouse was still working or had already retired. They will help you determine what benefits you are eligible to receive in the form of pension income, life insurance proceeds, and health insurance. Send a letter similar to the one below to the employee benefits department.

                                                            _____(Date)_____

ABC Corporation
Employee Benefits Department
Street Address
City, State, Zip Code
RE: _____(Your spouses' Name)_____

Dear Employee Benefits Department:

Please be advised that my (husband/wife), _____,
Social Security number _____ died on _____(date)_____ .
Please provide me with full information regarding all employee benefits I am eligible for as his/her surviving spouse. In particular, please provide information on the following:

1) Life Insurance benefits
2) Continuation of health insurance for 18 months
3) Payments of unused vacation time and/or unpaid payroll
4) Pension benefits
5) Payout options on available retirement plans

I may be reached at the address and phone number below. Thank you for your prompt attention.

Sincerely yours,

Your street
City, State, Zip code
Phone No. _____

NOTE: If your spouse was still working at the time of death, you and your family are entitled to receive health insurance benefits at group insurance rates for the 18-month period following his/her death.

UNDERSTANDING PENSION BENEFIT CLAIMS

The terms "pension" and "qualified plans" are used to refer to a variety of investment benefit programs to which your spouse, and perhaps your spouse's employer, made regular contributions. These plans can include, for example, pension, profit sharing, stock option, 401(k), target benefit, stock purchase, thrift savings and 403(b) plans. In addition, a spouse who was self-employed may have had a form of profit sharing plan known as a Keogh (HR10) plan.

You may not know what all these terms mean, but recognizing them will allow you to ask questions that will help you determine what is rightfully yours. Call your spouse's employer and find out what benefits are available through retirement plans, and whether they are available in a lump sum or in periodic payouts.

Every lump sum held by your spouse in a qualified plan of which you're the named beneficiary can be rolled over to an IRA in your name. You may receive the proceeds yourself. You will have 60 days to place them in your own IRA, or the proceeds can be transferred directly from the custodian of your spouse's account to the custodian of your IRA. In most cases, the best format will be what is called a "self-directed IRA," which allows you to place the funds in a variety of investments.

Any after-tax dollars your spouse contributed to company plans are available to you tax-free, but this only applies to *after-tax* contributions. When you receive the after-tax dollars invested in a qualified plan, a sheet will accompany the check showing both the before-tax and after-tax contributions made by the employer and by your spouse.

Here are some related issues to consider:

1. If you're receiving periodic pension benefit payments, do they have a provision for cost of living increases? If so, how often are the adjustments made?

2. If your mate's previous marriage ended in divorce, the former spouse may qualify through the divorce decree for part of your partner's pension benefits. Check the divorce papers if you're not sure.

3. If your spouse was already retired at the time of death, and was receiving pension benefits, what are the terms of the

CHAPTER 3

survivor provisions? For example, if the benefits are available to you, will they be smaller than what your spouse received? Or, are survivor benefits available to you, but not until a certain age? If so, when can you begin receiving the payments and approximately how much will they be?

Up to $5,000 of death benefits from an employer qualified retirement plan may be tax excludible as an employer paid death benefit. If the benefit is a lump sum distribution, the full exclusion is available. If the benefit is in the form of periodic payments, the $5,000 exclusion is available only to the extent that the employee's benefit was non-forfeitable prior to the employee's death. If the death benefit is payable under a life insurance contract held by the qualified plan, the pure insurance amount of the death benefit is excluded from income taxes. The pure insurance amount is the difference between the policy's face amount and its cash value at the date of death.

If IRA accounts are paid to you, as the beneficiary, you will have to declare the IRA payments, whether lump sum or periodic, as ordinary income since they are received just as though you were the original owner of the IRA. The IRA distributions are considered income. If you take the IRA account as a lump sum distribution, be aware that you may have to pay income taxes as well as estate taxes on those proceeds.

Even if you are under age 59-1/2, the *deceased spouse's IRA* can be taken without the 10% IRS penalty. (There is no penalty after age 59-1/2 on your IRA).

As an IRA beneficiary, you may elect to roll the funds over into your own IRA, avoiding current taxes. (You can also make your own deductible IRA contributions to that IRA account if you qualify). You also have the option of leaving the funds in your spouse's name. Distributions from that IRA account do not have to begin until your spouse would have reached the age of 70-1/2. If your deceased spouse was already receiving payments according to a schedule and you are the beneficiary you must receive distributions at least as rapidly.

A *rollover IRA* means taking receipt of the assets for up to 60 days before reinvesting it into a new retirement IRA plan. A *transfer* means moving the assets from one IRA custodian to another IRA custodian. Rollovers are allowed once a year. Transfers can occur as often as you wish and as many times a year as you wish. Losses that are incurred in an IRA account are not deductible.

There are two types of rollovers for IRAs. One is an IRA-to-IRA rollover. In this case, all or a portion of the existing funds are withdrawn and checks come to you. The funds are not subject to current income taxes as long as they are deposited into another IRA within 60 days. Each IRA can be rolled over once every 12 months.

The other type of rollover is from a qualified retirement plan to an IRA. If your spouse was a participant in a company retirement plan, such as a pension or profit sharing plan, you may take the proceeds from that plan and roll them into an IRA. Again you may receive those proceeds yourself and then have 60 days in which to roll that money into an IRA. If you use the rollover, at least 50% of the amount in the company retirement program must be rolled over into an IRA. Also, be aware of a new IRS ruling that requires 20% withholding on rollovers. Use a direct custodian-to-custodian transfer to avoid the 20% withholding.

There are different tax treatments of IRA withdrawals depending upon your age:

1. *Before Age 59-1/2*: Withdrawals are taxable as ordinary income plus a 10% penalty for early withdrawal. Withdrawals from deceased spouse's IRA escape the 10% penalty.

2. *Age 59-1/2 to 70-1/2*: Withdrawals are taxable as ordinary income and there is complete flexibility on amounts and timing of withdrawals.

3. *Age 70-1/2 and later*: Withdrawals are taxed as ordinary income. Minimum distributions must begin by age 70 1/2 and are based on life expectancy. A 50% penalty is imposed if minimum distributions are not withdrawn. Distributions can exceed the minimum requirement.

TAXES ON LUMP SUM DISTRIBUTIONS

As a surviving spouse, you normally have two choices when a lump sum distribution is received from your deceased spouse's retirement program: 1) You can rollover part or all of it into an IRA (see the preceding discussion) or 2) pay tax on the distribution. If you elect to pay taxes, the lump sum distribution may qualify for a 5- or 10-year averaging. If your spouse made non-deductible contributions to a company pension or annuity plan, those parts of the distributions will be considered non-taxable.

If you wish to use the five year averaging, all five of the following requirements must be met for a lump sum distribution:

1. The lump sum distribution must represent the entire account balance from the employers plan [need more explanation].

2. Your spouse must have been 50 or older on January 1, 1986. If so, you have the option of choosing either the 10-year averaging using 1986 tax table rates or 5-year averaging using the current year tax rates. Both the 5-year and 10-year averaging tax tables are shown in the accompanying charts.

5-Year Averaging
Tax Computation at 1992 Rates

Taxable Lump-Sum Distribution	Multiply By This %	Subtract This Amount	
$ 0 to $20,000	x 7.5%	–$ 0 =	Tax
20,001 to 70,000	x 18.0%	– 2,100 =	Tax
70,001 to 107,250	x 15.0%	– 0 =	Tax
107,251 to 259,500	x 28.0%	– 13,942.50 =	Tax
259,501 & Over	x 31.0%	– 21,727.50 =	Tax

This table does not include any capital gain allocations or excise tax on excess contributions.

10-Year Averaging
Tax Computation at 1986 Rates

Taxable Lump-Sum Distribution	Multiply By This %	Subtract This Amount	
$ 0 to $ 20,000	x 5.5%	–$ 0 =	Tax
20,001 to 21,583	x 13.2%	– 1,540 =	Tax
21,584 to 30,583	x 14.4%	– 1,799 =	Tax
30,584 to 49,417	x 16.8%	– 2,533 =	Tax
49,418 to 67,417	x 18.0%	– 3,126 =	Tax
67,418 to 70,000	x 19.2%	– 3,935 =	Tax
70,001 to 91,700	x 16.0%	– 1,695 =	Tax
91,701 to 114,400	x 18.0%	– 3,529 =	Tax
114,401 to 137,100	x 20.0%	– 5,817 =	Tax
137,101 to 171,600	x 23.0%	– 9,930 =	Tax
171,601 to 228,800	x 26.0%	– 15,078 =	Tax
228,801 to 286,000	x 30.0%	– 24,230 =	Tax
286,001 to 343,200	x 34.0%	– 35,670 =	Tax
343,201 to 423,000	x 38.0%	– 49,398 =	Tax
423,001 to 571,900	x 42.0%	– 66,318 =	Tax
571,901* to 857,900	x 48.0%	– 100,632 =	Tax
*Over 857,900	x 50.0%	– 117,900 =	Tax

Does not include any capital gain allocations or excise taxes on excess distributions.

3. The plan must have been a qualified pension plan, profit sharing plan or stock bonus plan.

4. Your spouse must have participated in the plan at least five years before the year of the distribution, or the distribution is to be paid to a named beneficiary at death.

5. Also, one of the following conditions must be true:
   a) The distribution is to be paid to a beneficiary of the employee who died.
   b) The employee quit, retired or was laid off or was fired before receiving a distribution.
   c) Your spouse was self-employed or an owner-employee and became disabled, or was age 59-1/2 or older at the time of distribution.

Finally, besides the above requirements, note that averaging can only be used once. If you choose the averaging method you have to use it for all qualifying lump sum distributions you receive in that year.

ROLLOVER OR FORWARD AVERAGING

Should the lump sum distribution from your spouse's retirement plan be rolled over into an IRA, or should you elect the 5- or 10-year averaging on the lump sum distribution? Here are some considerations when making the choice:

Consider the current tax rate, and that future tax rates may rise. Also, if you pay the tax now you have unrestricted after-tax use of the funds in the future. This eliminates the uncertainty about any future tax laws and possible tax problems for you and for your heirs.

If you pick the IRA rollover you will effectively be deferring paying taxes until a future date. More wealth will be available to accumulate without taxation during that period. Higher taxes in the future may be offset by the investment values accumulated over the intervening years in the IRA.

IN SUMMARY

Although applying for these claims may seem burdensome and unnatural to you, remember that you or your spouse contributed to these programs so that, some day, one of you would receive the promised benefits. Think of it as your money—it just hasn't been transferred to you yet. If you don't fill out the forms, file the claims and follow the procedure, what is rightfully yours will just sit there, maybe forever.

MASTER INSURANCE CLAIMS TRACKING FORM

Policy No./ Description	Co. Name, Address	Contact Person/ Phone No.	Date Submitted	Follow-Up Dates	Date Acknowledged	Notes	Final Action

MASTER EMPLOYER BENEFITS TRACKING FORM

Benefit	Company	Contact Person	Phone No.	Date Contacted	Notes
Pension					
Profit Sharing					
Thrift Savings					
401(k)					
Medical Insurance					
Vacation					
Unpaid Payroll					
Life Insurance					

CHAPTER 3

CLAIMING EVERYTHING THAT'S YOURS FROM GOVERNMENT SOURCES

In addition to benefits through private resources discussed in Chapter 3, such as insurance policies, pensions and profit sharing plans, self-employment plans, IRAs, and other benefit programs, it's likely that you're entitled to a variety of government related benefits through Social Security, Veterans programs, and, if applicable, your spouse's government employment. This chapter will show you how to file with Uncle Sam to get everything that's yours from the government, starting with Social Security benefits.

The term "Social Security" conjures up all sorts of misinterpretations. As dispensed by the Social Security Administration, four basic areas of survivor benefits may be available to you:

- survivor insurance benefits;
- disability insurance benefits;
- supplemental income benefits; and
- Medicare.

Let's explore each one in order:

SOCIAL SECURITY SURVIVOR BENEFITS

If your mate paid into Social Security, you, and perhaps other family members as well, may qualify for survivors' benefits. Eligible family members include the surviving spouse, children, dependent parents and, in certain circumstances, surviving divorced spouses.

45

Benefits could include a one-time funeral payment, monthly survivors benefits, retirement income, disability income, and Medicare. It may be possible for a widowed person of any age, no matter how young, to qualify for Social Security benefits. Keep in mind that benefits are never sent to you automatically—you must apply for them.

General Eligibility For Benefits

Benefits are available to those who qualify under one of the following circumstances:

1. As the surviving spouse, you can receive full benefits—one hundred percent—at age 65 or older. Between ages 60–64, benefits range from 71–94 percent. If you are disabled, you can start receiving benefits as early as age 50.

2. As the surviving spouse, you can receive benefits at any age if you are caring for your children who are under age 16, or disabled. You will receive 75 percent of full benefits for each child.

3. Surviving children up to age 18.

4. Surviving children age 18–19, if they attend school full-time.

5. Surviving children over age 18 who became disabled before age 22.

6. Surviving divorced spouses age 60 or older, if married to the deceased spouse for ten years or longer.

7. The surviving parents of your spouse age 62 or older, if they were being supported by your spouse. You and any qualifying children are entitled to a percentage of your spouses age-65 benefit, even if he or she did not live to age 65.

There is a limit to the amount you can receive for yourself and for other family members. It can vary but it is usually between 100 to 180% of the full benefit rate. The amount paid to all of you is limited to what is called a family maximum benefit. This currently can range from a low of $576/month to as high as $2,299/month. Your Social Security office can give you an accurate determination of your family maximum.

Children's benefits are not affected if you remarry, even if your new spouse adopts them and contributes to their support. No adoption of a surviving child by any other person causes benefits to stop. Your children's benefits stop when they marry or they reach the age of 18. When your youngest surviving child marries or reaches age 16, your benefits also stop, but you can pick them up again at age 60 (or age 50 if you are disabled). Note that payments received from Social Security for children are considered the child's income, not yours.

You can receive survivors' benefits only if your spouse accumulated enough credits for work done as an employee or in self-employment; most workers earn four credits per year. The number of credits needed to receive benefits as a survivor depends on the age of your spouse at death, but the average is 40. However, under a special rule, benefits can be paid to you and your children even if your spouse had only 1-1/2 years of credit accumulated within the three years just before death.

Credit for work under Social Security had to be earned by your spouse before he/she was eligible for benefits. Social Security credits are earned during employment that is covered by the law after 1936 and for self-employment after 1950. Social Security coverage is measured by quarters of coverage. Wage earners and self employed people are credited with one quarter of coverage for each $520 earned (1990).

It does not matter when it is earned during the year and no more than 4 quarters of coverage may be credited during a calendar year. One quarter of coverage is credited for each dollar amount listed up to a maximum of 4 quarters per year. Once your spouse earned 40 quarters of coverage they are considered fully covered. The term fully insured means that your spouse and you and your dependents are eligible for most Social Security benefits. This does not govern the amount of the benefits. Only that you qualify for benefits.

Also, if your spouse was fully covered when he or she died, a one time $255 lump sum death benefit can be collected. However, it can only be paid to you if you were living with your spouse at the time of death, or to you as the widow or widower if you were not living with your spouse, but you demonstrate eligibility on your spouse's earnings records. As with all Social Security benefits, you need to apply for the one-time death benefit in order to receive it. They don't just send it!

Any Social Security checks addressed to your spouse that arrive after his or her death should be returned to the Social Security Administration. If the checks were directly deposited to a bank account, notify the bank to return them. The law requires that such checks be returned, and it's also an important part of establishing a legitimate basis for your own claims.

Staking Your Claim

Here's a summary of what you need to do to get what's coming to you from the Social Security Administration:

1. If you are not currently receiving Social Security benefits, act promptly. In some cases, benefits are not retroactive. Visit any Social Security office or phone the toll-free number, 1-800-772-1213, from 7 a.m. to 7 p.m., to find the office nearest you.

2. Have the following information handy; if you don't have it all available, apply anyway. You will need to submit original documents, or copies certified by the proper issuing office. You can mail or bring them to the Social Security office; the staff will make copies for you and return the documents if you request that they do so.

   a) Your Social Security number and your spouse's Social Security number.

   b) A death certificate.

   c) Proof of your spouse's worker earnings from the last year before death. W-2 forms are usually sufficient.

   d) Your birth certificate.

   e) A marriage certificate, if you're applying for benefits as a widowed individual or a divorced spouse.

   f) A divorce decree if you are a divorced spouse.

   g) Children's birth certificates and Social Security numbers, if you are applying for benefits for your offspring.

   h) Your checking or savings account information, if you want direct deposit of Social Security benefits made to one of those accounts.

3. If you're already receiving Social Security benefits from your spouse's account, report your spouse's death to the Social Security office; your payments will be changed to survivor benefits.

4. If you're receiving Social Security benefits from your own account, you'll need to fill out an application to receive survivors' benefits. The Social Security Office will calculate whether you would receive more as a widowed individual than you would receive under your own primary benefit, and will give you the plan that provides the highest payout.

A sample letter you can use to file a claim with the Social Security Administration is located on page 49. Feel free to photocopy it and adapt its language to your situation.

Sample Letter to Social Security Administration

_____(Date)_____

Social Security Administration
Department of Health and Human Services
Washington, DC 20201

Re: Name of Deceased:_____
     Social Sec. No.: _____
     Claimant:_____

Dear Staff:

The person whose Social Security number appears above passed away on ____(Date)____ at _____(City/State)_____ .

As a claimant under this Social Security account, I hereby request that you send the necessary forms to initiate a Clearance Claim and a Survivor's Claim.

Listed below are the names and dates of birth of our children:

_____(Name)_____	_____(Date of Birth)_____
_____(Name)_____	_____(Date of Birth)_____
_____(Name)_____	_____(Date of Birth)_____
_____(Name)_____	_____(Date of Birth)_____

Sincerely,

_____
(Your Signature)

_____
(Your Street Address)

_____
(Your City/State/Zip Code)

Divorced?—If you are divorced and your deceased ex-spouse was covered under Social Security you may still be eligible for Social Security benefits. To be eligible you must be at least 60 years old, or 50 and disabled, and had been married for at least 10 years. You can be any age if you are caring for a child that is eligible for benefits. Another qualification is that you cannot be currently married, unless the remarriage occurred after age 60, or 50 if you are disabled.

The easiest way to reach the Social Security Administration is to call their toll free number which is 1-800-772-1213. You can call anytime from 7:00 a.m. to 7:00 p.m., any business day. If you prefer to talk to someone in person, just call the "800" number; they will be happy to give you the address and phone number of the closest office.

Social Security benefit statement—You can obtain a detailed document from the Social Security Administration which gives an accurate estimate of your Social Security benefits by calling toll free 1-800-234-5772 and ask for form SSA-7004. The form requests some personal information such as your name, Social Security number, date of birth, previous years earnings, estimate of current year's earnings, planned age of retirement and projected earnings until retirement. However, you can get the estimate of your benefits due to your spouse's death by just giving the information on your deceased spouse, if the death occurred in this calendar year. Additionally, you may obtain information on your earnings, if you wish, by filling out a separate form.

SOCIAL SECURITY DISABILITY INSURANCE

If you are a disabled widow or widower, 50 years of age or older, you may also qualify for disability coverage from Social Security. Your disability must have started before your spouse's death or within seven years after it if you are a surviving ex-spouse and you are 50 years or older and your marriage lasted 10 years or longer. In addition, if you have dependent children they may be eligible for disability benefits if they are under age 18.

Call Social Security and ask for the following publication that covers disability; Social Security and SSI Benefits for Children with Disabilities, Publication #05-10026 or Publication #05-11000.

It is important for you to understand the definition of disability that the Social Security Administration uses. You are considered disabled only if you are unable to do any kind of work for which you are suited, and only if your inability to work is also expected to last for at least one year or result in death. Physical evidence from a physician or other source should show how severe the condition is and to what extent it prevents you from working.

NOTE: If you can do any other job that provides substantial gain you would not be considered disabled under Social Security law.

If you become disabled you should file for disability benefits as soon as possible. Do this by calling or visiting your local Social Security office. It may take as long as five or six months before disability benefits begin, so you need to plan accordingly.

SUPPLEMENTAL SECURITY INCOME

Supplemental security income, called SSI for short, is another program administered by the Social Security Administration. SSI makes monthly payments to people who have low incomes and very few assets. To obtain SSI you must be living in the United States or the Northern Marianna Islands, and you must be a U.S. citizen or living in the U.S. legally. In addition, you must be 65 or older, be blind, or disabled.

Your children also can qualify for SSI benefits if blind or considered disabled under Social Security rules. To qualify for SSI, your income and the value of your possessions must be below very low limits. Income here means *any* kind of income that you receive, such as Social Security or government checks, pensions, etc. Also non-cash items such as the value of free food and shelter may be counted.

Most people who receive SSI also get food stamps and Medicaid assistance. Medicaid, a different program than Medicare, helps pay doctor and hospital bills. (See Chapter 9). For more information, call Social Security and ask for Publications 05-10026, 05-10100 or 05-10095.

Correct Monthly Payments

How can you determine if you are receiving the correct amount of monthly payments from Social Security? William M. Mercer, Inc., the world's largest compensation/employee benefits consulting firm, publishes a pamphlet titled, *Guide to Social Security and Medicare*, which describes how Social Security benefits are computed. It includes worksheets for you to make calculations for yourself, however the calculations are complex and you'll need accurate records of your annual earnings before starting these calculations.

To get a copy of the Mercer pamphlet, send a check for $4.00 to William M. Mercer, Inc., 15 Hunter Meidinger Tower, Louisville, KY 40202-3415. Mark the envelope to the attention of Social Security Division.

If you calculate your earnings yourself, check your records against the Social Security Administration's figures. If their figures are wrong notify them immediately. You will need copies of your statements showing what your records state.

MEDICARE

The rising cost of health care has become a critical concern in our country. The ability to obtain quality health care service at cost-effective prices is a dilemma for many widowed persons. National statistics cite that senior citizens, of which widowed persons make up a large segment, is the fastest growing population segment in our country. Medicare is the health care alternative available through the government.

Offered for almost 20 years, the Medicare health program is ad-

CHAPTER 4

ministered under the Social Security Administration. There are two major parts to the program:

Hospital Insurance, and
Medical Insurance.

Hospital Insurance pays for in-patient hospital and certain follow-up care. Medical Insurance helps pay for doctors and many other medical services.

If you are 65 or older and receive either Social Security or Railroad Retirement Benefits, you are automatically eligible for the Medicare Hospital Insurance. As a surviving spouse, you are eligible if your spouse qualified under Social Security. The Medical Insurance is available for eligible Medicare recipients for a monthly premium of $31.80, currently. These premiums can be deducted automatically from your Social Security check.

If you have Medicare and have little income or assets you should know about a program that will help save you money. It is called the Qualified Medicaid Beneficiary or "QMB" program. If you qualify for help from the QMB program, your state will pay your monthly Medicare premiums, deductibles, and co-insurance. The rules vary from state to state, but in general you may qualify for the QMB program if your income is limited and your resources do not exceed certain limitations. Contact the Medicaid Agency, Social Security Office or Welfare Office for additional information.

Medical Insurance pays 80% of the reasonable and customary charges after a $75.00 per year deductible. Often there is a discrepancy between what Medicare pays and what you are charged. For example, suppose you have a major operation and the charges look like this:

Doctor's charge for operation	$40,000
Medicare's definition of reasonable payment	25,000
Medicare pays 80% of the $25,000	20,000
You pay	20,000

In this case Medicare pays only 50% of the total charges and you pay the difference. To protect yourself, consider buying a Medicare supplemental insurance policy. (See Chapter 9 on Insurance). This is purchased after you turn 65. Coverage and cost vary so you should shop for these "Medigap" policies.

With the hospitalization part of Medicare (Part A), Medicare pays hospitals according to what are called diagnosed illness. Each illness has a pre-determined hospital charge which Medicare is willing to pay to the hospital, regardless of how long you use a facility. For example, if the pre-determined cost of a heart operation is $30,000 and the hospital can get a patient out at a cost of $15,000, the hospital will make a $15,000 greater profit.

The final result is that you as a patient may be forced to leave the hospital perhaps before you should, and find you must have supplemental nursing care. Medicare will not pay for supplemental custodian nursing home care, yet these costs can be very high. Consider buying long term health care insurance to cover such unusual costs unless you have substantial assets.

CLAIMS IF YOUR SPOUSE WORKED FOR THE FEDERAL GOVERNMENT

Here's a checklist of government employee benefits and programs for which you may be eligible:

1. *Federal Employees Group Life Insurance (FEGLI) Claims*: Federal Employees Group Life Insurance is provided with various options for coverage including:

a) *Basic Insurance Amount*. This is coverage equal to the greater of a) your spouse's annual basic pay (rounded to the next $1000) plus $2,000, or b) $10,000. For employees age 35 or younger the basic benefit is double; beginning with age 36, the extra benefit decreases 10 percent each year, until at age 45, the extra benefit disappears.

b) *Accidental Death*. This feature doubles the amount payable under the Basic Insurance Amount if your spouse died as a result of bodily injury received solely through violent, external or accidental means.

c) *Option A—Standard*. If your spouse enrolled in 1) above, then this option, in the amount of $10,000, could have been purchased. Accidental Death benefits are available also on this coverage, thereby doubling it in the event of accidental death.

d) *Option B—Additional*. This option makes available amounts equal to one, two, three, four or five times the basic insurance amount.

A more complete description of insurance benefits is available in the *Federal Personnel Guide*, published by Key Communications Group Inc., Post Office Box 42578, Washington, DC 20015-0578.

Filing a Claim: Contact the employing office where your spouses' Official Personnel Folder, or its equivalent, is maintained. A claim form and instructions will be furnished to you.

2. *Survivor Claims Procedures after the Death of Your Spouse for Civil Service Retirement System (CSRS) or Federal Employees Retirement System (FERS) Annuities:*

a) Return any uncashed annuity checks to the return address shown on the envelope in which the check was delivered. If annuity payments have been sent directly to the bank or other financial institutions, promptly notify that institution of your spouse's date of death. Ask that any payments received after the date of death be returned to the Treasury Department.

b) Notify the Office of Personnel Management, Employee Service and Records Center, Boyers, PA 16017, of your spouse's death so they can send an application (Standard Form 2800) for survivor benefits. Use of this address will expedite your claim.

c) Obtain a certified copy of the death certificate to enclose with the application that the Office of Personnel Management will send. OPM prefers that the applicant wait for the official application, and that it be completed and returned promptly after receipt. While awaiting return of the application, OPM will have completed certain preliminary actions so that the application can be expedited.

The sample letter on page 55 is supplied by the National Association of Retired Federal Employees, 1533 New Hampshire Avenue, NW, Washington, DC 20036 (202-234-0832). It can be used to expedite your claims for funds from the federal government.

Sample Notification Letter
Federal Government Employee Claims

_____(Date)_____

Office of Personnel Management
Employee Service and Records Center
Boyers, PA 16017

Dear Staff:

This is to report the death of the following named annuitant:

Name of Annuitant:_____

Claim Number: _(CSA/CSF)_____

Social Security Number:_____

Birth Date: _____ Date of Death:_____

Send application forms to: _____

_____

I will return all uncashed Treasury checks payable to the deceased, and any which may hereafter be received.

If the payments have been directed to a bank, I have asked that such payments be returned.

Sincerely,

_____(Your Signature)_____

NOTE: Add the following paragraph, if applicable:

The deceased had "Self and Family" health benefits coverage, which I wish to be reduced to "Self Only" with the premium rate adjusted accordingly, unless I notify you that minor children also survive, for whom I want coverage.

VETERANS BENEFITS

If your partner was a veteran, you and your children may qualify for veterans benefits. These include burial in a national cemetery (there are over 100 throughout the country), an allowance for burial expenses, transportation of the remains to the nearest national cemetery, a headstone or grave marker, and an American flag to drape the casket.

In the event your spouse has been buried in a private cemetery, either by preference or because you were unaware of the veterans benefits, you can still apply for burial reimbursement and other benefits, but you must do so within two years of the date of death.

Veterans Life Insurance. There are several life insurance programs under which a veteran may be covered. If you wish to file a claim, or receive information about veterans life insurance benefits, be sure to provide the insured's full name, policy number, date of birth and Social Security number.

For those who served prior to 1965, there are five plans, listed below, administered by the Veterans Administration regional office and insurance centers in St. Paul, Minnesota, and Philadelphia, Pennsylvania:

1. *United States Government Life Insurance.*

2. *National Service Life Insurance.*

3. *Veterans Special Life Insurance.*

4. *Service-Disabled Veterans Insurance.*

5. *Veterans Reopened Insurance.*

For more specific information, Call the Veterans Administration at 1-800-827-8244, or write directly to the VA office closest to you.

Also, here are two life insurance programs for those who were on active duty:

6. *Servicemen's Group Life Insurance,* set up in September, 1965, to provide group coverage to members on active duty. Benefits have since been extended to ready reservists, retired reservists and National Guard members. The maximum coverage is $50,000. If your spouse was covered under one of these policies, call your local Veterans Administration office, *not* the Philadelphia or St. Paul offices.

7. *Veterans Group Life Insurance,* established in August, 1974, to provide for the conversion of SGLI to five-year, non-renewable term coverage. If your spouse owned a VGLI policy, call the Veterans Administration office closest to you to make a claim.

These two types of coverage are administered by the Office of Servicemen's Group Life Insurance, 213 Washington Street, Newark, New Jersey 07102, to which you can write if you have questions about either of these programs.

Educational Assistance for Dependents. If your spouse's death was service-connected, or if death occurred while your spouse was completely disabled from service-connected causes, the Veterans Administration will pay a monthly allowance to help educate you or your children. Payments are usually provided for children 18–26 years of age. The benefits to your children are not canceled if they marry, but your remarriage would terminate educational benefits to you.

Dependency and Indemnity Compensation. Payments are available for surviving spouses and/or the surviving children due to veterans dying on or after January 1, 1957 from:

1. a disease or injury incurred or aggravated in line of duty while on active duty or active duty for training.

2. an injury incurred or aggravated in line of duty while on in-active duty training.

There are many possible ways to obtain payments and the subject should be followed thoroughly to see if benefits apply.

Non-service Connected Death Pension. Death pension may be paid to eligible surviving spouses and children of veterans who had 90 days or more of wartime service or who had less than 90 days of wartime service but were separated from such service for a service-connected disability, who have died of causes not related to their service.

Making A Veterans Administration Claim

If your spouse was in the military and you believe you have a valid claim in one or more areas, assemble the following information before contacting the Veterans Affairs office.

1. Certified copy or original Form DD214, Enlisted Record and Report of Separation.

2. Certified copy of your original marriage certificate.

3. Certified copy of your spouse's death certificate.

4. The amount of life insurance proceeds you expect to receive as a result of your spouse's death.

5. Paid receipts for funeral and cemetery expenses.

6. Paid receipts for hospital and doctors' bills incurred during your spouse's last illness.

7. Social Security numbers for yourself and your dependent children.

8. If your spouse was previously married, you will need an original or certified copy of the divorce decree, or the former spouse's death certificate.

9. If you have dependent children under age 18, or children who are over 18 but still in school, you'll need originals or certified copies of their birth certificates. In addition, if your children are over 18 and still in school, you will need to complete a form for possible benefits for them.

CHAPTER 4

10. If you are currently receiving Social Security benefits, you will need to show the exact amount of benefits you receive.

11. Your VA claim number, if you already have one, has to be furnished to Veterans Administration staff.

Gathering these documents is an essential part of your overall strategy to secure your financial future. You may not like doing it—few people do—but once you're armed with the proper documents it's much easier to claim what's rightfully yours.

SOCIAL SECURITY AND RETIREMENT

The United States Congress in 1975, disturbed by the high rate of inflation, passed a law that allows Social Security benefits to rise automatically with inflation. The adjustment for next year is the rate of inflation based on the Consumer Price Index in the third quarter of the previous year. It is announced in October and begins in January. In 1991 the adjustment for 1992 was set at 3.7%. For 1991 it was set at 5.4% and for 1990 it was set at 4.7%. This is an important feature of your benefits—without it, your benefits could be diminished by 50% or more in less than 10 years, due to inflation.

The usual retirement age in America remains at age 65. The Social Security Administration regards this as the age at which those qualifying may receive full retirement benefit. In the year 2000, retirement age will be moved up to 67 and will affect people born in 1938 and thereafter. The table below shows the ages that full retirement Social Security benefit is available.

Your Year of Birth	Full Benefits available when age:
1938	65 years, 2 months
1939	65 years, 4 months
1940	65 years, 6 months
1941	65 years, 8 months
1942	65 years, 10 months
1943–1954	66 years, 0 months
1955	66 years, 2 months
1956	66 years, 4 months
1957	66 years, 6 months
1958	66 years, 8 months
1959	66 years, 10 months
1960 & Later	67 years, 0 months

Taking early benefits—You can start your Social Security benefits as early as age 62 but the benefit amount you receive will be permanently less than your full retirement benefits. Early retirement reduces your monthly benefit by 5/9ths of one percent per month prior to age 65. For example, at age 62 you would currently receive 80% of your age 65 benefit; at age 63 you would receive 86-2/3%; at age 64 you would receive 93-1/3%.

> **NOTE:** When the phase-in to normal retirement age of 67 is complete, early retirement at age 62 will yield only 70% of what the full benefit would generate.

As a general rule, early retirement gives you about the same total Social Security benefits over your lifetime, assuming you live to your life expectancy. The smaller amount at early retirement takes into account the longer period you would receive them. Assuming everything remains constant, if you wait until age 65 to receive normal retirement benefit, you will be 77 years old before you reach a break-even point.

If you take the retirement benefit at age 62 and invested that money for the 3-year early retirement period, the interest earned on that money would more than offset the money lost due to drawing early retirement benefits. In other words, by waiting until age 65 until you start receiving benefits, you would never catch up. Hence, if you have the discipline to invest the early benefits, you'll fare better.

Delaying your benefits—If you delay taking your full retirement benefit by a year or more, you can increase your Social Security benefit in two ways:

1. If you are working, you could be adding a year of high earnings to your Social Security record. Your higher lifetime average earnings may result in higher benefits.

2. Your benefits will be increased by a certain percentage for each year you delay retirement. These increases are added automatically from the time you reach your full retirement age until you begin taking your benefits up to age 70. The percentage varies depending on your date of birth.

For example, if your were born in 1935, 6% will be added to your benefit for each year you delay Social Security retirement benefits.

> **NOTE:** Should you decide to delay your retirement, make sure you sign up for Medicare at age 65. In some cases the medical insurance costs more if you delay applying for it. See the section on Medicare in Chapter 9.

C
H
A
P
T
E
R

4

If you're under age 70, there is a limit on the amount you can earn and still collect full Social Security retirement benefits. Under age 65 your benefits are reduced by $1 for each $2 earned over $10,440. Between the ages of 65 and 69 you will loose $1 of Social Security for every $3 earned above $10,200.

DOES IT PAY TO WORK BEYOND AGE 65?

Suppose you're age 65, and earn $20,000 in 1992. You will lose $1 for every $3 of earnings over $10,200.

$20,000
–10,200
$ 9,800/3 = $3,266 lost Social Security

You'll also have to pay taxes (assume 15% federal and 5% state on the total $20,000) as well as FICA taxes on the income:

Federal at 15%	$3,000
State at 5%	1,000
FICA at 7.65%	1,530
	$5,530

Hence, your total "taxes" equal $8,796 ($3,266 + 5,530) on the $20,000 and your net after-tax is only $11,204.

If you'd only earned the $10,200 limit, you'd keep $8,160.

$10,200
–1,530 federal tax
–510 state tax
$ 8,160

To make $3,044 additional in net earning, you have to earn a gross of $9,800 more—not much of an incentive for most people!

There is no limit over age 70 on the amount of money you can earn. You can earn as much as you want without having benefits reduced.

GETTING ORGANIZED— BRINGING ORDER TO YOUR FINANCIAL HOUSE

A key to making your money last is developing a well-thought-out approach to financial management. Your first step to building a plan is to organize your finances according to a step-by-step procedure. Right now your future is full of financial questions. The secure feeling you had when your spouse was with you is probably gone. One way to begin alleviating your concerns is to determine where you stand financially.

Like most people, you've probably thought you'd be in better financial shape if you had a workable financial plan. However, just the thought of where to start and how to do it was enough to make you shudder. Developing a plan was something you'd do "later," but "later" never came. Now, with your spouse gone, "no planning" might mean that you will run out of money before you run out of life.

As mentioned in Chapter 2 you should set up a filing system to keep everything organized. Here are some suggested file topics:

Suggested File Headings

Bank statements	Social Security records
Automobile insurance	Divorce agreement
Charge accounts statements	Birth certificates
IRA statements	Death certificates
Health insurance information	Marriage certificate
Life insurance information	Military discharge papers
Wills	Stock brokerage statements
Living wills	Certificates of deposit
Powers of Attorney	Real estate titles and deeds
Trusts agreements	Mortgage statements

Investment statements   Title Insurance
Income tax information   Auto registrations, etc.
Property and Casualty insurance information   Mutual fund info
Pre-nuptial/Post-nuptial agreements   Stock option plans
Pension accounts   Partnership Info
401(k) accounts   Business real estate
Safe deposit box information

It takes motivation, time and effort to put your financial house in order. The method and the worksheets in this chapter will guide you, but first you must learn about, and generate, two important documents:

1. *A Net Worth Statement*, also sometimes called a balance sheet. This is a listing, first, of all the assets you own or are about to receive, and their established or estimated value; second, your liabilities—that is, what you owe; and, third, your "net worth" which is determined by subtracting your liabilities from your assets.

Your net worth is an important statement about you. It reveals crucial financial information to which you will refer again and again for future planning. Not only does your net worth indicate what you and your spouse accomplished financially during your life together, it is the critical amount you have available to plan for your future.

2. *A Cash Flow Statement*. This is simply a list of all the incoming funds from every source, along with a record of all your expenses, usually by category. The cash flow statement will show you how much money is coming in, where it is going, and the impact of taxes on your cash flow resources.

DETERMINING YOUR NET WORTH

The first step in determining your net worth is difficult but important: assembling and organizing all your financial data to calculate your net worth. A sample net worth statement appears on the next page, completed for "Martha Young."

Your net worth statement can be general or very detailed. Following the "Martha Young" sample, is a blank net worth form that is simplified and another that is detailed; which sample you use depends on the amount and variety of your assets and on your level of financial sophistication. Regardless of which form you use, be sure you include everything. If you don't know the exact value of an asset, estimate its worth.

—SAMPLE—
MARTHA YOUNG
NET WORTH STATEMENT

ASSETS		TOTALS
Cash Reserves (less than 12 months maturity)		
Checking Accounts	$ 20,000	
Money Market Funds	20,450	
Life Insurance Proceeds	125,000	
Other: Series EE Bonds	7,000	
		$172,450
Invested Assets		
Tax Deferred Annuities	$ 90,000	
Municipal Bonds	86,000	
Individual Stocks	22,500	
Stock Mutual Funds	150,000	
Investment Real Estate	150,000	
401(k) Proceeds	17,500	
		516,000
Personal Use Assets		
Home @ Market Value	$200,000	
Household Furnishings	40,000	
Automobiles	15,500	
		255,500
TOTAL ASSETS		$943,950
LIABILITIES (Debts)		
Mortgage on Residence	$ 12,500	
Mortgage on Rental Unit	70,000	
		–82,500
NET WORTH		
Total Assets Less Total Liabilities		$861,450

Simplified Net Worth Statement

A. What You Own:	Current Value	% of Total Assets
Liquid Assets		
Checking Accounts	$_____	
Savings Accounts	_____	
Money Mkt. Funds	_____	
Cash Value of Your Life Insurance	_____	
Other	_____	
TOTAL LIQUID ASSETS	$_____	_____ %
Investment Assets		
Stocks	$_____	
Bonds	_____	
Mutual Funds	_____	
Certs. of Deposit	_____	
Retirement Plans:		
IRAs	_____	
401(k)	_____	
Pension Plans	_____	
Other	_____	
Miscellaneous	_____	
TOTAL INVESTMENT ASSETS	$_____	_____ %
Personal Assets		
Residence	$_____	
Vacation Property	_____	
Jewelry	_____	
Art/Antiques	_____	
Other	_____	
TOTAL PERSONAL ASSETS	$_____	_____ %
B. What You Owe (Liabilities):		
Credit Cards	$_____	
Banks	_____	
Car Loans	_____	
Personal Installment Loans	_____	
Education Loans	_____	
Mortgages	_____	
Other	_____	
TOTAL LIABILITIES	$_____	_____ %

Total Assets	$ _____
Less: Total Liabilities	− _____
YOUR NET WORTH	$ _____

Detailed Net Worth Statement

	Current/ Est. Value	Total		Current/ Est. Value	Total
ASSETS			**Personal Use Assets**		
Cash Reserves			Home (Market Val)	$ _____	
Checking Accts	$ _____		Household Furn.	_____	
Cred. Union Shares			2nd Residence	_____	
Savings Accts	_____		Motor Vehicles	_____	
Money Mkt.Funds	_____		Camper/RV	_____	
U.S. Sav. Bonds	_____		Jewelry/Furs	_____	
Treasury Bills	_____		Art/Antiques	_____	
Life Ins. Cash	_____		Time Share	_____	
Values	_____		Other	_____	$ _____
Other	_____	$ _____	TOTAL ASSETS	_____	$ _____
Investment Assets					
Stocks	$ _____		**LIABILITIES**		
Bonds			Home Mortgage	$ _____	
Stock Mutual Funds	_____		Other Mortgages	_____	
Bond Mutual Funds	_____		Auto Loans	_____	
Bond Unit Trust	_____		Credit Cards	_____	
Certs. of Deposit	_____		Install. Loans	_____	
Notes Receivables	_____		Private Loans	_____	
Deferred Annuity	_____		Taxes Owed	_____	
Series E Bonds	_____		Brokerage Margin Accounts	_____	
Investment R.E	_____		Education Loans	_____	
Limited Partnerships	_____		Retirement Plan Loans	_____	
Collectibles	_____		Other	_____	$ _____
Business Value	_____				
IRA Accounts	_____		TOTAL LIABILITIES	$ _____	_____ %
Keogh Accounts	_____				
401(k)/403(b)	_____		Total Assets		$ _____
Pension/Profit Sharing	_____		Less: Total Liabilities		− _____
Other	_____	$ _____	YOUR NET WORTH		$ _____

CHAPTER 5

As you can see, the basic factors that make up your net worth statement include:

1. *Cash Reserves*, or money set aside for use in an emergency. These are liquid funds that can be obtained on very short notice.

2. *Investment Assets* are all the assets you set aside to generate long-term streams of income, or build toward a particular financial goal, such as your retirement, inflation hedges, college for children, and travel.

3. *Personal Use Assets* are resources you use every day—your home or your car, for example—or assets you use for enjoyment, such as a boat or a camper.

4. *Liabilities* are simply what you owe or what you and your spouse owed together.

As a widowed person, you're likely to have need for liquidity and safety. Often the dollars left to you are all the money there's going to be, and those funds have to last for your lifetime. Your desire for liquidity and safety is counter-balanced by your need for inflation-fighting growth in some of your assets. There is really no "correct formula" to determine how much cash you should have available for emergencies, but the following approach has worked well for many:

1. Retain, in an interest-bearing checking account, sufficient cash to cover all of one month's expenses. This means that after you have paid all your expenses for one month, you still will have the equivalent of one month's funds left in your checking account.

2. Keep a minimum of five additional months' expenses in a money market account, or other fairly liquid investment. For example, if your monthly expenses are $3,000, you would keep $15,000 in an easily accessible account. Many widowed persons keep up to a year's equivalent in this type of account.

3. If you have other assets to which you have quick access, such as certificates of deposit, insurance or securities, you can reduce somewhat the amounts mentioned in paragraph 2. However, it is wise to stay within your comfort zone; this is intended to be "peace-of-mind" money.

Analyzing Your Net Worth Statement. First, look at what you have. If you have a high percentage of your assets in easily accessible cash reserves, they may not be producing enough growth for the long term.

If your assets are largely in speculative stocks—perhaps those inherited from your spouse—you may be fighting inflation, but risking the loss of principal.

Next, take a look at your liabilities. How do your liabilities compare to your overall assets on a percentage basis? For example, Joan has $90,000 in debts and only $140,000 in assets, mostly in her home. Her debt-to-asset ratio is $90,000 to $140,000, or 64 percent. One of Joan's goals might be to restructure her debts and build up her assets by refinancing her home, using the savings generated from lower mortgage payments to reduce debts, or build investments.

Your assets may contain a large amount of cash reserves because of the lump sum life insurance payment resulting from your spouse's death. This is a temporary situation, because a portion of these funds will probably become investment assets to provide growth and income to you in future years.

DEVELOPING A CASH FLOW STATEMENT

Most of your cash inflows will be what is usually considered income. The term "inflows" is used because it's all-encompassing—including, for example, a loan that someone is repaying that might not necessarily represent taxable income to you. The same applies for the term "outflows." Everything you pay in a given year is an outflow. Some are deductible expenses on your federal and state income tax returns, and some are not. For purposes of tracing what's happening to your cash, the term "outflows" yields a more useful picture of where you stand.

Check your most recent pay stubs if you work outside the home, as well as brokerage accounts, tax returns, bank statements and retirement survivor statements. Include any rents you receive on real estate, tax refunds and proceeds of any stocks. If you know the monthly amounts from pensions, annuities, Social Security or other benefits, enter them. If not, you may need to make a few calls to come up with a close estimate.

Total all these items so you will have a total cash inflow figure for the year. On page 69 you will find a simplified cash flow worksheet, followed by a detailed cash flow worksheet. Use the one that's best for your situation to plot the cash that's coming in, versus the cash that's going out on an annual basis.

What you want from your cash flow worksheet is a representative "snapshot" of your best "guesstimate" for the coming year. Outflows have a way of escalating—be sure to include a healthy guesstimate in each area.

C
H
A
P
T
E
R

5

Now that you have the numbers, look for categories or expenses that can be controlled. Can you cut back, or is there an unusual expense that won't recur? Will some expenses drop or increase dramatically? High cost in certain areas may indicate that you need to consider a financial step, such as refinancing your home, consolidating loans or streamlining insurance costs.

Actual Versus Estimate. Your net cash flow can be either positive or negative. As you receive the inflows and spend the outflows, you're actual experience may, and in all likelihood WILL differ from what you put on the planning sheet. If the planning sheet indicates that you will have a surplus of, say $5,000 at the end of the year, and it's clear by May that you've fallen behind, perhaps you understated one or more of your outflow items or overstated one or more of your inflow items.

Examine your checkbook, looking especially at the amount of cash you're withdrawing every week for spending money; perhaps there's "seepage" somewhere—an outflow that you did not include in your planning. In any case, continue to revise your cash flow plotting sheets, so that they more closely reflect reality, and you always have the latest figures to use in financial planning.

A Cash Flow Control Plan. One way to put yourself in control of your cash flow is to establish two separate checking accounts.

The first account can be a money market fund or traditional checking account. This account is to handle all the expenses that always seem to come at the wrong time or in the wrong amounts. These expenses are usually ones that do not reoccur monthly, but can still be programmed. Examples are once-a-year and occasional expenses such as auto insurance, travel and leisure activities, real estate taxes, and estimated tax payments.

One of the first steps in setting up this approach is to identify all these occasional expenses. Most widowed persons feel comfortable with keeping a 6-month or one-year reserve in this account to cover these occasional programmed expenses. If you don't have an interest-bearing checking account, you can place some of the funds in a money market fund so that temporarily idle funds are earning some interest. As expenses are covered from this account, the account is replenished to always keep the reserve intact.

The second checking account—a traditional checking account or "Regular Account"—will be used to pay most of your regular bills and recurring monthly expenses, including cash you withdraw to spend on incidentals.

This system is simple and effective, because it helps you separate monthly living costs from occasional expenses, as well as money used for savings and investments. Meanwhile, the programmed account is drawing interest while you are writing fewer checks on it, and the Regular Account is also drawing interest while you are drawing more checks against it. In this way, you're optimizing the use of your checking accounts.

Simplified Annual Cash Flow Planning Sheet

	Amount	Total
Cash Inflows		
Wages, Salary, Commissions	$ _____	
Dividends and Interest	_____	
Annuities, Social Security, Pensions	_____	
Rents	_____	
Other	_____	$ _____
Cash Outflows		
Housing	$ _____	
Food	_____	
Clothing	_____	
Transportation	_____	
Utilities	_____	
Taxes	_____	
Insurance	_____	
Education	_____	
Child Care	_____	
Entertainment	_____	
Vacations/Travel	_____	
Gifts/Donations	_____	
Other	_____	_____
Net Cash Flow		$ _____

Subtract your estimated cash outflows from your estimated annual cash inflows. If the result is a plus, you'll likely finish the year in a positive cash flow situation. If the result is a minus, you are spending more than your income, and you are headed for trouble.

CHAPTER 5

Detailed Annual Cash Flow Planning Sheet

	Amount		Amount
Income		Housing Expenses *(continued)*	
Salary	$ _____	Insurance: Fire,	$ _____
Self-Employment Income	_____	Liability,	
Interest:		Homeowners, Theft	
Savings	_____	Assessments,	_____
Money Market Funds	_____	Special Taxes	
Credit Union	_____	Other	_____
Certificates of Deposit	_____	Total Housing Expenses	$ _____
Bonds	_____		
Other	_____	Household Expenses	
Dividends:		Gas	$ _____
Stocks	_____	Electricity	_____
Bonds	_____	Phone	_____
Mutual Funds	_____	Water/Sewer	_____
Rental Income	_____	Trash/Garbage Pickup	
Partnership Income	_____	Groceries/Supplies	_____
Annuity Income	_____	Cleaning Costs	_____
Pension Income	_____	Water Softener Service	_____
IRA Income	_____	Gardening/Lawn Service	_____
Civil Service Benefits	_____	Cable TV	_____
Social Security Income	_____	Home Maintenance	_____
Veterans Benefits Income	_____	Home Improvements	_____
Child Support/Alimony from		Appliance Repair	_____
previous marriage	_____	Major Purchases: Rugs,	
Tax Refunds	_____	Furnishings, etc.	_____
Bonuses, Gifts	_____	Other	_____
401(k) or 403(b) Income	_____	Total Household Expenses	$ _____
Other	_____		
		Personal Expenses	
TOTAL INCOME	$ _____	Misc. & Pocket Cash	$ _____
		Clothing	_____
Expenses		Drycleaning/Laundry	_____
Housing Expenses		Cosmetics/Hair Care	_____
Rent/Mortgage/		Entertainment/Hobbies	
Condo Fee	$ _____	Vacations/Travel	_____
Property Taxes	_____	Education	_____
Homeowner's Fees	_____	Dues/Membership Fees	_____
		Pets/Pet Care	_____

Amount

Personal Expenses *(continued)*

Charity	_____
Gifts/Religious Inst.	_____
Other	_____
Total Personal Expenses	$ _____

Children's Expenses

Tuition	$ _____
Room/Board at School	_____
Travel To/From School	_____
School Visitations	_____
Books & Supplies	_____
Summer Camp	_____
Lessons: Music, Dance	_____
Sports Activities	_____
Lunch Money	_____
Allowance	_____
Entertainment	_____
Child Care/Babysitters	_____
Other	_____
Total Children's Exp.	$ _____

Medical Expenses

Doctors	$ _____
Dentists	_____
Specialists	$ _____
Prescription Drugs	_____
Lab Fees	_____
Glasses	_____
Other	_____
Total Medical Expenses	$ _____

Transportation Expenses

Car Loan/Lease	$ _____
Car Insurance	_____
Gas/Oil	_____
Maintenance	_____
Tires	_____
Tolls, Fares	_____
License Fees/Tags	_____
Other	_____
Total Transp. Expenses	$ _____

Amount

Insurance Expenses

Life	$ _____
Disability	_____
Group	_____
Accident	_____
Health	_____
Other	_____
Total Insurance Expenses	$ _____

Taxes (If Not Included Elsewhere)

Federal Income Taxes	$ _____
FICA (Social Security)	_____
State Income Taxes	_____
State Sales Taxes	_____
City/Local Taxes	_____
Personal Property Tax	_____
Other	_____
Total Tax Expenses	$ _____

Category Expense Totals

Housing	$ _____
Household	_____
Personal	_____
Children	_____
Medical	_____
Transportation	_____
Taxes	_____
Miscellaneous	_____
TOTAL EXPENSES	$ _____
List Your Total Income	$ _____
Subtract Total Expenses	– _____

NET CASH FLOW REMAINING $ _____
FOR SAVINGS & INVESTMENT

VALUABLE DOCUMENTS AND SAFE STORAGE

Another aspect of getting organized is physically securing valuables and important documents. Such items should be sorted and kept in a fire-proof safe or safety deposit box. A safety deposit box is the best choice for storage outside your house, though it's wise to keep photocopies of original papers in a file at home.

In general, store only those documents and valuables which are irreplaceable in the safe deposit box; if they're replaceable, they can be covered by insurance. Here is a list of items to keep in a safe deposit box:

- Adoption papers;
- Automobile titles;
- Original birth certificates;
- Valuable books;
- Certificates of deposit;

- Citizenship papers;
- Coin collections;
- Contracts;
- Copyrights;
- Court decrees;

- Death certificates;
- Deeds and titles;
- Divorce decrees;
- Employment contracts;
- Household inventory for insurance purposes;

- List of life and disability insurance policies;
- Jewelry;
- Valued letters;
- Original marriage certificates;
- Military discharge papers;

- Mortgages;

- Naturalization papers;

- Patents;

- Pension certificates;

- Treasured photo negatives;

- Promissory notes;

- Savings certificates;

- Social Security card;

- Stock or bond certificates;

- Trust agreements;

- Veterans Administration papers;

- Videotape of household contents;

- Copies of your will.

If you have a power of attorney agreement, which gives someone else the right to act in your behalf should you become incapacitated, then don't keep the power of attorney document in your safe deposit box. It's a better arrangement for the person to whom you grant the power to retain one copy of it, and for you to retain another in your personal files at home.

If you've computed your net worth, determined your cash flows, and safely stored what needs to be stored, you can take a deep breath and relax a bit now. The preliminary planning is a great deal of work, but it's done and out of the way.

Estate Income/Expenses Record Book

Any income received that was due your spouse prior to death should be deposited in a separate bank account (also see Chapter on Estate Settlement). This could include dividends, work related income, etc.

During your visit to your local bank, discuss what is involved in setting up an estate account. Until then, keep track of any checks you receive, including date, amount and who the payer is. Also keep receipts and record them for expenses incurred to settle the estate.

CHECKLIST OF
LOCATION OF IMPORTANT DOCUMENTS

	Safe Deposit Box	Office	Residence
Wills			
Trust Agreements			
Powers of Attorney			
Burial instructions			
Cemetery deeds			
Safe combination			
Employment benefits			
Employment contracts			
Pension records			
Social Security records			
Life insurance policies			
Home & car insurance			
Birth certificates			
Passports			
Naturalization papers			
Military discharge			
Marriage certificates			
Partnership agreements			
Checking accounts records			
Savings accounts			
Credit card records			
Certificates of deposit			
Record of investments			
Stock & bond certificates			
Tax returns			
Real estate titles and deeds			
Mortgage papers			
Notes payable/receivable			
Ownership records:			
Auto			
Boat			
Recreational property			

SETTLING YOUR SPOUSE'S ESTATE

The burden of settling your spouse's estate usually rests entirely with you, but don't let that scare you. Following the death of a spouse, the surviving spouse most often is named as executor or personal representative, and is responsible either for carrying out the terms of the will, or for settling the estate according to the laws of the state in which you live.

The term "settling the estate" describes the process of collecting assets, filing inventories of accounts, paying claims, completing administrative details and distributing any remaining assets. More broadly defined, "settling the estate" is the process of legally transferring title to property currently in your spouse's estate to the heirs, or confirming title to property the heirs already have in their possession.

> **NOTE:** Don't be intimidated by the phrase "settling the estate," or by the tasks involved. When you have taken care of the basic items discussed here, in essence, you will have settled your spouse's estate.

Estate administration can be extremely complex or relatively simple —it largely depends on how many and what type of assets are involved. It is not the purpose of this book for you to prepare a complete estate administration by yourself, although that may be possible if the estate is simple and has few assets. However, few surviving spouses have the training or temperament to do so, especially in the aftermath of their loss. In many cases, the best advice is to seek competent legal assistance.

Even if an expert does most of the work, you need to be familiar with estate administration so that you will know what your attorney is doing and you won't feel threatened by the process.

Whether you bring in professionals or initiate the proceedings yourself, you'll need to collect certain information about your spouse, about the estate and about yourself. Much of this information is described in Chapter 2, but it is presented here, in brief form, to aid you. All official documents—for example, birth, marriage and death certificates, military papers, deeds, etc.—should be originals or certified copies.

1. Your spouse's will. Find it and read it right away. Studying a copy of the will is okay, but you'll need the original to start the settlement process.

2. Any trusts established by your spouse or any trust for which your spouse may have acted as trustee.

3. Retirement plan information, including pension, profit sharing, 401(k), IRAs and self-employment plans.

4. Any business agreements to which your spouse was a party, and accompanying company books and records.

5. Birth certificates for you, your spouse and your children.

6. Military discharge papers.

7. Marriage certificate.

8. Any existing prenuptial agreements.

9. Divorce papers.

10. Adoption papers for your children, if applicable.

11. Deeds to property owned or co-owned by you and your spouse.

12. Registration papers for your spouse's motor vehicles, boats, etc.

13. Bank account statements.

14. Securities certificates and account statements.

15. Tax returns for the last two years, and the most recent W-2 forms from your spouse's employer, and 1099 forms.

16. Any loan documents, including mortgages.

17. Life insurance policy information, both those on the life of your spouse and any your spouse may have owned on the lives of others.

18. Health, travel and accident, disability, property and auto insurance policy information.

19. Membership statements and benefit descriptions for all clubs and organizations.

20. Credit card information.

21. Citizenship papers, if applicable.

22. Social Security cards.

23. Death certificates.

24. Inventory of all assets in the estate.

25. Inventory of safe deposit box, if available (also covered in Chapter 3).

SIMPLIFIED PROCEDURE ONCE THE WILL IS READ

- Determine who is the executor, or personal representative.

- File the will with probate court.

- Have the court issue Letters of Appointment certifying the authority of the personal representative.

Helpful Pointers

1. Prepare yourself to answer a lot of questions, even some that may seem pointless. You can expect questions about:
   - property owned individually or jointly by your spouse;
   - how to contact your legal or financial advisors; and
   - Social Security numbers for you, your spouse and, possibly, your children.

   Depending on who's asking—for instance, court officials, your attorney, accountant or financial planner—it may be appropriate to provide the names, addresses, phone and Social Security numbers of your spouse and of all your spouse's beneficiaries.

2. If you think your spouse had life insurance, but you can't find the policy and don't know the name of the issuing company, send a stamped, self-addressed envelope to:

   American Council of Life Insurance
   (Policy Search ACCI)
   1001 Pennsylvania Avenue, N.W.
   Washington, DC 20004

   They will initiate a free search for you.

CHAPTER 6

3. Contact the state Office for Inheritance Tax, usually listed under state agencies in the phone book. If your state imposes an inheritance tax—a tax on people receiving property from a decedent—ask for the release forms.

4. If you can't locate your spouse's will, perhaps you can find the attorney who drafted it. The attorney's name may be in an address book, a pile of business cards, the personal papers in your spouse's office or desk, the checkbook register, or on a canceled check. Original wills are often kept in the safe of the attorney who prepared them.

   If the will is in a safe deposit box, you may be permitted to open the box if you have the key and you were a joint signer on the box. If state law requires that the box be sealed upon death, you will probably have to file a petition with the probate court for permission to open the box and search for the will.

Professional Advisors

Once you've found the will and have read it, you may want to hire an attorney or other professionals to help you settle the estate and get your legal and financial affairs in order. If you follow the steps already outlined, you will be giving your advisors a "head start," and you will probably reduce the time they will need to spend and the cost of their services. Chapter 17 specifically discusses the qualifications of various advisors, but a synopsis is provided below.

Lawyers can do everything required to settle an estate, including probate. They also can help to collect survivors' benefits, deal with creditors, prepare or modify your own will, and draft other estate planning documents.

Accountants can prepare estate and income tax returns, advise about financial matters, minimize taxes, and help with financial decision-making.

Financial Planners can assist you in choosing financial goals, developing strategies to reach them, and can help to invest insurance proceeds to achieve your objectives.

A major factor in hiring an expert, one that will be essential to your working relationship, is trust. You also need to feel comfortable about asking questions and voicing your concerns, and secure that your advisors can provide answers, educate you if necessary, and won't push you to take actions about which you feel ill at ease. If you're not happy with a professional advisor, say so. Then, after weighing all the factors, if you're still unhappy, feel free to change advisors.

Understanding Probate

Probate is the process of law that proves the authenticity of your spouse's will (or that there is no will) and oversees the distribution of probate property to the creditors and rightful heirs. It is usually handled by the office of the registrar of wills or the clerk of the court.

Assets may be considered "probate" or "non-probate." Non-probate holdings are those that pass to survivors independently of the will, and, with the possible exception of federal and state death taxes, are not subject to claims of your spouse's creditors.

You do not need to report non-probate assets to the court. If your spouse's entire estate is composed of non-probate assets and there are no minor children to consider, no probate is required, and the assets may be distributed. However, if there was any property held in your spouse's own name, it is necessary to submit the will for probate.

Here are some examples of *non-probate* property:

1. Property owned by you and your spouse in "joint tenancy with right of survivorship" (JTWRS).

2. Property owned by you and your spouse in "tenancy by the entirety," a designation used only for real estate. The property in this case will pass to you.

3. Life insurance proceeds. Almost all life insurance proceeds are received federal income tax-free at the death of the insured (unless the proceeds are payable to your spouses estate or the named beneficiary has died). Thus, you don't have to file any federal income tax forms on life insurance proceeds.

4. Property held by a trust established during your spouse's lifetime, known as a "living trust" or an *inter vivos* trust.

5. Qualified plan benefits of which you are the beneficiary (unless your spouse's estate was named as beneficiary, or the beneficiary has died). These may include your spouse's IRA, pension, 401(k) or similar plans.

6. Savings bonds co-owned by you and your spouse, or those that are payable to a named beneficiary.

7. In many states, wages, vacation pay, sick leave pay and the like, that were earned by your spouse but not paid at the time of death, can be paid to you without having to go through probate.

8. Totten Trusts—joint bank accounts set up with your spouse, or set up by your spouse with you as beneficiary.

INFORMATION NEEDED WHEN PROBATING A WILL

1. The will.

2. The contents of the safety deposit box.

3. A listing of all real estate.

4. A listing of all securities, government bonds and bills, certificates of deposit, or other financial instruments.

5. A listing of all corporations owned in whole or in part, especially closely-held corporations.

6. A listing of all money accounts such as checking, savings, money market, and wrap accounts.

7. A listing of all judgements (whether owed or owing), accounts receivable, notes receivable, and notes payable.

8. A copy of all insurance policies, including life, health, disability, and property and casualty.

9. A listing of all limited partnerships and partnerships.

10. A listing of all personal property.

11. A listing of all business and governmental benefits.

12. A listing of all debts and claims against the estate.

13. A listing of the last five years' tax returns.

14. A listing of all pension funds, IRAs, or other retirement accounts.

15. A listing of medical and funeral expenses.

16. A copy of any buy-sell agreements.

17. A copy of all trusts, revocable and irrevocable.

Suppose the estate of Jane's husband, George, was comprised of the following assets:

- the family house, held as joint property in tenancy by the entirety;

- pension and 401(k) plans, and IRAs, which all name Jane as beneficiary;

- three life insurance policies, including a company group policy naming Jane as beneficiary;

- securities owned by Jane and George as joint tenants with right of survivorship; and

- three stocks that George owned in his name only.

The *only assets requiring probate* in this case are the three stocks owned in George's name. The entire balance of the estate, amounting to more than $500,000, passes to Jane outside of probate.

Some states require any will to be filed with the proper court; but, if there is no probate estate to settle, no administration may be necessary. Also, probating the will is a separate procedure from the administration and settlement of the estate, and is separate from the payment of inheritance or estate taxes.

A GLOSSARY OF ESTATE PLANNING TERMINOLOGY

The average surviving spouse can feel overwhelmed by the complexities of our legal system. Many of the terms are in Latin, or have special meanings in the context of settling an estate that are different from their usual definitions. The following is a scorecard of "legalese" you may encounter:

Administrator (male) or Administratrix (female): the person named by the court to handle an estate if no one was named in the will, or if the person named in the will cannot serve.

Assets: money or value in any form owned by the deceased.

Beneficiary: a person named in the deceased's will to receive assets, and who is entitled by law to receive them.

Bequest: a gift of personal property given through a will; a legacy.

Codicil: a supplement, amendment or addition that modifies an existing will or possibly revokes only a portion of the will.

Crummey Power: a right given to a beneficiary of an irrevocable trust. Allows the contribution to qualify for the present-interest test and also for the annual exclusion.

Decedent: the person who has died.

Devise: to give real estate through a will.

Disclaimer (Qualified): a complete refusal to accept property where one is entitled to receive it. It must be made timely and no direction as to ultimate disposition may be made. No receipt of property can be made previous to a qualified disclaimer. Must be made within nine months of death.

CHAPTER 6

Estate: all the assets and the liabilities left by the person at death.

Executor (male) or Executrix (female): the person(s), or sometimes institution(s), named in a will to handle an estate.

Fair market value: value at which estate assets are measured for calculating the gross estate tax and gift tax; price at which a willing buyer and a willing seller will transfer property.

Fiduciary: person who is in a legally defined position of trust.

Gift: property transferred for less than adequate and full consideration; a gratuitous transfer from one individual to another either in trust or outright.

Gift splitting: spouses' ability to split a gift to an individual with the assumption half the gift is made by each spouse.

Guardian: person named to represent the interests of minor children or incompetent individuals. Also known as a conservator; may represent financial interests or caretaking interests.

Insurance Trust: irrevocable trust created to hold life insurance policies for estate planning purposes.

Intestate: died without a will. Each state has specific laws as to how an estate is to be divided when there is no will.

Legacy: a bequest.

Liabilities: money owed.

Marital Deduction: may be made outright or through a trust; either a marital deduction trust or a qualified terminable interest property (QTIP) trust. All assets transferred from one spouse to another either while alive or at death are free of transfer taxes.

Probate: the process by which property is transferred in accordance with the terms of a will.

Power of Appointment: a right created by the donor, enabling the donee to designate the ultimate owner of the property; can be general or limited. General power of appointment gives the donee the ability to transfer the property to anyone, including himself. Limited power of appointment allows the assets to be transferred to a certain class of individuals, typically not the donee. This power can be testamentary or created while the donor is alive.

Principal: the assets making up the estate or property inside the trust; otherwise known as *corpus*.

Qualified Domestic Trust (QDOT): a trust that meets the requirement for a marital deduction for property left to a surviving resident non-citizen spouse. The trust must have at least one U.S. trustee who approves of distributions.

Qualified Terminable Interest Property Trust (QTIP): a trust that allows property to be transferred to the surviving spouse in trust and qualifying for the marital deduction. The surviving spouse must be given the exclusive right to all the income derived from the property in the trust at least annually during the surviving spouse's life. The deceased spouse's executor must make the irrevocable election on the decedent's federal estate-tax return to qualify the property for the marital deduction. An affirmative election must be made. All property remaining in the trust will be included in the surviving spouse's estate at this death. Property will be distributed according to the deceased spouse's wishes.

Reciprocal wills: when spouses have mirror-image wills.

Right of Dower: a widow's interest, for the remainder of her life, in the property of her deceased husband.

Shrinkage: the amount of property that will be reduced due to estate settlement costs at the first or second death.

Step up in basis: property held in a revocable trust or outright at the time of death will receive a tax basis equal to fair market value. This will cause no capital gains to be recognized on the sale of the assets immediately following the death. Gifted property does not receive a stepped-up basis.

Testate: died with a will.

Trust: property or money set aside for a particular person or persons, and managed by a trustee.

Trustee: the person or institution attending to the management and distribution of a trust.

Unified Credit: a credit to which every individual is entitled either at death as a credit against estate taxes or during the life of the individual with a credit against gift taxes. The credit is equal to $192,800, which is equal to $600,000 worth of property.

Will: a legal instrument providing for an orderly distribution of property from one individual to many individuals. It has provisions choosing an executor to administer all aspects of the estate, including the post-mortem period. Each state varies the requirements necessary for executing a valid will, but most require witnessing the signature.

The executor of an estate has four major duties:

1. Listing, assembling and safeguarding the deceased's assets.

2. Managing the estate while the settlement is being processed.

3. Paying taxes and debts of the estate.

4. Distributing the assets to the proper beneficiaries.

An individual can serve as executor and also be a beneficiary of a will.

NO WILL OR NO EXECUTOR NAMED IN THE WILL

If your spouse died intestate (i.e., without a will) or if your spouse did not name an executor, you will probably be appointed as personal representative of the estate. You do not have to accept the appointment, but being involved will help speed settlement and protect your interests and future needs.

Again, it is recommended that you retain an attorney for these procedures. However, if you choose to do it on your own, you can call the clerk of the probate court or the clerk of the circuit court for guidance. Their numbers are listed in the white pages or in the city or county directory section of the phone books in most cities.

Thus far you've gathered all the estate information, read the will, determined which assets, if any, require probate, and chosen an attorney, if you need one. The total value of the assets requiring probate, and the relationships of the surviving beneficiaries to your spouse, will determine which probate procedures to follow in your state. You, or whomever the court has approved as executor, must continue managing the estate while the settlement process is being completed.

APPOINTMENT AS PERSONAL REPRESENTATIVE

To make the text easier to follow, hereafter, assume that you have been named as executor or executrix in your spouse's will, and that you have agreed to serve in that role.

Your state may require you to petition the probate court for official appointment as the estate's personal representative. If so, you must apply within a certain period of time—thirty days following death is typical—or the court will assume you have waived the right to act.

If you file a petition you may preclude the estate from using the simplified probate procedures available in many states. A quick review of the estate's assets can tell you which probate procedures may be best. Often, you can get the answer by calling the county probate office; the staff will tell you which of the following procedures to follow:

1. Small estate or affidavit procedure;

2. Summary or abbreviated probate, also called mini-probate; or

3. Full, formal probate.

As executor or administrator, you must be bonded for an amount equal to the value of all the estate's personal property, plus any annual income that will be generated by the estate. The bonding requirement may be waived by a provision in your spouse's will. If there is no provision for waiving bond, courts will often allow a reduced bond if the estate's representative is also the sole or principal beneficiary. However, even the reduced bond must be an amount large enough to protect potential creditors or tax authorities.

The court will determine the amount of the bond. Your insurance agent can help you through the procedure of being bonded or, if you have hired an attorney, he or she can set up the bond. The premium for the bond, which is regulated by law in most states, can be an expense of the estate.

If your spouse owned motor vehicles solely in his or her name, check with the department of motor vehicles to learn whether your state's law allows vehicles of less than a certain value to be transferred directly to you. In effect, this procedure removes the property from the category of probate assets.

You will have to contact creditors and inform them of your spouse's death.

NOTE: Do not feel compelled to pay creditors right away.

Creditors are given three or four months in which to file a claim. Once formal claims have been made, you can pay them and make distributions to beneficiaries of the estate. Even if you think it's proper to pay creditors promptly, and even if you don't like to have outstanding debts, don't make payments before you legally must; *there may be downstream repercussions from prematurely disbursing the estate's funds.*

Basic Responsibilities of the Personal Representative

1. File an inventory with the court of all assets, i.e., money and property, owned on the date of death.

2. File reports with the court periodically indicating a description of property received and funds spent from the estate.

3. Open a bank account in the deceased estate's name.

4. Set up separate accounts for each minor child who is a beneficiary.

5. Obtain the court's permission to spend the estate's funds.

6. Obtain the court's permission to dispose of property of the estate.

7. Obtain appraisals of estate property, if required.

8. Notify and deal with creditors.

9. Oversee the filing of income, estate and inheritance tax returns.

10. Be completely accountable for all assets collected and amounts paid from the estate.

11. Distribute the estate assets.

12. Provide a final accounting to the court.

Estate Management

As executor, you have a fiduciary position—a position of trust—to manage, for yourself and the benefit of others, all the assets and financial affairs of your spouse's estate. As a fiduciary you cannot favor the interests of one party over another, nor can you put your own interests before the interests of the estate and its beneficiaries. The estate must be managed and administered fairly and prudently.

While the estate settlement is proceeding, you may be required to keep records, revise inventories, provide detailed accounting, examine insurance contracts, collect rents, pay taxes, review investments or make investment decisions, and a host of additional, day-to-day management tasks.

Before you can pay any bills, you need to open an estate checking account. The bank you choose should be convenient to you and your attorney, and should be federally insured. Look for a checking account that requires a small minimum balance with low, or no, fees.

The estate account will be mainly a "parking place" for funds that will be distributed as the estate is settled. If it turns out that you have substantial funds in the account for a lengthy period of time, you might want to switch some money to a higher yield savings account or money market fund. Before moving funds into a new vehicle, you may be required by state law to obtain permission from the court.

When you open the estate account, title it as follows:

Estate of (Your Spouse's Name), Deceased,
(Your Name), Executor/Executrix

Persons or businesses who are unaware of your spouse's death may send checks made out to your spouse. You can endorse, as executrix or executor, these checks made payable to your spouse, and deposit them into the estate account. Any estate debts or bills should be paid from this account, not from your personal checking account. Again, you will be required to keep careful records of every item that goes into the account, as well as what is paid out of it.

Debts and Claims Against the Estate

As executor, you are responsible for determining the truthfulness of claims against the estate, and for paying the debts of the estate. These may include funeral expenses, medical bills, phone bills and mortgage and loan payments. If you have an attorney, he or she can do any or all of the tasks listed below:

1. Pay bills;

2. Publish death notices to notify creditors of the death; such notices are usually printed in the local newspaper;

3. Re-title and re-register your spouse's assets to your name as personal representative;

4. Keep track of estate expenses that may be deductible on various tax returns, such as legal and accounting expenses for work done to settle the estate.

Before any bill is ever paid, you or your attorney need to establish whether it is:

1. your debt,

2. your spouse's debt, or

3. a jointly held debt—such as the following:
   a) Charges on credit card accounts that you are authorized to use;
   b) Loans signed by both you and your spouse;
   c) Property taxes, if both of you owned a piece of real estate;
   d) Household expenses.

CHAPTER · 6

Remember, you are not required to pay your spouse's debts; the estate is responsible for these.

Filing Tax Returns and Paying Taxes

As the surviving spouse, you may have to file a profusion of tax forms, as well as pay taxes. First, there are the regular federal and state income taxes, if applicable; these are the same forms you would have filed if your spouse had not died.

Then there may be estate income tax returns to file, as well as inheritance and fiduciary returns, all with accompanying taxes to be paid. If you have these tasks to face, an accountant or tax attorney can be extremely helpful.

The following is a list of the types of tax returns involved in estate settlement and an explanation of what you or your professional advisors must do in each case:

1. *Form 1040, U.S. Individual Income Tax Return*, should be filed as usual. This form will show your income and deductions for the whole tax year, and your spouse's income and deductions until the date of death. When you file this form, include a notice to the IRS, stating that this Form 1040 is your spouse's "final income tax return."

   As a surviving spouse, you may file a joint return for the year in which your spouse died, and you may get special consideration for the two following years if you meet special IRS requirements for a qualifying widowed person. See Chapter 8 for more information.

2. *Form 1041, Fiduciary Income Tax Return*, if required. For tax purposes, you can consider your spouse's income in two parts. The first was income generated while your spouse was alive, which is reported on the Form 1040 discussed in paragraph 1, above. The second, income generated after your spouse's death, is considered income of the estate, and is reported on Form 1041.

3. *Form 706, U.S. Estate Tax Return*, is filed only when the gross estate is valued at more than $600,000. The return is due within nine months of death, unless you obtain an extension. The form must be accompanied by the following:
   a) A copy of the will certified by the local probate court;
   b) IRS Form 712, "Life Insurance Statement" for each life insurance policy;
   c) A certified copy of the death certificate;
   d) Appraisals of real estate and personal property;

    e) Certification by the state that death and inheritance taxes were paid, and;

    f) Additional documents as needed to support any schedules accompanying Form 706.

The Unified Tax Credit: Only for the Rich

A Federal law enacted in 1981 provides a unified tax credit for each person's estate. This tax device is called "unified" because it combines credits for estate and gift taxes, and gives you a credit on your federal estate tax bill.

Basically, the law allows your spouse's estate to take a credit against the first $600,000 of the taxable estate; the amount of the credit being $192,800. Consider this example:

> Let's say the taxable estate is valued at $750,000. The federal estate taxes on that amount are $248,300, less the credit of $192,800. Thus, the amount you would have to pay is $55,500.

> If the taxable estate was valued at $500,000, the tax would be $155,800, less the unified credit of $192,800, which would equal zero.

If tax on the estate is less than $192,000, you don't get to re-apply the unused tax credit elsewhere—the remaining amount cannot be applied against any other taxes.

Your spouse's estate may also qualify for the unlimited marital deduction, which allows you, as a surviving spouse, to deduct up to 100 percent of the value of the gross estate, depending on what portion of your spouse's estate is given outright to you by will or other devices. The marital deduction alone might eliminate any federal estate tax owed to the government.

Distributing the Estate

While distribution of assets is often considered to be one of the last steps in estate settlement, the process actually may have started soon after death. Non-probate assets may have passed automatically to survivors and may already be in their possession.

Once claims and taxes have been paid, and debts settled, you are ready to distribute the remaining probate estate. You or your attorney must follow the instructions in the will, and any other procedures required by the probate court. If the estate is large, you may need professional help to distribute the assets.

Once the distribution is complete, the executor must file a final accounting with the court for all income, expenses and administration of the estate. The actual termination of the estate may require a court-issued decree, if you are involved in formal probate procedures; for informal probate procedures, you may only have to prepare a signed closing statement, stating that the estate has been fully administered.

Settling an estate can be complex, legally demanding and time consuming. As executor, you will be called upon to make a multitude of decisions that can affect your life and the lives of others for years to come. Your actions in hiring competent professionals, directing the settlement, and understanding what the professionals are doing will give you the confidence to proceed.

Knowing that everything was done correctly, costs were minimized, and assets protected and preserved is not only personally satisfying, it's a major part of making the money last.

Post-mortem Estate Planning Techniques

Although your spouse is no longer with you to plan the distribution of the estate, there are a number of techniques your attorney may suggest that are still available to you to facilitate the estate settlement.

Post-mortem techniques may do some or all of the following:

1. Provide a more equitable distribution of the estate

2. Result in lower estate tax liability

3. Provide lower amount of gift tax liability on lifetime gifts

4. Result in lower income tax liability

5. Facilitate the transfer of property from your spouse to intended beneficiaries

6. Preserve and protect certain property from creditors of your spouses' estate

7. Possibly lower probate costs and administrative expenses

There are over 25 different post-mortem techniquest that can be used by an estate in an effort to redistribute property and/or provide estate, gift, and income tax savings. Following is a brief description of the major techniques:

1. *Qualified Disclaimer*—Used where the estate of your spouse has overqualified the estate for the marital deduction, thus avoiding wasting some of the unified credit.

2. *Homestead Allowance*—This technique protects the homestead against the claims of creditors in recognition of the custom

that the surviving spouse (and children) should not lose their principal place of living due to the spouse's death.

3. *Exempt Property Award*—Most all states have laws which provide the surviving spouse with the right to receive certain personal property free from the claims of creditors.

4. *Election against the will by the surviving spouse*—This is also known as "the elective share statute", and ensures that the surviving spouse will be entitled to at least some minimal part of the estate in the event the deceased spouse leaves an amount of property by will that is less than that prescribed by the state statute.

5. *Will contest*—If successful this technique can effectively redistribute an estate.

6. *Family settlement agreements*—This is an informal means of redistributing the estate, where shortly after the death all the family members and heirs gather to determine how the estate should be distributed.

7. *Use of Alternate Valuation Date*—This allows assets to be valued 6 months after the date of death, rather than on the date of death, which is especially valuable if the assets have depreciated significantly since the date of death.

Here are some other post-mortem planning techniques to run by your attorney:

1. Section 303 stock redemption

2. Use of the installment method of paying estate taxes

3. Election to report administration/sale expenses on either form 706 or 1041

4. Waiver of executor's commission and fees

5. Election of the QTIP by executor

6. Election by the surviving spouse to split gifts made by your spouse

The selection of appropriate post-mortem planning techniques depends on a great many factors and requires expert legal assistance. While those techniques listed above are a few of the better known ones, your attorney may suggest others that will also provide benefits and tax reductions.

PART II:

A LOOK AT THE BIG PICTURE

RETIREMENT PLANNING— MAKING THE MONEY LAST

Retirement income planning is much like Aesop's fable of the goose and the golden egg. The fable relates the story of a poor farmer who discovers one day in the nest of his pet goose, a beautiful glittering golden egg. At first he's suspicious, thinking it must be some kind of trick. He starts to throw the egg away, but has second thoughts and instead has it appraised.

He is delighted to learn it is pure gold. He can't believe his good fortune. His delight and wonderment grow the following day, when the goose lays another golden egg. Each day the experience is repeated and the farmer becomes tremendously wealthy.

But with wealth comes impatience and greed. The farmer is unable to wait for the golden eggs arriving each day. He decides to kill the goose and get all the eggs at once. When he does, he finds the goose is empty and now there is no way to get anymore. The farmer has destroyed the goose and thereby any future eggs.

An easy transition can be made to your assets (the goose) and the income produced (golden eggs) by those assets. If you begin to spend the assets the income will be reduced, and if you kill the goose the income will stop altogether. Once you add the impact of inflation, increased longevity, and the increased probability of nursing home care, then solving your income/ retirement planning needs seems overwhelming.

Think of income and retirement planning as a stool which is held up by three legs:

1. Income from government benefits

2. Income from pensions (either survivor benefits and/or your own pension.

3. Income from personal investments.

Income and retirement planning is an essential part of Making the Money Last. In this chapter you see how to determine how much income you'll need, how much you'll have available, and how to meet your needs.

THREE MAJOR FACTORS AFFECTING INCOME/RETIREMENT PLANNING

Inflation, *Social Security and pensions*, and *long term care needs* will likely have a profound impact on you.

Today, on average, everyone is living longer. You need to plan for more years of retirement than people did in the past. A few years ago the average person retired at age 65 and died seven years later at 72. Widows who reach age 65 today can expect to live to age 89; widowers to age 83. Also, people are retiring earlier than they used to. *An increasing number spend as many years or more in retirement as they do working.* Your retirement money may need to last 25 to 30 years!

Let's take a quick look at inflation, Social Security and pensions, and long term care in the context of your long term income and retirement planning needs, and then explore their impact on retirement.

Inflation

Inflation seems likely to always be around, digging away at your carefully acquired and accumulated retirement dollars. Inflation will make the task harder unless you invest to stay ahead of rising prices. Your retirement funds will buy less and less each year.

Suppose you need $30,000 of income annually from your investments to live on, you have $200,000 of investment assets, the yield on the investments is 6%, and inflation is 5% (see table, page 97).

During the first year, your investments (Column C) generate $12,000 of income (Column D). This is $18,000 (Column E) short of the $30,000 needed (Column B). The $18,000 comes out of the $200,000, leaving $182,000 at the end of the year. In the second year, the investments generate only $10,900; meanwhile, the income need has risen 5% to $31,200 (Column B).

You spend more of your assets to meet current needs (the goose is being eaten alive!). Eventually the assets are completely spent and the income disappears by the eighth year.

Income/Retirement Analysis—Adjusted for Inflation

Investment Income Required ..... $ 30,000/yr	Investment Return 6%
Investment Assets $200,000	Inflation Rate 5%

A	B	C	D	E	F
	Income Need Adjusted for	Value of Investment	Investment	Use of Investment	Investment Assets Value
Year	Inflation	Assets	Income	Assets	End of Year
1	$30,000	$200,000	$12,000	$18,000	$182,000
2	31,200	182,000	10,900	20,300	161,700
3	32,448	161,700	9,702	22,746	138,954
4	33,330	138,954	8,337	24,992	113,961
5	34,247	113,961	6,837	27,409	86,551
6	35,201	86,551	5,193	30,007	56,544
7	37,959	56,544	3,792	34,167	22,377
8	39,478	22,377	1,742	22,377	0
9	41,057	0	0	0	0
10	42,699	0	0	0	0

Social Security and Pensions

At age 65, the *maximum* Social Security benefit for a surviving spouse today is $17,376. This number is automatically raised each year to reflect rising prices. For someone needing $30,000 a year, Social Security will only go a short way towards meeting post-retirement needs. What's more, Congress has begun taxing Social Security benefits (up to 85% of benefits are now taxable).

It is possible to start receiving Social Security benefits before you are age 65, but those benefits at age 62 are reduced by 20%.

If employed, any company-sponsored pensions that may be forthcoming, obviously, will also favorably impact your long term cash flow.

Long Term Care

One out of four Americans over 65 will spend time in a nursing home. Nursing homes cost anywhere from $25,000 to $70,000 each year and by the year 2020 may run as high as $160,000. Medicare health insurance pays only a tiny fraction of America's nursing home bills.

An increasing number of insurance companies offer long term care policies (see Chapter 13 on Long Term Care). The premiums depend on

C
H
A
P
T
E
R

7

your age, the deductible, the amount of daily benefit, and how long you want to receive benefits.

Medicaid pays a big portion of nursing home expenses. However, Medicaid is a welfare program and to qualify you must be poor. Some financial advisors tell people to qualify for Medicaid by giving away their assets. Others warn of losing control of finances and becoming dependent on welfare.

> **CONCLUSION:** With the prospects of a long post-worklife, inflation, and the need for long term care, you have every reason to wonder how you are going to pay for your retirement.
>
> Plan on a combination of Social Security, pension and savings. If those aren't enough, you may have to continue working longer than you had hoped, or return to work.

RETIREMENT PLANNING ANALYSIS FOR WIDOWED PERSONS

One of the most perplexing problems surviving spouses face is that of determining whether they will have enough income to survive over their lifetime.

While not perfect, a retirement analysis can give you a strong indication if you are headed for trouble or have a rosy future. Obviously the assumptions used in any retirement analysis cannot be carved in stone. This is an excellent reason for you to redo your retirement analysis on at least an annual basis, using new assumptions for inflation, investment yield, etc.

Step 1
Determining Your Average Rate of Return

A valuable number for you to know is the average rate of return of all your income-producing investments. This will give you one current number to work with, and should you need to increase your income, you can simply use this number for your new calculations.

How Average Rate of Return Is Calculated

An example of an average rate of return (ROR) analysis is provided below:

Asset Category	Value	Rate of Return %		Percent of Total %		Weighted Avg ROR%
Savings Account	$ 5,000	4.0	x	5	=	0.200
CD's	25,000	5.5	x	25	=	1.375
Common Stocks	25,000	6.5	x	25	=	1.625
IRA	10,000	8.0	x	10	=	.800
Municipal Bonds	25,000	6.0	x	20	=	1.200
Credit Union	15,000	5.0	x	15	=	.750
	$100,000			100%		5.95%

In this example, the rate of return is determined for each income-producing asset, then the percentage of that asset versus the total assets is determined (ex., the $5000 savings account is 5% of the total $100,000). Each rate of return is then multiplied times the percent of the total, resulting in the *weighted* rate of return for each asset. These weighted rates of return are then added, providing a *total* average rate of return. A worksheet is provided on page 100.

Step 2
Determining Income Needs at Various Years

If you've already done a budget analysis, the initial work in determining your income needs is already done. If not, you need to do a realistic appraisal of your expenses, both current and future. This requires making estimates of expected dollar outlays for each budget item. It is important to recognize that over the years some expense items will increase, and some will decrease or even disappear.

Here's an example:

Martha, age 66, has examined her expenses, and determines them to be $2000/month. She had read that inflation is currently at 2.7%, but feels it will be higher over the years ahead. She decides that 4.0% for inflation is realistic. Also, using the life expectancy table on page 113 she sees that she could live 18 years longer, or more.

CHAPTER 7

Using the Table of Inflation Factors on page 114, she quickly determines her future expense estimates as:

Age	Year	Current Expenses	x	Inflation Factor (4%)	=	Future Expenses
67	1	$2000	x	1.04	=	$2080
71	5	2000	x	1.22	=	2440
76	10	2000	x	1.48	=	2960
81	15	2000	x	1.80	=	3600
86	20	2000	x	2.19	=	4382

Thus, Martha can see that her income needs will be increasing if she wishes to maintain her current standard of living. A worksheet is provided for your use on page 102.

AVERAGE RATE OF RETURN WORKSHEET

Asset Name	Value	Rate of Return	Percent of Total	Weighted Rate of Return
Totals	$		100%	%

A GUIDE TO SOME FUTURE RETIREMENT EXPENSES

Expenses That Usually Decrease:
Mortgage payments (eventually eliminated)
Food
Clothing
Taxes (income/social security)
Debt repayment (eliminated)
Life insurance (if any)
Household furnishings
Personal care
Medical insurance (Often reduces at age 65, but increases later)
Savings and investments

Expenses That Usually Increase:
Rent
Property tax
House upkeep (repairs)
Utilities and telephone
Auto, home and liability insurance
Long-term Care insurance
Vacation and travel
Recreation and entertainment
Contributions and gifts
Medical costs (in later years)

Step 3
Determining Income

Now that you know the future expenses, you need to determine the income you can expect as you go through your retirement years.

Identifying your sources of income should be fairly straightforward, especially if you've already read the chapter on organization (Chapter 5). Now you need to develop a comprehensive sheet of all your income sources.

CHAPTER 7

FUTURE EXPENSE WORKSHEET

Age	Year	Current Expense	Inflation x Factor	Future = Expense

Here's a list of possible sources of income. Set up your own list and add the monthly income you expect from each source (or annual income, if that's easier). If the income will not start until a specific date, note the date.

SOURCES OF INCOME DURING RETIREMENT

Item	Amount ($)	Date Begins
Wages	_____	
Self-employment	_____	
Monthly pension	_____	
Social Security	_____	
Interest	_____	
Dividends	_____	
IRA distributions	_____	
401(k) distributions	_____	
403(b) distributions	_____	
Real estate income	_____	
Trust income	_____	
Miscellaneous	_____	
Total	$_____	

Employment Income

There are many questions to poise to yourself in this area:

- If you are working now, will you continue at retirement age?

- If you continue, how long is it reasonable to expect you will work?

- Will you go from full-time to part-time?

- If you continue to work for the same employer, will you endanger your retired status, particularly the treatment of lump sum distributions?

Although it may not be financially necessary, it may be desirable for you to work during some part of your retirement years.

Social Security

Working during retirement can reduce your Social Security income. Under the existing rules you can only earn a limited amount (called earned income) before Social Security benefits are reduced.

In 1995, if you are under Age 65, you're allowed to earn up to $8160 of working income and keep all of the Social Security benefit. Above $8160, you lose one dollar for every two you earn. At age 65 through age 69 the amount changes to $11,280. Above this amount you lose one dollar for every three you earn. At age 70 you can earn any amount of income you wish from employment without losing any Social Security retirement benefits.

It is important to remember that, for Social Security retirement income purposes, earned income is income generated by you, working at a job or being self-employed. It does not include pension income, interest, dividends, capital gains, IRA distributions, or rental property income.

IRA Income

Withdrawals from IRA's (and most other retirement plans) must begin by age 70-1/2. The rule is that you must withdraw the required amount from the *total value* of all your IRA accounts each year after you reach 70-1/2.

First, add the values of all your IRA's together as of the year-end. Apply the proper life expectancy number (see page 113) to determine the minimum withdrawal amount. Then pick which IRA, or IRAs to pull the money from.

Make sure to allow yourself enough time to withdraw the money. The IRA trustees have forms that you must complete before they will release the funds.

Interest and Dividends

Most interest and dividends are paid on a quarterly basis. Capital gain dividends from mutual fund holdings are usually paid once a year (typically in December). Many municipal bonds pay twice a year, quarterly, or even once a year. Some certificates of deposit pay at various times, some only after several years. If you do your retirement planning on a monthly basis you need to convert these figures to monthly income as shown on page 105.

INTEREST AND DIVIDEND CONVERSION WORKSHEET

1) Interest Bearing Accounts:	Current Rate	Annual Income	Monthly Income
a) _____	_____ %	$ _____	$ _____
b) _____	_____ %	_____	_____
c) _____	_____ %	_____	_____
d) _____	_____ %	_____	_____
e) _____	_____ %	_____	_____
Totals:			

2) Dividends and Capital Gains:			
a) _____		_____	_____
b) _____		_____	_____
c) _____		_____	_____
d) _____		_____	_____
e) _____		_____	_____
Totals:			
Total of 1 and 2:		$ _____	_____

A Master Income Worksheet

You may wish to list all the income you receive by the month you receive it. The worksheet on page 106 can be a guide.

A more valuable tool is the long-range estimate of your income in future years. For this item we need to develop an income spread sheet.

MASTER MONTHLY INCOME WORKSHEET   Year _____

Income Source	Jan	Feb	Mar	Apr	May	Jun	Jly	Aug	Sep	Oct	Nov	Dec	Totals
Wages													
Self-Employment													
Monthly Pension													
Social Security													
Interest													
Dividends													
IRA Distributions													
401(k) Distributions													
403(b) Distributions													
Real Estate													
Trust													
Miscellaneous													
Total													

Step 4:
Determining Future Income Projections

This step requires a little more work on your part, but is worth it. We now need to list the components of your income and factor in any cost of living (COLA) increase for each component. For example, if you feel that Social Security will have an annual 3% cost of living increase, then that must be factored in for the particular future years you have in question.

An example may help you walk through these calculations.

Jane has the following income sources:
- Social Security = $1200/month, COLA applies
- Pension Benefit = $1500/month, COLA applies
- Investment Income = $1000/month; growing at 2.5%/year
- Interest bearing savings account = $400/month (4%)
- IRA account with interest at 5% = $300/month

Jane feels that 3% for the cost of living increase (COLA) is appropriate. Using the inflation factors on page 114, she is able to calculate the following:

	Now	1 yr	5 yrs	10 yrs	15 yrs	20 yrs
Social Security	$1200	$1236	$1391	$1612	$1869	$2167
Pension Benefit	1500	1545	1738	2015	2337	2709
Investment Inc.	1000	1025	1131	1280	1448	1628
Interest	400	400	400	400	400	400
IRA account	300	300	300	300	300	300
Totals	$4400	$4506	$4960	$5607	$6254	$7204

If Jane's estimated expenses in 15 years are greater than $6254/ month, she will need to consider making some changes now to either decrease expenses or increase income. Otherwise, she may face the problem of diminishing assets.

Step 5:
Putting the Long-range Income and Expenses Together

Now you are ready to do the final number-crunching on your retirement plan. (A financial planner may be of value here if you don't wish to do this step yourself). There are many software programs available to provide the spreadsheet information, but you can also do it yourself with a hand-held calculator.

Here are the steps to follow in building your retirement-planning master worksheet:

1. Set up a long-range retirement plan worksheet as shown on page 111.

2. Using the Inflation Factors Table, calculate your future income for each year for columns 4, 5, 6.

3. List in column 3 the future expenses determined on page 102.

4. List the actual investment income you expect for each year in column 8 (see page 98, Average Rate of Return).

5. Subtract the total of columns 4, 5, 6 from column 3. That will provide you with the income required from investments, which is entered in column 7.

6. If the amount in column 7 is greater than that shown in column 8, determine that difference and list it in column 9 as a negative. If the amount in column 7 is less than column 8, list that difference in column 9 as a plus.

7. Add or subtract the amount in column 9 from your investment assets, listed in column 10.

TAKING A HARD LOOK AT YOUR RETIREMENT ANALYSIS

If your retirement plan doesn't work out the way you had hoped, here's a few suggestions to improve it:

1. Work additional year(s) before retiring.

2. Delay or advance Social Security payments.

3. Delay or advance IRA, 401(k) or other pension benefits.

4. Sell your personal residence and buy a less expensive home or rent.

5. Consider working part-time.

6. Cut back expenses.

7. Increase your investment yield.

You may also wish to play what are called "what if" scenarios with retirement factors that you can't control. These include:

1. Higher or lower inflation rates than expected

2. Cost of living adjustments being modified

3. Increase/decrease in income taxes

4. Better or worse return on investments

SUMMARY

You may be one of the fortunate surviving spouses whose retirement income is sufficient to satisfy all your needs. Usually there are no easy answers for shortfalls that are often evident once the preceding analysis is complete. However, by completing the process of examining your retirement picture, you should feel you have done the best job possible and know what steps are required to face the future.

SAMPLE INCOME FORM

Year	Age	Investment Income	Social Security	Job Related	Gifts Or Other	Pension, IRA	Total Income
1							
2							
3							
4							
5							
6							
7							
8							
9							
10							
11							
12							
13							
14							
15							
16							
17							
18							
19							
20							

LONG-RANGE RETIREMENT PLANNING WORKSHEET

(1) Year	(2) Age	(3) Required Income	(4) Social Security	(5) Pension	(6) Employment Income	(7) Investment Income Required	(8) Actual Investment Income	(9) Add or Subtract to Col. 10	(10) Investment Asset Balance
1									
2									
3									
4									
5									
6									
7									
8									
9									
10									
11									
12									
13									
14									
15									
16									
17									
18									
19									
20									
21									
22									
23									

CHAPTER 7

SAMPLE: LONG-RANGE RETIREMENT PLANNING WORKSHEET

(1) Year	(2) Age	(3) Required Income	(4) Social Security	(5) Pension	(6) Employment Income	(7) Investment Income Required	(8) Actual Investment Income	(9) Add or Subtract to Col. 10	(10) Investment Asset Balance
1	66	$39,710	$11,053	$12,360	–0–	$16,297	$16,940	$ 643	$279,443
2	67	41,496	11,440	12,730		17,326	16,979	(347)	279,096
3	68	43,364	11,841	13,112		18,411	16,958	(1453)	277,643
4	69	45,315	12,255	13,506		19,554	16,869	(2684)	274,958
5	70	47,355	12,684	13,911		20,759	16,706	(4052)	270,905
6	71	49,406	13,030	14,328		22,128	16,400	(5668)	265,237
7	72	51,712	13,486	14,758		23,468	16,115	(7853)	257,884
8	73	54,041	13,958	15,201		24,881	15,669	(9212)	248,672
9	74	56,471	14,657	15,657		26,368	15,109	(11259)	237,413
10	75	59,013	14,952	16,126		27,935	14,425	(13510)	223,903
11	76	61,668	15,475	16,610		29,583	13,604	(15979)	207,924
12	77	64,443	16,010	17,109		31,324	12,633	(18691)	189,233
13	78	67,343	16,578	17,622		33,143	11,498	(21845)	167,588
14	79	70,374	17,158	18,151		35,067	10,182	(24885)	142,703
15	80	73,540	17,756	18,695		37,089	8,670	(28419)	114,284
16	81	76,850	18,519	19,256		39,075	6,944	(32131)	82,153
17	82	80,308	19,167	19,834		41,307	4,991	(36316)	45,837
18	83	83,922	19,837	20,429		43,656	2,785	(40871)	4,966
19	84	87,698	20,532	21,042		46,124	301	(45823)	0
20	85	91,645	21,251	21,673		—	—	—	—

Life Expectancy Tables

Age	Male	Female	Age	Male	Female	Age	Male	Female
41	34.2	39.6	56	21.5	26.0	71	11.5	14.5
42	33.3	38.6	57	20.8	25.2	72	10.9	13.8
43	32.5	37.7	58	20.0	24.4	73	10.4	13.2
44	31.6	36.7	59	19.3	23.5	74	9.9	12.5
45	30.7	35.8	60	18.6	22.7	75	9.4	11.9
46	29.8	34.9	61	17.9	21.9	76	8.9	11.3
47	28.9	34.0	62	17.2	21.1	77	8.4	10.7
48	28.1	33.1	63	16.5	20.4	78	8.0	10.1
49	27.2	32.2	64	15.8	19.6	79	7.5	9.5
50	26.4	31.3	65	15.2	18.8	80	7.1	9.0
51	25.6	30.4	66	14.5	18.1	81	6.7	8.4
52	24.7	29.5	67	13.9	17.4	82	6.3	7.9
53	23.9	28.6	68	13.3	16.6	83	6.0	7.4
54	23.1	27.7	69	12.7	15.9	84	5.6	7.0
55	22.3	26.9	70	12.1	15.2	85	5.3	6.6

Tables are furnished by the Department of Health and Human Services and reflect life expectancies for all races in the year 1989, the latest available.

CHAPTER 7

Compound Sum of $1.00

EXAMPLE: You invest $100 in a savings account that pays 7% a year, compounded annually. At the end of the tenth year you will have $196.70 in your account ($100 x 1.967).

Year	4%	5%	6%	7%	8%	9%	10%	11%	12%	13%	14%
1	1.040	1.050	1.060	1.070	1.080	1.090	1.100	1.110	1.120	1.130	1.140
2	1.082	1.103	1.124	1.145	1.166	1.188	1.210	1.232	1.254	1.277	1.300
3	1.125	1.158	1.191	1.225	1.260	1.295	1.331	1.368	1.405	1.443	1.482
4	1.170	1.216	1.262	1.311	1.360	1.412	1.464	1.518	1.574	1.630	1.689
5	1.217	1.276	1.338	1.403	1.469	1.539	1.611	1.685	1.762	1.842	1.925
6	1.265	1.340	1.419	1.501	1.587	1.677	1.772	1.870	1.974	2.082	2.195
7	1.316	1.407	1.504	1.606	1.714	1.828	1.949	2.076	2.211	2.353	2.502
8	1.369	1.477	1.594	1.718	1.851	1.993	2.144	2.305	2.476	2.658	2.853
9	1.423	1.551	1.689	1.838	1.999	2.172	2.358	2.558	2.773	3.004	3.252
10	1.480	1.629	1.791	1.967	2.159	2.367	2.594	2.839	3.106	3.395	3.707
11	1.539	1.710	1.898	2.105	2.332	2.580	2.853	3.152	3.479	3.836	4.226
12	1.601	1.796	2.012	2.252	2.518	2.813	3.138	3.498	3.896	4.335	4.818
13	1.665	1.886	2.133	2.410	2.720	3.066	3.452	3.883	4.363	4.898	5.492
14	1.732	1.980	2.261	2.579	2.937	3.342	3.797	4.310	4.887	5.535	6.261
15	1.801	2.079	2.397	2.759	3.172	3.642	4.177	4.785	5.474	6.254	7.138
16	1.873	2.183	2.540	2.952	3.426	3.970	4.595	5.311	6.130	7.067	8.137
17	1.948	2.292	2.693	3.159	3.700	4.328	5.054	5.895	6.866	7.986	9.276
18	2.206	2.407	2.854	3.380	3.996	4.717	5.560	6.544	7.690	9.024	10.575
19	2.107	2.527	3.026	3.617	4.316	5.142	6.116	7.263	8.613	10.197	12.056
20	2.191	2.653	3.207	3.870	4.661	5.604	6.727	8.062	9.646	11.523	13.743
25	2.666	3.386	4.292	5.427	6.848	8.623	10.835	13.585	17.000	21.231	26.462
30	3.243	4.322	5.743	7.612	10.063	13.268	17.449	22.892	29.960	39.116	50.950

THE SURVIVING SPOUSE'S GUIDE TO TAXES

One way to help make your money last is to reduce the amount of taxes you pay. There is an old saying in financial circles: "It is not what you earn, it is what you get to keep." This concept can help you to retain more money to invest or spend, depending on your personal financial situation.

This chapter is not intended to replace the services of your CPA or accountant tax preparer—tax laws change often and the information given here is based on the latest information available from reliable sources.

The aim of recent tax reforms was to simplify the tax system but Congress was not successful in their endeavors. The system is still highly complex. Most taxpayers feel compelled to have even the most basic tax returns prepared by professionals. Also, there are many types of taxes including Social Security, state, excise, property, sales, and estate and inheritance taxes.

TAX PLANNING TIPS

There are things you can do in general to make the job of preparing your tax return easier:

1. If you are a younger widower and haven't done so already, obtain Social Security numbers for your children who will be a year old or older by the end of the year. These numbers need to be listed on Form 1040. Call your nearest Social Security office and ask them to send you Form SS-5, the application for a Social Security number card.

2. Keep track of all tax exempt income you receive. You need to report it on Form 1040 even though it is not taxable.

3. Obtain Form 8615 from the IRS if you have children under the age of 14 with more than $1,300 unearned income. Note that if your child's gross income is less than $5,000, you can choose to report it on your own tax return. If you do, use Form 8814.

4. Sort out your records of interest payments. The Tax Reform Act made big changes in this area. Talk with your tax preparer if you're unsure how to separate these payments.

5. Convert your consumer interest payments. Interest paid on consumer debt is non-deductible. However, interest paid as part of your home equity mortgages, up to *$100,000* on your principal residence plus one other residence, remains 100 percent deductible, regardless of how the loan proceeds are used. I would suggest, instead of using your credit card or taking out a consumer loan, that you re-mortgage your home. That way you'll be able to fully deduct the interest payments. (See Chapter 11 for a rundown of mortgage interest rules).

6. Set up a separate bank account for any money you borrow to make investments. Because you need to substantiate any deductions for investment interest expense, you need to be ready to prove that the money you borrowed was actually spent on investments rather than personal use.

7. Pay close attention to miscellaneous expenses, such as job-hunting costs, professional dues, etc. Some miscellaneous expenses are fully deductible and others are deductible only if they total more than 2 percent of your adjusted gross income.

8. Keep accurate records of the income and expenses of any rental real estate. Keep separate records for units that you yourself actually manage and for those that you don't. The tax rules on deducting losses are different. For vacation homes that you rent out for part of the year, keep a diary showing when you use it personally and when you rent it out.

9. Fill out a sample tax return for the coming tax year as soon as possible. An estimate will help you project taxes for the next year. In addition, you will see where mistakes may be and have plenty of time to correct them for the coming year.

10. Notify IRS when you move. Use Federal Form 8822, Change of Address, when you need to change your address. This form

helps eliminate the risk of not receiving an IRS notice soon enough so that you can respond to it.

11. Medical payments paid by the estate within one year after death may be treated as deductible on the final return. A statement must be attached confirming the fact that the same expenses were not deducted for federal estate tax purposes and that an estate tax deduction for them is waived.

Also, set up your record-keeping. Once you have figured out your tax bill for the current year, it will probably be obvious where you lacked sufficient records to substantiate your deductions. Set up and improve your record-keeping system to accommodate your current needs.

FILING STATUS

It is important to file your status correctly since your tax rate is dependent on it. You can qualify as a surviving spouse for two tax years following the year in which your spouse died under the following conditions:

1. you maintain a household for certain dependents;

2. have not remarried; and

3. filed or could have filed a joint return with your spouse for the year in which he/she died.

As a surviving spouse, you compute your tax using the same rates as married couples use when filing joint returns. If your spouse died before filing a return for the current year, you or a personal representative will need to file and sign the return for your spouse.

If your spouse did not file a return, but had tax withheld, you or someone acting in your behalf will need to file a return to get a refund. The person who files the return needs to write "deceased" in capital letters, the deceased's name, and the date of death across the top of the tax return.

A joint return must show your spouse's income for the current year up to the date of death, and all of your income for the current year. Write "filing as surviving spouse" in the area where you sign the return. If someone else is your spouse's personal representative, he or she will need to sign as well.

The surviving spouse rate schedule initially allows more taxable income to be taxed at the 15 percent and 28 percent rate than the rate schedules for heads-of-household, or single individuals. Here's a simple comparison:

Comparison of taxes at $34,000 taxable income:		
	TAX	"WIDOW(ER)" TAX SAVINGS
STATUS:		
Qualifying widow(er), joint return	$5104	—
Head of Household	$5562	+$458
Single	$6570	+$1466

The surviving spouse tax status is a nice tax break, but is available to you for only two tax years after your spouse's death. If more than two years have passed, you will have to file as single, unless you are able to file as a head-of-household, meeting all five of the following criteria:

1. You were not married at the end of the filing year;

2. You maintain a household for your children, dependent parent or other dependent relative;

3. The household has to be your home and it must also be the main home for a qualifying relative, as outlined in (2), for more than half of the filing year;

4. You provide more than 50% of the cost of maintaining the household;

5. You were a U.S. citizen or resident alien during the entire tax year.

UNDERSTANDING YOUR MARGINAL TAX BRACKET

It is not what you earn that really counts in the accumulation and preservation of wealth; it is what you keep. This statement leads to a fundamental principal for making the money last. *Rates of return before taxes are meaningless*—it is after-tax rates of return that are all-important.

It is also important to realize that overall aggregate tax rates are not the same as marginal tax rates. For example, a person paying $25,000 in taxes with an income of $125,000 has an "overall" tax rate of 20%. However, their real tax rate is probably 31%. Every dollar above $115,000 will be taxed at 31% (the marginal tax rate).

Conversely, it is equally important to realize that a low or non-existent tax bracket may provide advantages unavailable to high tax bracket persons. For example, if you are in a zero tax bracket, you might wish to accelerate your IRA income, thus removing it from the confines of your IRA.

Here's a tax measuring table to help you see what marginal tax bracket your income reaches (use the specific tax tables to determine your actual income tax):

How To Determine Your Marginal Tax Bracket

Joint Return		Single Return	
Taxable Income	Marginal Tax Bracket	Taxable Income	Marginal Tax Bracket
Above $250,000	39.6%	Above $250,000	39.6%
$250,000		$250,000	
	36%		36%
$140,000		$115,000	
	31%		31%
$91,850		$55,100	
	28%		28%
$38,000		$22,750	
	15%		15%
—0—		—0—	

ESTIMATED TAXES

Most people pay their taxes to the Internal Revenue Service during the course of the year when withholding taxes are deducted from their salaries or pension payments. As a widowed person, you may have income which is not subject to regular withholding, such as interest, dividends, capital gains, certain pension income, self-employment wages, partnership income, and so forth. It is likely you will need to make estimated tax payments. The tax rules require that you pay this tax in quarterly installments during the year rather than in a lump sum on April 15.

How do you know if you must file an estimated return? You will need to pay estimated tax for the following:

1. if you expect to owe at least $500 in tax after subtracting any regular withholding and tax credits;

2. you expect your withholding to be less than 90 percent of the tax shown on your tax return;

3. you anticipate your withholding to be less than 100 percent of the tax shown in your prior year's tax return.

Also you will need to file if:

4. Your adjusted gross income is more than $75,000;

5. Your current adjusted gross income exceeds the current year's adjusted gross income by more than $40,000.

Estimated taxes are due in four equal installments. For instance, if you owe $1,000 of estimated tax, you would pay $250 each on April 15, June 15, September 15 and January 15. Note that these dates are not spaced evenly. There are two months between the April and June filings and four months between September and January filings. If you work, you can also adjust your W-4 form so that enough money is withheld by the end of the year to equal your anticipated tax liability. This way, you can avoid estimated filings. Estimated payments are files on vouchers (Form 1040-ES), which you can obtain from the IRS.

A non-deductible penalty established by the IRS is charged for failure to make estimated tax payments as required and must be paid at the time your tax return is filed. Although the computations are somewhat complicated, Form 2210 (Underpayments of Estimated Tax by Individuals) does provide directions.

Taxpayers sometimes intentionally underpay the first payments for the estimated tax for the year and then make up the difference with a large final payment. The danger in this is that the penalty applies from the date of each underpayment. The IRS may not detect the ploy, but, if it does, the penalty will be imposed.

A Tracking Form is provided on page 128, for estimated payments.

CLAIMING DEPENDENTS

If you are a widowed person, claiming an exemption for a dependent can be important in your tax computations. There are five tests that you need to apply in order to claim a dependent and obtain an exemption:

1. *A support test:* You need to provide over 50 percent of the dependent's total support, including food, lodging, clothing, education, medical expenses, recreation, transportation, and other necessities. If you share the support with other persons, it needs to be more than 50 percent of the total spent for the dependent. If less than 50 percent is provided, either by you alone or you with contributors, you will not be able to claim any exemptions.

2. *A gross income test:* Your dependent must have less than $2,150 in gross income, unless he or she is your child and is (a) under 19 years of age, or (b) a full-time student during five months of the year *and* is under the age of 24.

3. *A citizenship test:* Your dependent must be a U.S. citizen, resident or national, or a resident of Canada or Mexico.

4. *A joint return test:* Your dependent cannot file a joint return with anyone else.

5. *A relationship or member of household test:* Your dependent must live in your household for the entire year, or be related to you (i.e., child, grandchild, etc.).

Since each exemption for a qualified dependent is worth $2,450 in deductions it is important to claim every exemption you can.

IRAs, Taxes, and Surviving Spouses

IRA accounts are usually payable to you, the surviving spouse. As the beneficiary, you will have to declare the IRA payments (unless you elect other options), whether lump sum or periodic, as ordinary income since they are received just as though you were the original owner of the IRA. The IRA distributions are considered income. If you take the IRA account as a lump sum distribution, be aware that you may have to pay income taxes as well as estate taxes on those proceeds.

If you are under age 59-1/2 your deceased spouse's IRA can be taken by you without the 10% IRS penalty. (There is no penalty after age 59-1/2).

As an IRA beneficiary, you may elect to roll the funds over into your own IRA, avoiding current taxes. (You can also make your own deductible IRA contributions to that IRA account if you qualify). You also have the option of leaving the funds in your spouse's name. Distributions from that IRA account do not have to begin until your spouse would have reached the age of 70-1/2. If your deceased spouse was already receiving payments according to a schedule and you are the beneficiary you must receive distributions at least as rapidly.

A *rollover* IRA means taking receipt of the assets for up to 60 days before re-investing it into a new retirement IRA plan. A *transfer* means moving the assets from one IRA custodian to another IRA custodian. Rollovers are allowed once a year. Transfers can occur as often as you wish and as many times a year as you wish. Losses that are incurred in an IRA account are not deductible.

There are two types of rollovers for IRAs. One is an IRA-to-IRA rollover. In this case, all or a portion of the existing funds are withdrawn and checks come to you. The funds are not subject to current income taxes as long as they are deposited into another IRA within 60 days. Each IRA can be rolled over once every 12 months.

The other type of rollover is from a qualified retirement plan to an IRA. If your spouse was a participant in a company retirement plan, such as a pension or profit sharing plan, you may take the proceeds from that plan and roll them into an IRA. Again you may receive those proceeds yourself and then have 60 days in which to roll that money into an IRA. *Also, be aware of a new IRS ruling that requires 20% withholding on rollovers. Use a direct custodian-to-custodian transfer to avoid the 20% withholding.*

There are different tax treatments of IRA withdrawals depending upon your age:

1. *Before Age 59-1/2*: Withdrawals are taxable as ordinary income plus a 10% penalty for early withdrawal. Withdrawals from deceased spouse's IRA escape the 10% penalty.

2. *Age 59-1/2 to 70-1/2*: Withdrawals are taxable as ordinary income and there is complete flexibility on amounts and timing of withdrawals.

3. *Age 70-1/2 and later*: Withdrawals are taxed as ordinary income. Minimum distributions must begin by age 70-1/2 and are based on life expectancy. A 50% penalty is imposed if minimum distributions are not withdrawn. Distributions can exceed the minimum requirement.

TAXES AND LUMP SUM RETIREMENT PLAN DISTRIBUTIONS

As a surviving spouse, you normally have two choices when a lump sum distribution is received from your deceased spouse's retirement program: 1) You can rollover part or all of it into an IRA (see the preceding discussion) or 2) take the money and pay tax on the distribution. If you elect to pay taxes, the lump sum distribution may qualify for 5- or 10-year averaging. If your spouse made non-deductible contributions to a company pension or annuity plan, those parts of the distributions will be considered non-taxable.

If you wish to use the five year averaging, all five of the following requirements must be met for a lump sum distribution:

1. The lump sum distribution must represent the entire account balance from the employer's plan.

2. Your spouse must have been 50 or older on January 1, 1986. If so, you have the option of choosing either the 10-year averaging using the 1986 tax table rates or 5-year averaging using the current year tax rates. Both the 5-year and 10-year averaging tax tables are shown on page 40.

3. The plan must have been a qualified pension plan, profit sharing plan or stock bonus plan.

4. Your spouse must have participated in the plan at least five years before the year of the distribution, or the distribution was to be paid to a named beneficiary when your spouse died; and,

5. One of the following conditions also needs to be true:
   a) The distribution is paid to a beneficiary of the employee who died;
   b) The employee quit, retired, was laid off, or was fired before receiving a distribution;
   c) The person was self-employed or an owner-employee and became disabled;
   d) The employee was age 59-1/2 or older at the time of distribution.

In addition to the above requirements, you can use averaging only once, and you will need to use it for all qualifying lump sum distributions you received in that year.

The only requirement to use ten-year averaging is that your spouse needs to have been age 50 or older on January 1, 1986. Ten-year averaging allows you to use 1986 tax tables, while five-year averaging requires the use of current tax tables.

Rollover or Forward Averaging

Would it be best for you to roll the lump sum distribution from your spouse's retirement plan into an IRA, or to elect 5-year or 10-year averaging? Here are some things to consider when you are making the choice for 5- or 10-year averaging:

1) The current tax rate may be lower than future tax rates. Also, if you pay the tax at this time, you have unrestricted after-tax use of the funds now and in the future. This eliminates uncertainty about the effect of future tax laws;

2) If you do pick the IRA rollover, however, you will defer paying taxes until a future date. You will accumulate more wealth without taxation during that period. Higher taxes in the future may be offset by the investment values you accumulate within your IRA.

NOTE: If your spouse made non-deductible contributions to a company pension or annuity plan, those parts of the distributions received are considered non-taxable. Also, up to $5,000 of the benefit from an employee qualified retirement plan may be excluded from income tax as an employer paid death benefit.

BEFORE FILING YOUR RETURN

Before you mail your return, double check everything. Don't forget to:

1. Include your name, address, Social Security number on the first page of the return. If you use the IRS pre-addressed label, correct any incorrect information.

2. Write your name and Social Security number on every page you send to the IRS.

3. Attach a copy of your W-2 form using copy B.

4. Sign and date the return.

5. Staple your check or money order to the return. Don't forget to sign the check and write your Social Security number on it.

6. Make a copy of the return for your own records.

7. Make certain every form and related schedule is included.

8. Re-check your arithmetic, using a calculator.

9. Address the return to the IRS Center in your state.

10. Mail the return on or before April 15th. IRS won't accept an office postage meter as proof of your date of mailing if there is any doubt as to when the return was actually filed.

GIFTING

If you wish to give money and, again, can afford it, consider setting up a gift giving program (covered in detail in Chapter 16) for your children or grandchildren. You can still shift a certain amount of income to your family members in lower tax brackets. The best time to do this is early in the year.

Children under the age of 14 who have investment income below $1,300 in 1992, pay tax at their own lower tax bracket. Their investment income over that amount, regardless of its source, will be taxed at their parent's tax bracket. So it may be better to have $1,300 taxed in the child's lower bracket. If you have children who are age 14 or over, consider shifting even more than $1,300 income to them. The entire amount may be taxed in their lower bracket.

Many times the surviving spouse will have two cars and wish to dispose of one of them. If it's an old car and you can't sell it, consider making a charitable contribution. Find a high school or community college with an automotive trades or studies program and donate it. You'll obtain a valuation based on the Blue Book. This will give you a charitable contribution deduction and you'll have exercised your civic responsibility by helping public education.

HANDLING WORTHLESS SECURITIES

Joan found some old stock certificates of the Empty Hole Oil Well Company that her husband had acquired. He paid $10 per share for them. Joan called her financial planner and learned that the shares had been worthless since 1989. Since a taxpayer can go back seven years to claim deductions, she can file an amended return (Form 1040X) for the year 1989 to claim the deduction and receive a refund.

Securities are deductible only for the year in which they became worthless. The IRS keeps a list of companies whose stock has become worthless for each year. If the company is not on the list, the IRS will not accept the deduction unless there is a real transaction or the worthlessness can be otherwise proven.

ARE SOCIAL SECURITY BENEFITS TAXABLE?

A portion of Social Security benefits may be included in your gross income if your modified adjusted gross income exceeds a base amount. "Modified adjusted gross income" is your adjusted gross income plus tax-exempt interest, such as municipal bonds.

The base amount for a modified adjusted gross income is $25,000 for individuals. In your first and second years as widow(er), you may be able to file joint return for which the base is $32,000. The benefits, if they are taxable, are included in your gross income.

To illustrate: Assume you file an individual return, have an adjusted gross income of $25,000, and also receive $9,000 of municipal bond interest. You receive $12,000 of Social Security benefits during the taxable year. Your modified adjusted gross income plus one-half of the Social Security benefits is, $40,000 ($25,000 + $9,000 = $34,000, + 1/2 of $12,000 = $40,000), $15,000 greater than your base amount of $25,000.

The amount of Social Security benefits that will be included in your gross income is $6,000. That is the lesser of one-half of your Social Security benefits ($6,000), or one-half of the excess of your combined income over the base amount (1/2 x $15,000 = $7500).

The maximum amount that will be subject to tax is now up to 85% of the Social Security benefits you receive. This applies only to the extent that adjusted gross income exceeds $44,000 for joint returns or $34,000 for single and head-of-household returns. If your adjusted gross income falls between the old and new threshold amounts, only 50% will be subject to tax. Tax-exempt interest is only used to figure the amount of benefits that will be included in your gross income. It will remain free of taxation.

A form is shown on page 127 to help you compute any taxable Social Security income.

It is important to note that as a qualifying widow(er) with dependent children, you can file using joint return rates, even though you need to use the $25,000 base amount.

ARE LIFE INSURANCE PROCEEDS TAXABLE?

Life insurance proceeds paid to a named beneficiary due to the death of your spouse are not taxable income for federal or state income tax purposes. If you take the proceeds of a life insurance policy in installment payments, each non-taxable installment equals the total amount payable at death divided by the number of installments to be paid. Anything paid over this amount in each installment is taxable income.

DETERMINING TAXES ON SOCIAL SECURITY BENEFITS

HOW MUCH WILL YOU PAY? This worksheet will help you estimate if you'll pay taxes on your Social Security benefits.

List your income to determine if you exceed either of the Social Security thresholds.		
1. List toal income reported on Form 1040, excluding Social Security benefits.	1.	
2. List 50% of your annual Social Security benefits.	2.	
3. List all tax-exempt interest.	3.	
4. Modified Adjusted Gross Income (add Lines 1 through 3).	4.	
5. First Threshold Subtract $32,000 from Line 4 ($25,000, if single).*	5.	
If Line 5 is zero, STOP. You'll pay no taxes on your Social Security benefits.		
6. Second Threshold Subtract $44,000 from Line 4 ($34,000, if single).*	6.	
This section will help you estimate how much of your Social Security benefits will be taxed.		
7. Multiply Line 5 by 0.50 (50%).	7.	
8. Multiply Line 6 by 0.35 (35%).	8.	
9. Add Lines 7 and 8.	9.	
10. Multiply annual Social Security benefits by .85 (85%).	10.	
11. Multiply annual Social Security benefits by .50 (50%).	11.	
12. Multiply Line 6 by .85 (85%).	12.	
13. Add Lines 11 and 12.	13.	
14. Enter whichever amount is smaller: Line 9, 10 or 13.	14.	
Line 14 is an estimate of how much of your Social Security benefits will be considered taxable income.		
15. Multiply Line 14 by your estimated tax rate.	15.	
Line 15 is an estimate of how much your taxes will be.		

SETTLING UP WITH THE IRS

If you're unable to pay your federal income taxes, call 800-829-1040 well before April 15 and explain your situation. If the tax bill is under $10,000 you will be sent a one-page form (9465), "Installment Agreement Request," to attach to your regular return. The Internal Revenue Service promises to respond within 30 days. Those who owe more than $10,000 must complete a financial statement and provide additional documentation.

The IRS usually allows payments to extend for 2 or 3 years if the tax owed is less than $10,000, with the average agreement lasting 1 to 1.5 years. Interest and late penalties on the unpaid tax continue to accrue, but they are less than the penalty for not filing a tax return at all. If back taxes are so high it is likely they will never be repaid, taxpayers can file an offer-in-compromise. How much the IRS will settle for varies with each case.

KEEPING TRACK OF ESTIMATED TAXES

Internal Revenue Service Payment Record				
Qtr	Date Paid	Amount	Check Number	Due Date
1				
2				
3				
4				

State of _____ Payment Record				
Qtr	Date Paid	Amount	Check Number	Due Date
1				
2				
3				
4				

INSURANCE—UNDERSTANDING THE GREAT MYSTERY

The insurance industry is one of the largest industries in the world and provides hundreds of millions of dollars each year in claims and benefits. Yet it remains a mystery to most people. An insurance policy is simply a contract between you (the insured) and an insurance company (the insurer), under which the insurance company promises to pay for your losses according to the specified terms of your contract.

You are transferring your risk of monetary loss to the insurance company. The insurance company accepts your risk because it hopes to make a profit by collecting money—premiums—from a large number of people it insures. Then, it invests the money. From the money collected and the earnings on that money the insurer pays claims and operating expenses. Hopefully, for the insurer these expenditures will be less than the total from collected premiums plus the invested earnings from those premiums.

The Concept Of Risk—Whenever you have a financial interest in something, whether it be your life, your health, your possessions or your job, you face risk. You face the possibility that your budget will be upset or that your net worth will be reduced drastically. Because of the great effect that losses could have on your financial health, you must devise ways of dealing with risk. You have several options:

> You can ignore the risk;
> You can lessen it by some action you take to lower the risk;
> You can share the risk, or
> You can assume the risk.

When you weigh the potential costs of ignoring or assuming the risk entirely, insurance often becomes a bargain.

LIFE INSURANCE

Why is it called life insurance? This is one of the great misnomers in our society because life insurance proceeds are paid upon the death of the insured. You buy life insurance to provide funds for costs which may befall your benefactors after your death. (As a widowed person, you are probably more aware of this than other people). If your spouse owned life insurance policies, you know the benefits of this coverage.

Life insurance is an intangible, and even if you own it, you can't see it, touch it, smell it, or taste it. The only thing that makes it ultimately real is the event that causes the payout of the benefit. Deciding whether or not, and in what amounts, you need life insurance is an important issue. Here are some reasons why you should consider owning life insurance:

1. If you have anyone, children or an aging parent, dependent on you for an income, life insurance might be a wise investment. If you were taken out of the picture, and it would affect the income flow to your beneficiaries, life insurance would help minimize their income loss;

2. If you feel that the debts you have would be a burden to your heirs, then you may want to consider life insurance;

3. If your estate is larger than $600,000, you might want to think about using life insurance to pay the estate taxes;

4. If you want to leave an inheritance for your beneficiaries, life insurance is an easy way to do it.

The Right Amount

You will want to have enough coverage to bridge the gap between what your dependents will need and the current resources available after your death. Figure the costs your dependents will face—mortgage payments, other loans, college expenses, health costs and everyday living expenses. Also, consider your present resources: employer-provided life insurance, if it is available, your liquid assets, potential pension benefits, Social Security survivor benefits and so forth.

Now you're ready to use the form on page 132, "The Widowed Persons Capital Needs Worksheet," as a guide to determine the right dollar amount for your insurance.

1. Estimate how much money your survivors will need if you are not in the picture.

CHAPTER 9

2. Figure how much debt payment you will have to make, how much emergency reserve money you need, and any estate settlement costs.

3. Add all these items together to determine your total capital needs.

4. Determine your total capital available by adding your existing insurance, any current assets available that can produce income, and any other lump-sum distributions available to your heirs at *your* death.

5. Take that total, the total capital available, and subtract it from your total capital needs to determine how much net capital you need.

In the example provided on the next page, the total capital need is $558,943, and the total capital available is $490,700. The net capital needed in this case is $68,243. Notice that in the first line item listing, called "After tax income needs," you need to include mortgage or rent payments, utilities, food, clothing, installment payments, medical/dental payments, educational payments, entertainment, child care, home/auto maintenance, etc.

Once you determine the amount of insurance coverage you need, it is important to pick the right kind of policy for your situation. Basically, there are only four types of life insurance available today—term, whole life, universal life and variable life.

Term Insurance

Term insurance is pure protection against financial loss resulting from death occurring during a specified period of time. Term insurance offers the most coverage for the least amount of initial premium. It is not designed to meet a permanent lifetime need.

There are three types of term insurance:

1. annual renewable term;
2. level term;
3. decreasing term or mortgage insurance.

1. *Annual renewable term insurance*, also called yearly renewable term, is the simplest form of life insurance available. It requires an annual charge which provides you with a specific death benefit for the following year. There are no cash values or side funds available.

Quality contracts provide you with both a renewable and a convertible clause. This means you may renew the contract each year by paying the premium without taking any medical exam. You may con-

WIDOWED PERSON'S CAPITAL NEEDS WORKSHEET

	Yours	*Example*
A. Family Income Needs (yearly):		
1) After-tax income needs		$ 43,500
2) Less: Estimated Social Security Benefits		−12,000
3) Less: Pension Survivor Benefit Income		−3,600
4) Equals: Income Needed from Investment Capital		26,400
5) Capital needed assuming 7% after-tax return (Divide A4 by 7%)		$377,143
B. Debt Repayment Needs:		
1) Home Mortgage(s)		$ 47,000
2) Charge and Credit Cards		1,500
3) Bank loans (cars, etc.)		4,800
4) Other		0
5) Total		$ 53,300
C. Other Funding Needs:		
1) Emergency Reserves (6 months)		$ 21,000
2) College Education (See Chapter 12)		100,000
3) Other		0
4) Total		$121,000
D. Estate Settlement Costs:		
1) Funeral Expenses		$ 5,000
2) Administration/Probate Fees		1,500
3) Federal Estate Tax (See Chapters 6, 15)		0
4) State Death Tax (See Chapters 6, 15)		0
5) Uninsured Medical Costs		1,000
6) Other		0
7) Total		$ 7,500
E. Summary of Total Capital Needs:		
A. Family Income Needs		$377,143
B. Debt Repayment Needs		53,300
C. Other Funding Needs		121,000
D. Estate Settlement Costs		7,500
E. Total		$558,943
F. Assets Available to Produce Income:		
1) Investments and Cash Reserves		$400,000
2) Pension		0
3) Profit-Sharing and 401(k)		21,700
4) IRA, Keogh (HR-10)		19,000
5) Life Insurance on your life		50,000
6) Total Assets Available		$490,700
G. Capital Needs/Assets Summary:		
1) Total Capital Needed (E)		$558,943
2) Total Assets Available (F6)		490,700
3) Net Capital Needed		$ 68,243

vert the contract to any cash value or universal life contract by completing a form provided by the insurance carrier. Because term policies have no cash values, premiums are determined mainly by mortality costs. This means that your premium increases annually as the probability of your death increases. As you become older, this type of coverage eventually can become expensive and usually renewable only until age 75, with a few exceptions, making them unsuitable for estate or post-retirement planning.

2. With *Level Term Insurance*, premiums and coverage remain level for a certain period of time. This period, stated in the policy, can be 5, 10, 15 or perhaps even 20 years. After the level premium period ends, renewal may be available for the next period, at which time a medical exam is often required.

Level term is best if you need 10 years or more of coverage. Over an extended period of time, level term plans are generally more cost effective than annual renewable term policies.

3. The third type of term insurance is called *Decreasing Term* or *Mortgage Insurance*. This coverage usually decreases annually by a specified percentage over a pre-determined period during which time the premiums remain level. This is the most expensive type of term policy that you can buy. Your coverage ends when the policy face amount reduces to zero, or the term expires. This type of coverage is often sold in conjunction with mortgages through mortgage placement firms or banking institutions.

Since term insurance offers the most economic way to purchase a large amount of life insurance protection for a specific period of time, it is particularly advantageous for younger widowed persons who have elderly parents or children under eighteen. Let's say that you are a widowed person who has an elderly parent who is dependent on you for support and whose life expectancy is only another four or five years. If you should die first, there might be financial problems for that elderly person. You can buy a ten-year term policy in this case, just to put some cushion on the time frame.

You can also use life insurance if you have college bound children dependent on your income to pay for their education. You might want to buy some inexpensive term insurance to cover their college costs.

Shopping For Term Insurance—One way for you to shop for term insurance without an insurance agent is to call one of the insurance quote firms that provides computerized analysis. It will list four or five of the lowest cost policies from their database, for your particular situations. Such firms usually deal with insurance companies having quality ratings in the insurance industry. Here are some resources:

1. Insurance Information, 41 Pleasant Street, Suite 208, Mathuen, Maine 01844. Telephone: 800-472-5800. They provide comparisons of policies, but do not sell insurance.

2. Insurance Quote, 3200 North Dobson Road, Building C, Chandler, AZ 85224. Telephone: 800-972-1104.

3. Life Quote, 800 Douglas Road, Suite 450, Coral Gables, FL 33134. Telephone: 800-776-7873.

4. Select Quote, 140 Second Street, San Francisco, CA 94105. Telephone: 800-343-1985.

5. Term Quote, 2555 South Dixie Avenue, Dayton, Ohio 45409. Telephone: 800-444-8376.

Other Types of Term Insurance

Group term life insurance is life insurance that your employer buys on your behalf. As long as your coverage does not exceed $50,000 you are not taxed on the premiums the employer pays. If your coverage is more than $50,000, however, you are taxed on the premiums paid for the excess based on an IRS table. So you pay some tax for the extra coverage, but the tax cost is far less than the cost of similar coverage outside the company.

Whole Life Insurance

Some people continuously need some type of life insurance. Accordingly, whole life insurance, as its name suggests, is designed to offer financial protection for your whole life. In addition to death protection, whole life insurance has a savings feature called "cash value." You can borrow against this cash value, often at low interest rates. You can also set your own repayment schedule for any loan.

Because the policy offers permanent insurance coverage, premiums will be higher than for term insurance in the early years but lower over a long period of time. Whole life policies are most appropriate for those who want lifetime coverage, need the discipline of forced savings, and who will not need to cash in the policy for a minimum of at least 15 years.

After 15 years, the cash value is usually greater than the premiums paid into the policy. Another important feature of whole life insurance type policies is that the cash value in the policies does accumulate on a tax-deferred basis.

Universal Life

Universal life is a life insurance policy with an adjustable death benefit and flexible premiums. The pricing usually is based on current mortality and interest assumptions. A minimum premium is required in the first year, but afterwards the amount and frequency of your premiums are flexible.

Variable Life Insurance

Variable life combines the traditional tax deferred savings features of life insurance with the potential growth of equity type investments. Similar to traditional whole life insurance, variable policies have fixed premiums and usually a guaranteed minimum death benefit.

The variable life policy is an investment vehicle that let's you decide how the money in the savings part of the policy should be invested; stocks, bonds, money market accounts, or a combination. However, as the name implies, the amount of insurance coverage provided may vary with the investment profits (and losses) generated in the investment part of the policy.

Variable life is best only for those persons who need a tax shelter, have investment experience, and can tolerate the risk involved. It is not a product suitable for most widowed persons.

Compare Before Buying

It pays to shop for insurance. For example, a $100,000 universal life policy may cost a healthy 35 year old widow $650 in annual premiums with one company and over $900 with another. So after you pick the policy type that seems best suited to your needs, you need to compare the rates and policy features. If you are buying whole life or variable life, compare the death benefits and the annual premium payments.

Other features you need to compare include the total death benefit and the annual premium payments. Look at the guaranteed cash value growth or projected investment yields after one year, three years, five years, seven years and ten years. Check these yields for the number of years between your present age and 65.

Don't look *only* at the long term gain, even if you intend to keep this policy for twenty years or more. Compare the guaranteed rates to the projected rates. Consider the loan rates in the policy as well. Check to see how the annual dividends, if any, are paid, and how they may be used to offset your premium costs.

Also when examining policies, consider that Section 1035 of the Internal Revenue Code says that certain insurance policies may be exchanged for other insurance policies without any taxable gain or loss. In general, the following types of exchanges are non-taxable:

1. Exchanging one life insurance contract for another, for an endowment, or for an annuity contract;

2. Exchanging an endowment contract for another endowment contract or an annuity contract;

3. Exchanging an annuity contract for another annuity contract.

If you wish to exchange a life insurance policy, an endowment contract or a fixed annuity contract for a variable annuity contract with either the same or a different company, it will also qualify as a non-taxable exchange. In order to exchange life policies, each policy will have to be on the life of the same person. If you would like to exchange an annuity for another annuity, the contract will need to be payable to the same person or persons.

In light of this feature you should review any existing life insurance or annuity policies. If the return (i.e., yield) is low compared to other policies, consider a 1035 exchange. A competent insurance agent can be of value in these situations.

Who Should Own Your Insurance Policy?

If you own a policy yourself, or if you retain any ownership rights of a policy at your death, the proceeds at death will be included in your estate and may possibly be subject to estate tax. If your estate will be under $600,000, including the proceeds from your insurance policy, then estate taxes will not apply. If your estate will be over $600,000, however, you may wish to set up a trust for your beneficiaries and let the trust own the policy. You can make annual gifts to the trust to pay the premiums. The trustee then pays the insurance premiums from the trust.

Upon your death, the insurance proceeds go into the trust income tax free. The trust can then buy assets from your estate. In exchange for these assets, your estate receives cash. This cash can then be used to pay the estate taxes. The proceeds of the insurance policy into the trust are not included in your estate.

If your assets are concentrated in real estate or a business, for example, the availability of these invested dollars is limited. Plus, depending on your estate tax bracket, these assets may be subject to significant taxation upon your death. If your heirs do not have sufficient funds to cover your settlement costs and outstanding debts, they may be forced into a liquidation sale, sacrificing inherited belongings to raise quick cash. Proper insurance coverage can provide your heirs with immediate funds to meet such expenses.

However, if you transfer a life insurance policy to a trust within three years of your death, the proceeds will be includible in your estate.

Providing Life Insurance on Children

Most insurance advisors advocate insuring the parent, not the child. A parent normally needs insurance on his or her life and not on the child's. If the parent dies, the child will receive the funds for such things as college education.

Because a child's premium is fairly low, an insurance agent may suggest that an insurance policy will protect the insurability of the child in case he/she becomes chronically ill in the future. While this is true, the fact is that only 1.5 percent of applicants of all ages are denied insurance coverage for ill health. Consider buying your children life insurance only once your life is insured and your other needs are already met.

Life Insurance: Naming a Minor as a Beneficiary

Recently an agent had a client who unexpectedly died. There were two policies involved and the agent had the opportunity to work with the surviving spouse in helping her invest the proceeds. During the discussions it was determined that a minor child was named as a primary beneficiary for part of the proceeds in one of the policies (not sold by this agent).

The mother of the minor child was under the impression she would receive the monies outright on behalf of the child. In this case or in any situation where a minor is named as a primary beneficiary, the insurance company will not pay a death benefit directly to a minor because of the risk of double liability. Before the proceeds can be paid, a probate court must appoint a guardian of the minor's property before the insurance company will pay the death benefit.

A living parent is not a guardian of the child's property without court appointment.

To avoid any delays in having life insurance proceeds paid to a minor child who is named as a primary beneficiary, the beneficiary designation should name a custodian on behalf of the minor child in accordance with the resident State's Uniform Gift to Minors Act or Uniform Transfers to Minors Act. As an example, "Mary Jane, Custodian under the Maryland UTMA for Baby Jane".

Another solution is to set up a trust and name the trust as the recipient of the life insurance proceeds. A great deal of flexibility can be built into the trust and you can sidestep a number of legal restrictions imposed on outright distributions to minors. This is a safer and surer way to provide financial security for those who can't or don't want to handle large sums of money or other assets.

Choosing a Life Insurance Company

Let's discuss important criteria in choosing a company for your insurance or annuity needs.

You want a strong and secure company to meet your long time financial goals. You also want a company with significant experience, a good reputation, strong ratings and a high quality investment portfolio. The key factors to look at are:

1. Experience and reputation;

2. Independent rating services evaluation;

3. High quality investment portfolio (and philosophy!).

Your relationship with a life insurance company will likely be for many years. Therefore you want to make sure that the company will be there when you have a claim or are ready to retire. Consider how long the company has been in business and how the company has fared in difficult economic times. Look for a company known for its integrity, financial stability, and timeliness in claims payment and service.

Several major rating services evaluate the claims paying ability and financial strength of insurance companies. These services are experts in analyzing insurance companies and are familiar with the various companies' strategies and management:

1. *A.M. Best Co*. A.M. Best Company profiles hundreds of life insurance and annuity companies, rates their financial condition and lists the states in which they are licensed to do business. Because A.M. Best rates 3,800 insurance companies, it can provide an effective measure of a company's standing among its peers. A.M. Best Co., Inc., A.M. Best Road, Holdwick, NJ 08858 Telephone: 908-439-2200.

2. *Standard & Poors Corporation*. S & P has rated the claims paying ability of insurance companies since 1971. Their ratings show how companies can meet its obligations both now and in the future. The ratings range from AAA to C. Standard & Poors Corporation, 25 Broadway, New York, NY 10004. Telephone: 212-208-8000.

3. *Duff and Phelps Credit Rating Company*. Duff and Phelps combine quantitative and qualitative analysis. The key factors they examine include the amount of surplus, profitability and asset quality. This service also considers meetings with company managers highly important. These sessions measure top managers' experience and goals as well as their ability to match

investments with obligations. Duff and Phelps Credit Rating Company, 55 East Monroe Street, Chicago, IL 60603. Telephone: 312-368-3131.

4. *Moody's Investor Service Inc*. Moody's rates an insurer's credit quality. As such, the ratings are Moody's opinion of the ability of an insurance company to repay policyholder obligations and claims punctually. This service makes an effort to consider future worse case scenarios in assigning ratings. Moody's also includes quantitative as well as qualitative factors in its ratings. Moody's Investor Service Inc., 99 Church Street, New York, NY 10007. Telephone: 212-553-0300.

5. *Weiss Research, Inc*. Weiss has only evaluated insurance companies since 1989. To arrive at its ratings, Weiss uses numbers available through state insurance regulatory departments. It does not evaluate the management strength of a company. This service only considers the numbers as indicators of the company's ability to weather a deep recession. Weiss Research, Inc., 2200 North Florida Mango Road, West Palm Beach, FL 33409. Telephone: 407-684-8100.

If you have difficulty in finding the ratings for various insurance companies, a publication called *The Best Agent's Guide to Life Insurance Companies* is available in most libraries. Within this publication is a list of the phone numbers, many of them 800-numbers, for almost every company doing business in the United States. Most companies will provide their ratings information when you call them. They will even send you literature about the rating services and how their company stacks up in the overall rating of each particular service.

Other sources for additional information include these industry organizations:

1. The American Council of Life Insurance, 1001 Pennsylvania Avenue NW, Washington, D.C. 20004. Telephone: 202-624-2000.

2. The National Association of Insurance Commissioners, Suite 1100, 120 West 12th Street, Kansas City, MO 64105. Telephone: 816-842-3600.

3. The National Association of Life Underwriters, 1922 F Street NW, Washington, D.C. 20006. Telephone: 202-331-6000.

4. Your state insurance department is also a good source of information.

DISABILITY INCOME INSURANCE

Most widowed persons don't give much thought to what they'd do if a disabling illness or accident were to stop them from earning their livelihood. If you work and you become permanently disabled, your income, obviously, would be substantially reduced. Your cost of living, however, would remain the same and might even increase.

For the younger widow of about age 35, the chances of becoming disabled for 3 months or more is nearly 3 times as great as the chance of dying. At age 50, the odds are nearly 4 times as great. The greatest financial asset you have is your ability to generate an income. One of the most frightening situations that can happen to you is the loss of your ability to work for an extended period of time. Consequently, it is important to consider the financial consequences if your income is shut off as a result of a disability.

> **NOTE:** Unless you have enough income producing assets, disability insurance is a definite necessity for financial security. Income is required for basic needs—food, clothing, shelter—as well as the medical expenses connected with a disability.

In choosing a disability policy look for these features:

1. Non-cancelable and guaranteed renewability;

2. Monthly benefits that will replace 60 percent or even 70 percent of your income until age 65;

3. A cost-of-living adjustment rider which will protect the benefits from inflation;

4. A future insurability option to increase insurance as your income rises, regardless of your health;

5. A policy that eliminates premium payments while you are disabled. This is called a waiver of premium feature;

6. A residual benefits clause which allows partial payouts for partial disabilities;

7. A waiting period that will match your ability to pay for the policy along with your income needs (i.e., how long you can last before disability payments need to begin).

Group Disability Insurance

Your employer may provide protection for short-term illnesses or accidents. This type of coverage normally commences on the first or 14th day of your recovery and continues for 13 or 26 weeks. Employers may also provide long-term coverage with benefits to age 65. Both of these plans may have rigid definitions of disability and are more difficult for you to collect on than private policies.

Group plans typically cover no more than 60 percent of your salary. If the employer pays the premiums, the benefits are taxable to you. Disability insurance benefits are not taxable to you, though, if you pay the premiums.

HEALTH CARE INSURANCE COVERAGE

Health care insurance coverage is an essential element in making the money last. Without adequate health care insurance, all of your financial accomplishments and goals could easily be wiped out. Health care insurance coverage is a necessary part of their financial planning. Not only is it a way to meet the cost of illness and injury, but coverage is a vehicle to protect your existing assets and financial plans.

Types of Health Care Coverage

There are a wide variety of health care insurance products from which to choose. Understanding the basics of the various types of policies including hospital, surgery expense, physician expense, major medical and comprehensive major medical policies will make your choices easier. Following is a brief description of the types of health care coverage as well as terms used with medical insurance plans.

Hospital Insurance

Hospital insurance policies provide you with reimbursement covering the cost of hospital room and board and other expenses incidental to hospitalization. Basically, hospital insurance pays for a portion of the per day hospital room (semi-private) and board charges which typically include floor nursing and other routine services. Additional expenses such as operating room, laboratory tests, X-rays and medications you need while in the hospital are also covered.

Many hospital plans also offer reimbursement for some outpatient and out-of-hospital services. In most policies, hospital insurance is written to provide daily semi-private room and board charges up to a specified number of days such as 90, 120 or 360. The maximum reimbursement for the added expenses, however, may be a stated dollar amount or a multiple of the daily room rate.

Surgical Expense Insurance

Surgical expense insurance provides insurance for the cost of surgery in or out of the hospital. Typically, a list of scheduled benefits is provided which lists the dollar amount the insurer is required to pay for each surgical procedure.

Second Surgical Opinion

Most surgical expense plans fully cover the cost of a second surgical opinion. Some group health plans even require second opinions on specific procedures. Without second opinions, these health plans may reduce the surgical benefit they pay to you.

Physician Expense Insurance

Physician expense insurance, also called regular medical expense insurance, covers physician fees for non-surgical care in a hospital, including consultations with specialists. Also covered are X-rays and laboratory tests performed outside of the hospital. These plans usually provide the maximum amount payable as listed on a scheduled list.

Major Medical Insurance

Major medical plans provide benefits for nearly all types of medical expenses resulting from either illnesses or accidents. The amounts that you can collect under these policies are relatively large. Lifetime benefits of $100,000 to $1 million or more are common. Some policies have no limits at all.

Deductibles—Because major medical plans are designed to supplement basic hospital, surgical and physicians expense policies, they frequently include deductibles of $500 to $1000. Many plans currently offer an all-inclusive deductible for the calendar year. This allows a person to accumulate the deductible for more than one incident. In some plans, the deductible is on a per accident or per illness basis.

Co-insurance—This provision stipulates that the company will pay some portion, say, 70, 80 or 90 percent, of the covered amount of loss over the deductible rather than paying the entire amount. Because major medical limits now go up to $1 million or more, many plans have a stop-loss provision which places a cap on the amount of participation required. Without this feature a $1 million medical bill could still leave the insured with a large co-insurance cost.

Internal Limits—Most major medical plans are written with internal limits. Internal limits place boundaries on the amounts that are paid for certain expenses, even if the overall policy limits are not exceeded by a particular claim.

Comprehensive Major Medical Insurance

A comprehensive major medical insurance policy combines basic hospital, surgical and physicians expense policies with major medical protection in a single policy. The deductibles under a comprehensive major medical plan are usually low, often $100 or less. Most of these plans have a more favorable co-insurance clause than major medical policies, and they may require no co-insurance on basic hospital expense claims.

Dental Insurance

Some employers offer dental insurance through group policies. Dental insurance usually covers necessary dental health care as well as some dental injuries sustained through accidents. Dental work is covered under most policies, but policies vary greatly. Some dental plans contain deductible and co-insurance provisions. Others have first dollar protection and pay for all claims. Premiums are often large in light of the dollar amount of coverages paid.

Medigap Policies

In 1990, Congress passed a new law which requires all states to comply with certain standards for MediGap insurance with supplements to Medicare coverage. The new law protects consumers by restricting certain sales practices of insurance agencies and companies. It also simplifies policies by limiting the types of plans that can be sold and by specifying exactly what benefits each plan must contain. A detailed list of coverages is available from your local Medicare office.

AUTOMOBILE INSURANCE

If you own an automobile, you need auto insurance. In most states you can't drive without it. The following are the seven types of coverage which all auto insurers offer. You need to understand them before you make any decisions on buying automobile insurance or changing your existing policy:

1. *Bodily injury/liability injury.* If you are involved in an accident which kills or hurts other people, this part of your auto insurance covers legal cost and legal liability. You need to have this coverage. If you live in a no-fault state, you need less liability coverage because each insurance company pays for an accident no matter whose fault it is. If you can afford it, however, you should carry a minimum of $100,000. If you have substantial assets, carry a minimum of $300,000. Supplement

this policy with an umbrella policy. An umbrella liability policy is so called because it adds coverage over the existing liability coverage you have with your automobile policy. This normally can be added very cheaply. (See Liability Insurance on page 146).

2. *Collision coverage.* This coverage pays for the cost of repairing your car. Collision insurance is usually the largest part of your automobile insurance premium. However, the higher your deductible, the lower your cost. Please remember that insurance companies will pay only market or book value for your car. The older your car gets the less will be paid to fix it. Also, if you "total" the car, i.e., it is a complete loss, you may not receive enough cash back to buy another comparable car to replace it.

3. *Comprehensive coverage.* This includes theft, broken glass, vandalism, fire, flood or other acts of God.

4. *Medical payments coverage.* This pays for doctor and hospital bills that come about as a result of an accident. Both you and your passengers are covered.

5. *Property damage liability.* This part of your policy pays for property damage caused by you while driving your car. If, for example, you run into somebody's store, you are protected. You need to have at least $50,000 of property damage coverage.

6. *Uninsured motorists coverage.* Although it is against the law in most states to drive without automobile insurance, some people do. This insurance will protect you and your passengers if the other driver is uninsured or if you are the victim of a hit and run accident. It covers medical expenses, loss of wages, pain and suffering.

7. *Underinsured motorists coverage.* If you are in an accident which is somebody else's fault and that person is underinsured, this part of your policy will cover the difference for liability claims.

Some cars are expensive to insure and insurance companies know which cars have a high vulnerability to theft or mechanical breakdowns or are expensive to repair. *Before buying any car, check out the cost of a policy on it.*

Premium discounts are often available for factors such as good driving record, multi-car coverage, mature driver, anti-theft devices, defensive driving courses passed, restrictive mileage usage, non-smoker, and certain rural locations. Also included are discounts for seat belts or air bags. These discounts can add up to substantial savings, so be sure to ask your agent about them. Note, also, that if someone else is driving your car *with* your permission, your insurance coverage will normally cover everything it would have covered if you were driving.

HOMEOWNERS INSURANCE

Whether you are a renter or a homeowner, you need to understand what homeowner's insurance can provide for you. Homeowner's insurance usually covers much more than fire damage. Other coverage includes:

1. damage to your home or additional structures;

2. liability for that which you or your family is responsible, usually anywhere in the world;

3. damage and theft to any of your property except, perhaps, for your car;

4. living expenses while your house is being repaired due to fire or some other catastrophe;

5. injury to someone on your property.

In covering your home, make certain that you insure for the replacement value of your home, not the fair market value. This is important even for a partial loss. Often your home needs to be insured for at least 80 percent of its replacement value for you to recover the full amount of a partial loss by fire or other casualty.

If your home is insured for less than 80 percent of the replacement value, you effectively become what is called a "co-insurer." Consider this example for Linda Smith who had a major fire in one of her bedrooms.

Replacement value of home	$250,000
Fire policy limit of current policy	150,000
Bedroom fire resulting in damages of	40,000
Insurance company pays	24,000
Linda pays	$ 16,000

Because Linda was covered for only 60 percent of the replacement value of her home, $150,000, rather than 80 percent, $200,000, she became the co-insurer for 40 percent of the loss. Therefore, she was responsible for $16,000 in damages. Had she insured for 80 percent of the replacement value, her insurance would have covered the full $40,000 (less any deductible).

Protection of Personal Items

One of the quickest ways to ensure that your personal and valuable items will be protected is to take color snap shots of each room and its contents. Be sure to take close-up's of valuables including art, china, silver and glassware. You will want to have a written and photographic inventory to have in your safety deposit box.

Using a videotape is a good idea if you can sequence the date. For example, hold up a newspaper and make sure the date on the newspaper is legible. Also check with your insurer to see if discounts for smoke alarm, senior citizen, burglar alarms, non-smoker, sprinkler system, etc., are available.

If you have particular items of value that you would like to have appraised but can't find an appraiser, contact the American Society of Appraisers at P.O. Box 17265, Washington, D.C. 20041, Telephone: 1-703-620-3828. Ask for a free directory of Certified Professional Personal Property Advisors, and include a self-addressed stamped envelope.

LIABILITY UMBRELLA INSURANCE

The diversity of activities in which people now engage sometimes exceeds the limits of coverage for the policies discussed so far. Hence, the insurance industry has developed an umbrella policy that provides a broader scope of coverage with higher limits of liability than is normally encountered. The purpose of the liability umbrella policy is not to replace the other policies, but to provide excess liability coverage over and above what is referred to as the underlying limits.

The liability umbrella policy has two deductibles. The first deductible constitutes the limits of the underlying auto and personal liability policies. The second deductible, usually $250, is for any liability exposures beyond the scope of the underlying policies.

How much liability coverage is enough? Most insurance advisors agree that you need a lot more than you used to, and insurance is a very personal question. Look at what you can afford to pay and what assets you want to protect. You need to carry at least enough coverage to protect your total net worth.

It's an unfortunate aspect of our society today that if you are particularly successful or visible in your community, you are more likely to be sued and more likely to be hit with higher damage awards. "Financial visibility" greatly increases your risk. Therefore, you may want to increase coverage to protect the value of major assets such as your home or investment portfolio.

Liability rates vary from state to state. It may be cheaper for you to increase coverage with a one million dollar or larger umbrella policy than to significantly increase the limits on your existing homeowner and auto policies. In most states, you can expect to pay from $90 to $200 a year for a $1,000,000 umbrella policy.

While the insurance industry may change dramatically in the years ahead, your need for insurance protection remains. Deal only with the most stable companies, that are highly rated, and easily accessible by phone and mail. Ignore the rest.

PART III:

ENSUING CONCERNS

MONEY, CHILDREN
AND YOU

The last thing you probably expect at this time, or need, is problems from your children. Yet, it often happens that families bicker their way through their grief, and many shaky financial decisions are made during this period "for the good of the kids."

Children do need to be taken into account as you proceed through the bereavement and recovery period. After all, they're in mourning, too. Children sometimes exert pressure on widowed parents however, without meaning to do so, and the parents respond by focusing on the children while overriding considerations the parents need to make for themselves.

Ignoring your needs and thinking only of your children can blind you to what needs to be done. Take Donna's situation:

> A few months after John died, Donna began having money disagreements with her three grown children. Donna was thunderstruck; this wasn't what she expected.
>
> Donna and John had supported their oldest son, Bob, age 26, through most of his college education, and had also helped Bob purchase a car. Bob still owed $3,000 on a student loan, and he wanted his mother to pay it for him.
>
> Bill, age 20, had a year left in college; he wanted his father's pickup truck and enough money to spend the summer in Europe. Donna's daughter, Joan, age 24, was recently married, and made it known that she and her husband could use financial help to buy a new home.
>
> Donna gave each child $2,500 when John died, but the children seemed to want more, and Donna had a nagging feeling that she should do more. As one of her sons said, "Well, Mom, at least Dad left *you* well off."

Your financial situation may be of interest to your children, but it's vitally important to you. Wanting to help your children is natural and understandable, but doing it excessively and at the wrong times can create unfortunate results. If your money is used up, you will still have needs that must be met.

Remember that your primary objective is to make the money last. As you did in Chapter 7 on income planning, review your assets, liabilities and cash flow numbers to determine whether you'll have enough income for your continued well-being and future standard of living. Most parents and children don't want to be burdens to each other. If the numbers add up, and you can afford to make gifts to the children, go ahead; if your data suggest that meeting your children's desires is unwise, don't do it.

There is also the question of fairness. To avoid the implication between offspring that one received more in value than another, you may want to keep a private list of your giving. The relative value of your gifts may help to balance things out, as well as remind you what gifts already have been made. Your list should include such items as jewelry, cash, furniture, investment shares, stock certificates, bonds, life insurance or other items of value.

SAVINGS: A LEARNING EXPERIENCE FOR CHILDREN

If you're widowed and your children are minors, you have an opportunity to help them learn the habit of saving. Children save mainly for short-term goals—clothes, a concert or special events. Getting them into a savings pattern is your long-term goal. Once they form the habit, they can carry it into adulthood and save for longer-term objectives, such as a home, or even retirement.

Banks or credit unions are good places to start savings accounts, since most will waive fees on children's accounts; many banks even offer special youth savings programs. Take your children with you when you open the account. Let them actually deposit the funds and receive the receipt from the bank teller. Explain everything, or have bank officials do it. Participation is important; children who feel they are involved are more likely to respond to your training.

When the bank statement arrives, review it with your children and show them how the deposit earned money, even while they were asleep. Let your children take funds from their accounts if they wish, but examine with them the rationale for the withdrawal—if they feel they can't ever get to the funds, they may not wish to add to them.

Most experts agree that good money habits begin at home, starting with an allowance and continue by teaching young children how to earn and save. Some children develop such a strong feeling of responsibility that they use their allowance as an initial cash flow for their own businesses. In fact, the Young Americans Bank in Denver, Colorado, supplements allowances by lending money to businesses run by children.

Unfortunately, many parents use an allowance as a tool for discipline, which transfers the child's focus from learning money management to learning appropriate behaviors. Child guidance experts suggest giving children the opportunity to earn extra money apart from their allowance; if they don't do a good job for the additional funds, take the money back.

The other side of savings is how the money is spent. A spending plan, which is similar to an adult budget, is the way children learn to allocate money between savings and weekly expenses, such as lunch, field trips, gifts and clothing. Give your children the freedom to develop their plan, and then sit down and conduct regular evaluation sessions with them. Budgeting helps them identify the material goods they really want, and what it takes to achieve them.

By the time your children are 11 or 12, they will probably be mature enough to understand basic investments. You might consider starting an investment plan using a mutual fund, and then using the income earned from the fund to finance your child's allowance. Although this might mean you'll have to distribute the allowance quarterly, to coincide with the fund's dividend payout, the system would reinforce to the child the importance of developing excellent budgeting and spending habits.

Before long, your children will become interested in what you're doing with money that makes money. Since children are avid consumers, stocks may be even more exciting than mutual funds. For example, Walt Disney, McDonald's and Nintendo are three companies popular with children, because the appeal of their products is easy for children to understand. For older children, you might want to suggest shares of Apple Computer, Microsoft or Home Box Office.

WATCH THE CREDIT CARDS

Credit cards might seem to be an easy financial product for children to understand, yet many who have cards, or access to them, are surprisingly ignorant about them. Recently, college-age students have been the target of credit card issuers who are eager to build long-term customer relationships. These major credit card companies require only that individuals sign their names to obtain a card.

Parents can cause problems for their children, and ultimately for themselves, by co-signing for a separate card or by lending a card. Wise parents will explain how credit cards work, what the interest rates are, how interest is calculated, and how the repayment is scheduled. Next, set parameters: state clearly what the card can be used for and how much can be charged.

MAKING LOANS TO CHILDREN

Most people want to help their children and grandchildren, and you no doubt feel the same way. Naturally, you want the best for your offspring, and perhaps you feel that if you can assist them financially, you can make things easier for them.

There's a vast difference between making a gift to your offspring and making a loan. Lending money to your children or grandchildren, while a gesture of love and caring, is also a financial decision that deserves your careful concern and attention.

- Will there be good consequences for both you and the child?

- Will it be a "win-win" situation?

- Can you afford it?

- Is it a bona fide loan, or really just a gift?

You need to decide whether you can afford it. If you can't, you have to say, "No," even though you may find it difficult to do so. When you have to refuse a relative, one approach is to review again why the money is needed, and state in general terms why you can't lend it. Perhaps you can explore together some alternative solutions to solving the problem.

Next, if you decide that you can afford it, determine what the purpose of the loan is. For what purpose is the money going to be used? Is the purpose worthwhile? If so, proceed to the next question.

How trustworthy is the child? This is a hard but essential question. Everyone would like to trust their children and grandchildren equally, but there are always individual considerations of responsibility, maturity and integrity for each child.

- What's your child's past track record?

- How will the child repay you?

- Will the child willingly agree to sign a promissory note?

- What resources will the child use to repay the loan?

You may want to play the role of "lender" and check out the "creditworthiness" of the "borrower." Many credit advisors advocate getting a loan agreement in writing, especially if large sums of money are involved. Here's an example that illustrates why putting it in writing is a good idea.

Gloria lent her son a substantial sum to start a business. After two years the business failed, and the son had no way of repaying the loan.

Gloria could claim a tax write-off for the bad debt loss, but only if she can substantiate the loan with a document that states the terms of repayment and any collateral arrangements. Moreover, to claim a bad debt deduction on her tax return, Gloria has to prove that she attempted and failed to collect what was due her.

If you decide to lend money to a relative, say, $500 or less, you can use a simple letter of agreement such as the one presented here:

Simple Letter Agreement
For Loan to Family Member

_____(Date)_____

Name of Lender
Street Address
City, State, Zip Code

Dear _____

This letter is evidence that you have loaned me $_____, which I intend to repay as follows:

(Describe the loan repayments, any interest to be charged and dates of repayment.)

I am very appreciative of your willingness to loan the money to me, and I intend to repay it fully.

_____

Signature

For loans in larger amounts, say $500 or more, you may need a more formal letter that includes more provisions. I suggest using the promissory note on page 156. Despite the large number of blanks, is not difficult to handle and ready for you to complete.

Sample Promissory Note

_____
(Your City/State)

_____
(Date)

$ __(Amount of Loan)__

FOR VALUE RECEIVED, the undersigned jointly and severally promise(s) to pay to _____(Name of Lender)_____ , or order, the principal sum of ____(Amount of Loan, Written in Words)____ DOLLARS $ _____(Amount of Loan, Written in Numbers)_____ , with interest on the unpaid balance, from the date hereof until paid, at the rate of ___(Interest Rate, Written in Words)___ percent (_(Interest Rate, Written in Numbers) %)_ per annum. The said principal and interest shall be payable on or before __(Date By Which Repayment Is Due)__ at the office of __(Name of Lender)__ at __(Address of Lender, City, State, Zip)__ , or at such place as the holder may designate in writing.

Privilege is reserved to anticipate payment of this indebtedness in whole or in part at any time. Any partial prepayment shall be applied against the principal amount and shall not postpone the due date of the balance.

Presentment, protest and notice of dishonor are hereby waived. The maker(s) and endorser(s) of this Note also waive the benefit of any homestead exemption as to this debt, and agree to pay all costs of collection hereof, including attorneys' fees if, after default, this Note be placed in the hands of an attorney for collection, or if the holder deems it desirable to secure the services or advice of an attorney with regard to collection.

Security for this promissory note will be the following assets:_____.

_____(Signature of Borrower)_____ SEAL

_____(Signature of Borrower)_____ SEAL

INVESTMENT IDEAS FOR CHILDREN OR GRANDCHILDREN

Eileen wanted to give her children some money each year, to take advantage of the $10,000 annual gift exclusion, while moving the funds out of her estate. She wanted to do something dramatic, something that would make a real difference in the future of her 20 and 21 year old children.

Her financial advisor suggested that Eileen look at funding part of her children's retirement, by placing $10,000 in a variable annuity each year for five years. The estimated numbers look like this:

1. Invest $10,000 each year for five years, then stop. At a yield of eight percent, the variable annuity's value will then be $58,666.

2. Leave the accumulated funds invested in the variable annuity until the child becomes age 59-1/2. By then, at 8 percent, each account will have grown to $1,054,540 for the 20-year-old, and $967,166 for the 21-year-old.

Eileen chose the variable annuity to avoid all federal and state income taxes until the funds are withdrawn at age 59-1/2. Note that if Eileen's children take funds from the annuity before age 59-1/2, they'll have to pay a 10 percent penalty to the IRS. For this reason alone, Eileen's investment will probably last and achieve its original purpose—to fund her children's retirement.

Another investment idea might be appropriate for your children or grandchildren who recently graduated from college, and are now working at their first "real" jobs. Consider giving each of them a gift of $2,000 a year, with the idea that they fund their own IRA with the money. Most young adults qualify to have a tax-deductible IRA, because their income is still low enough. Single people can contribute $2,000, tax-deductible up to the first $25,000 in earnings. Then the deduction begins to phase out until, at $35,000 in earnings, it is completely gone. Here's an example:

Joe is 21, and works full-time earning $21,000 a year. His company doesn't provide a qualified retirement plan, but will probably start one in a few years.

You decide to give Joe $2,000 a year. Joe places the $2,000 into a tax deductible, self-directed IRA, using a growth mutual fund as his investment choice. If contributions are made for five years, and the fund earns an average of 12 percent a year, at age 59-1/2 it will be worth $575,782—not bad for a $10,000 investment.

The sooner you start, the larger the sum will be at age 59-1/2. For example, in Joe's case, waiting one year, until he's age 22, changes the total value at age 59-1/2 to $514,092, a difference of $61,690. The money compounds dramatically in the later years, so the sooner you start the better.

The downside to this overall strategy is the 10 percent IRS penalty levied if withdrawals are made before age 59-1/2. Thus, the money will not be available for other purposes, such as a house downpayment, until age 59-1/2. However, studies have shown that money left in an IRA for at least 10 years puts the owner ahead, even if the penalty is assessed.

TAXES AND YOUR CHILD'S INCOME

If you have dependent children who have income of their own, an income tax return will have to be filed if:

1. Your child has more than $3800 in earned income only;

2. Your child has more than $650 in unearned income only;

3. Your child has more than $650 in *both* earned and unearned income.

Note that children who can be claimed as dependents on your tax return cannot also claim a personal exemption for their return.

You may be able to reduce your total tax liability by giving your children income-producing property. Here's how the income from such property is taxed if your child owns it:

1. If a child is under the age of 14, the first $650 of income is not taxed, and the next $650 of income is taxed at 15 percent. Anything over $1,300 is taxed at the parents' highest marginal tax rate, which can be as much as 39 percent.

2. If a child is over age 14, the first $650 of income is likewise not taxed, but income above $650 is taxed at the child's actual bracket. In this case, the child's income does not fall into the parents' tax bracket at all.

Confusion often arises as to earned income versus unearned income.

Unearned income includes taxable interest, dividends, capital gains, rents, royalties, Social Security and pension benefits, some types of trust income to name a few.

Earned income is from wages or self-employment.

The distinction between unearned and earned income becomes important in determining whether the "kiddie tax" applies to your child.

Children age 14 and over are not subject to the "kiddie tax". Any child who reaches the age of 14 before the end of the tax year is no longer considered a minor for tax purposes. Unearned income in excess of the $650 standard deduction is taxed at the child's rate.

Children with unearned income under the age of 14 may be subject to the "kiddie tax". In this case, unearned income of more than $650 up to $1300 is taxed at the child's rate. Unearned income in excess of $1300 is taxed at your (the parent) rate—unless the child's rate is higher.

If the child is able to use itemized deductible investment expenses and they exceed $650, more than $1300 of unearned income may be exempt from your (the parent) rate.

THE "KIDDIE" TAX	
Unearned Income	*How Taxed*
$0–650	Fully offset by standard deduction
651–1300	Taxed at child's rate
over 1300	Taxed at your top marginal rate

The Tax Reform Act, by taxing the children's investment income at the parent's rate regardless of the income's source, discourages income shifting between parents or grandparents and children under the age of 14. In other words, if you give a grandchild money to be invested, and if those investments generate income, that income will be taxed at the parents' tax bracket—not the grandparents' or the child's tax bracket.

There are some methods of getting around the "kiddie tax." First, you can buy municipal bonds, which are free from federal income tax.

Second, you can buy growth stock or growth mutual funds that pay low dividends over the years but are expected to appreciate in value. If you sell the investment at a profit after the child reaches age 14, the gain would be in the child's tax bracket, not in yours.

Third, if you have your own business, you may "buy" your child a tax deductible allowance by hiring your child to work for the family-owned company. The child's earned income is taxed at the child's rate, which is likely to be much lower than yours. In addition, your company gets a business deduction for the child's salary.

Fourth, you can buy "education savings bonds." For certain tax-payers, the interest on U.S. Savings Bonds that are cashed in to pay for college expenses is tax-free. This applies to interest earned on U.S. Savings Bonds issued after December 31, 1989. Be aware that there are a number of restrictions on these so-called education savings bonds.

CUSTODIAL ACCOUNTS FOR CHILDREN

People who set up an investment plan for a child usually have three primary goals in mind:

1. Safety of principal;

2. Steady growth; and

3. Protection against taxes.

Most parents also would like to maintain control over the funds, so they will be used for the right purpose, such as college education. When you give money to a child and assist in setting up a savings account, you may ensure safety, provide growth and offer tax protection, but you don't maintain control.

Many investment programs for children are established under some kind of custodial arrangement that allows the parents to control the assets. The form of custody is usually a trust,—typically a 2503(c) trust, which will be explained later—the Uniform Gifts to Minors Act (UGMA), or, in some states, the Uniform Transfers to Minors Act (UTMA). Your local banker will know if your state has adopted the UTMA.

UGMAs and *UTMAs.* The UGMA and the UTMA are the simplest types of custodial accounts. You can set up either account inexpensively with virtually any bank, brokerage firm or mutual fund company. Both kinds of accounts allow you or other custodians to control the child's assets without being monitored by any court or other governmental body. Moreover, the UGMA and UTMA still provide tax advantages because they are based on the child's income tax bracket.

The kind of investments you are authorized to have in a UGMA account is limited to cash—certificates of deposit, savings accounts, and the like—or securities, such as stocks, mutual funds or similar investments. The assets automatically go to your child at the age of majority; in most states it is 18. When setting up a UGMA, title the account as follows:

> (Your Name), as Custodian
> for (Child's Name),
> Under the (Name of State)
> Uniform Gifts to Minors Act

The UTMA account, which is offered as an alternative in approximately 30 states, permits you a broader range of investments—including real estate and collectibles, such as paintings and antiques. In addition, under a UTMA, you can defer asset distribution until the child is at least age 21, and in California, age 25.

Both UGMAs and UTMAs allow "free switching of investments," meaning you can sell one mutual fund and buy another, or purchase a different investment entirely. You can withdraw money from either kind of account at any time, as long as the withdrawal is done for the benefit of your child.

Tax-Saving 2503(c) Minority Trusts. If you have substantial assets, you may want to consider setting up a 2503(c) Minority Trust, a vehicle that is designed primarily to help your children build a nest egg for the future. A 2503(c) Trust has some modest current income tax benefits, and it can be used to remove assets from your estate so they aren't taxed at your death. The Trust also has broad investment flexibility: there are no specific limitations on any kind of investments that can be made with it.

There are three main advantages to a 2503(c) Trust:

1. It is exempt from certain IRS rules covering gifts to trusts. Thus, as a parent, you can give up to $10,000 each year to a 2503(c) Trust without incurring any gift tax, allowing you to fund the trust without tax consequences.

2. The trust is taxed as a separate entity, so the first $5,000 of earnings is taxed only at the 15 percent rate, as long as those earnings are allowed to accumulate in the trust and not distributed to you or your child. This is important because of the "kiddie tax," which levies at your higher tax rate on investment income over $1,300 to a child under age 14.

3. It allows you to move assets out of your estate, a feature that is particularly important if your estate is large enough—over $600,000—to qualify for federal estate taxes.

The 2503(c) Trust does present some serious problems if you are worried about what your child might do with a large sum of money at age 21. Some trusts address this issue by incorporating a "window of time" provision, allowing a brief period during which the child can take assets at age 21. If your child does not take the assets within, for example, a 30-day or 60-day period, then the trust may continue until the child is 25 or 30. During the continuation period, the trust again qualifies for gift tax exclusion, so that you can continue to shift assets into the trust if you wish.

If you want to set up a 2503(c) Trust, you'll need the services of a competent attorney who is experienced in drafting trusts.

Remember, when you must deal with your children concerning finances, it's important to balance your emotional desire to help with the realities of your situation. Take an objective look at what you can and cannot do. Don't mortgage your future financial security to avoid a confrontation with your children today. Instead, find a way to maintain a harmonious relationship with them independent of finances.

CHAPTER 10

HOW TO DETERMINE IF YOUR
CHILDREN UNDER AGE 14 ARE SUBJECT
TO THE "KIDDIE TAX"

a) Your child's investment income $ _____

b) Less standard deduction   650

c) Your child's deductible investment expenses   _____

d) Add Lines b and c   _____

e) Enter the larger of Line d, or $1300   _____

f) Subtract amount on Line e from Line a   _____

If line f is zero, (or less), your child has no income subject to tax at your rate.

If line f is $1 or more, your child is subject to kiddie tax and your must file Form 8165 or 8814.

YOU AND YOUR HOME

Home ownership is part of the American dream. However, as a widowed person, due to pressures from family and friends, the American dream may not look so wonderful to you at this point in your life. You may feel a lot of anxiety about home ownership.

> You are wondering if you can take care of the property, if you should sell and buy a smaller home.

> You are wondering, if you have smaller children, is this the right place for you to live.

This chapter will help you decide whether to sell your property, buy another one, or just stay where you are. Also, it will enable you to take a look at refinancing, trade-offs between being a renter verses an owner of real estate. We'll also explore what's known as the $125,000 exemption, your home's "stepped-up," capital gains tax basis, and housing alternatives. We'll consider if should you rent to your children or sell your property to your children, reverse mortgages, and how to handle home repairs.

TAX ADVANTAGES OF OWNING YOUR OWN HOME

There are many reasons to own your home, but tax advantages are still the best. Here are some tax-related reasons for home ownership:

1. Taxation on the growth of your home is deferred until you sell it. If you and your spouse bought your house for $50,000 and today it is worth $100,000, until you sell, that extra $50,000 is not taxed. If you keep it till your death it may never be taxed.

2. The interest you pay on the mortgage for your home is tax deductible. Today you can carry up to $1 million in debt on your primary residence and as much as $100,000 on a second home.

3. If you sell your house and buy one with an equal or higher value within two years, you can continue to defer the unrecognized gain from your current residence.

4. If you are age 55 or older, you can exclude $125,000 in gains when you sell your primary residence.

5. Paying the mortgage helps you build equity. Each month you are placing a portion of your mortgage payment into paying off the principal of your loan. Some of it is interest, some of it is principal.

6. If you are an older widowed person who might be faced with unfunded long term care needs, you will be happy to know that in many states the home is exempt when trying to qualify for Medicaid benefits.

7. Depending on the state you live in, your home will provide varying degrees of protection from creditors.

8. In the event of your death, all unpaid tax on the appreciation of your home is forgiven, as is the portion of the house that was owned by your spouse.

As you can see, there are many advantages of home ownership. Your decision to buy, sell, rent or keep your home should be made only after careful consideration. If you stay in your house, here are a few areas you may need help with:

Should I Refinance?

Before you decide to refinance, you need to take a close look at your current financial picture. Don't refinance because everyone else is doing it, or because friends and relatives say you should. Seriously consider refinancing your home to consolidate expensive debt (getting rid of mounting credit cards charges, for example) and/or to improve your cash flow. If you plan to move in a few years, it won't pay to refinance or do a home equity loan because of the closing costs you will incur.

Is refinancing a good move for you? This depends on various factors including:

1. upfront costs;

2. how long you anticipate remaining in your home;

3. the amount you plan to refinance; and

4. the difference in interest rates between your existing mortgage and a new mortgage.

A good measure of whether or not refinancing is advantageous to you is to determine how long it will take you to recoup the costs. Refinancing a mortgage involves paying closing costs, which include appraisal fees, legal fees, and in most instances, a loan origination fee.

The origination fee, commonly referred to as "points", is based on a percentage of the amount you refinance and can represent a substantial expense. For example, refinancing a $100,000 mortgage at three points will cost you $3,000 in points alone.

Another cost to be considered is the possible payment of a penalty when you have an early payoff on a loan. Also, opportunity cost needs to be recognized. These costs equal the forfeited investment income on monies used to pay for the refinancing. In other words, if you pay $4,000 for refinancing costs, you have to realize the $4,000 could have been invested, earning income for you. Therefore, analyze the potential monthly savings very carefully. Here's an example of a refinance:

Rules for Deducting Mortgage Interest

Interest on mortgage loans (including only equity loans) that are secured by your main or second home is generally deductible in any of the following situations:

- Loans (regardless of amount) incurred on or before 10/13/87, and have not been increased since that date.

- Loans of not more than $500,000 (filing as single person) and the loan proceeds were used to buy, build or substantially improve your home.

- The proceeds of the loans(s) were not used as listed directly above, but is equal to or less than $50,000 (filing as single person).

CHAPTER 11

MORTGAGE REFINANCING ANALYSIS

Using the form below, you can see that Alice can replace her current mortgage balance of $113,900 (10% for 30 years) with a new 7.5%, 30-year loan. The break-even point is 24.6 months.

Item	Description	For Alice	For You
1	Current monthly payment (Principal and Interest)	$1000	_____
2	Anticipated additional years in house	10	_____
3	Additional months in house (Item 2 x 12)	120	_____
4	Total payment (Item 1 x Item 3)	120,000	_____
5	New Mortgage Payment	804	_____
6	New Total Payment (Item 3 x Item 5)	96,400	_____
7	Potential Savings (Item 4 – Item 6)	23,520	_____
8	Prepayment Penalty on current mortgage	0	_____
9	Closings costs on new mortgage	4,000	_____
10	Refinancing cost (Item 8 + Item 9)	4,000	_____
11	Total Savings (Item 7 – Item 10)	19,520	_____
12	Monthly savings (Item 1 – Item 5)	162	_____
13	Months to break even (Item 10 ÷ Item 12)	24.6	_____

Refinancing an existing mortgage can significantly alter your cash flow, lower your taxes and save you thousands of dollars in the long run. Tradition follows that the interest rate on a new mortgage must be 2 percent lower than the interest rate on the existing mortgage for refinancing to be favorable. However, do not take 2 percent as the ultimate rule as a basis for a final decision. If the new mortgage payments are lower, the property must be held long enough to recover closing costs in order to break even.

Choosing a Mortgage Broker

Whether you are shopping for a new mortgage or refinancing your current one, a good mortgage broker can ease the hassle of shopping for a mortgage. The quality of mortgage brokers varies widely. Picking the wrong one can be an exercise in futility. Here are some questions to ask when selecting a mortgage broker:

1. How many lenders does the broker represent? Good mortgage brokers generally represent at least ten lenders from different areas of the country, so they can shop nationwide to help you get the best deal. However, local lenders know you're area best and you may get the better deal through them.

2. What percentage of loans are actually funded? For a typical mortgage company, 70% or more of the applications submitted to lenders should lead to closing.

3. What references do you have from real estate agencies and banks. Find out if the broker has been in business for at least two years.

4. If your state requires that mortgage brokers be licensed, be sure that yours is licensed. Also, check with the licensing authorities to see if any complaints have been made.

5. Can you get a written estimate of closing costs? Most brokers will give you a written closing cost estimate, justifying every expense. Keep in mind these brokers typically get paid by the lender for originating the loan. About 80 percent of their income comes from origination fees and other commissions paid by the lender. In many areas borrowers pay up front application fees that range from $300 to $500 and at closing they pay processing and document preparation fees to the lender.

Reverse Mortgages

Reverse mortgages literally are mortgage loans that work backwards. They also go against most of the traditional principles of lending practice. Under a reverse mortgage, instead of sending a check to the lender every month to pay interest and reduce debt, you receive a check every month from the lender and the debt increases.

Reverse mortgages vary from lender to lender but most have several characteristics in common. First, they are generally available only to senior citizens including widowed persons (just who is a "senior" may vary from 62 to 70 years of age) who own their own home with little or no debt. Secondly, the type of loan is either a term loan (based on the life expectancy of the homeowner or a period certain) or a line of credit.

The amount of the monthly payment you'll receive depends on the term of the loan, interest rates, the value of the home, and the percentage of current equity eligible to be loaned out. With a line of credit arrangement there is no monthly check; you simply tap the line of credit for cash whenever needed. Generally, the loan is not repaid until the house is sold, or at your death. The risks to the lender are obvious. With a loan based on life expectancy, the loan could eventually be more than the amount recoverable on sale. Also, there is no current cash inflow to the lender. Given these and other disadvantages, its no wonder that lenders have not been flocking to offer reverse mortgages.

The risk to you, the homeowner, is also clear. The loan will eat away, and could wipe out, the entire value of your home. Deciding on a reverse mortgage is a serious step and often requires expert assistance. The advantages and disadvantages need to be carefully weighed before a lifetime commitment is made.

Two excellent resources are:

- AARP's free Home Equity Conversion Information Kit (D15601). Includes "Reverse Mortgage Lenders List"—state-by-state (except Alaska, South Dakota and Texas) listings of more than 125 lenders; Fact Sheet overview of home-equity conversion and reverse mortgages; *Home-Made Money* guide to risks and benefits. Address a postcard to kit name and number, AARP Home Equity Information Center EE0756, 601 E St. NW, Washington, D.C. 20049.

- *Your New Retirement Nest Egg: A Consumer Guide to the New Reverse Mortgages* by Ken Scholen (National Center for Home Equity Conversion, 1995). Compares reverse mortgages, including cash benefits, total loan costs, and leftover equity, in 300-plus pages. Send $19.63 (includes S&H) to NCHEC, 7373 147th Street W, Apple Valley, MN 55124.

IF YOU DECIDE TO SELL

The first step in selling your house is deciding where to live once it's sold. Everyone's housing needs differ. Some people prefer the quiet and private, while others like the hustle and bustle of big city life. Many want to live within walking distance to work, shopping and restaurants. Others don't mind 45-minute drives. Most everyone wants to be near their friends. Because you have your own unique set of likes and dislikes, the best way to start your search is to list your needs. Classify them according to whether they are essential, desirable or merely a plus. Such a classification is important for three reasons:

First, this procedure screens out housing that will not meet your minimum requirements. Second, it helps you recognize that you may have to make trade-offs since you will seldom find "the" single property that will meet all of your needs. Third, it can help you focus on those needs that you are willing and able to pay for.

In addition to *single-family homes*, *townhouses* and *patio homes*, you might wish to consider *manufactured homes*. These are factory-produced housing units that are transported to a desired location. You can place them on either a permanent or temporary foundation, connect them to utilities and use them as a residence. Because these homes were once more mobile than they now are, they used to be called mobile homes. Depending on size and features, their costs can range anywhere from $10,000 to $70,000.

You may also wish to consider *condominiums*. In these units, you own your own unit, arrange the financing, pay taxes, and pay for maintenance and building services. Typically you are assessed a monthly amount sufficient to cover your proportionate share of the costs of maintaining the common facilities. The cost of the condominiums are generally lower than single-family detached houses. They tend to be built with more efficient land use and lower construction costs. Also, many existing apartment projects have gone through what is called condo conversions. In effect, the apartments have been converted from rental to occupant owned units.

Before You Buy A Condo

In the long run, it pays to carefully check out the various operating and occupancy features of a condo before you buy:

- Thoroughly investigate the reputation of the developer through local real estate brokers, banks, or the Better Business Bureau, whether the building is brand new, under construction, or being converted.

- Read the rules of the organization.

- Investigate the condo government association, the restrictions on condo owners, and the quality of the property management.

- Check the construction of the building and its physical condition. If the building is being converted to condos, ask to see an independent inspection firm's report on the building's condition.

- Insist that any future changes in the building be put in writing.

- Ask occupants if they are satisfied with the living conditions.

- Determine how many units are rented; generally, owner-occupied units are better maintained.

- Determine if there is sufficient parking space.

- Watch for unusually low maintenance fees that will probably have to be increased soon.

- Consider the resale value (this was especially important in the mid-1980's when many condo units were impossible to sell without sharp price reductions).

- Compare the projected monthly assessment fees with those on similar buildings already in operation.

CHAPTER

11

Another housing option to consider is *cooperative apartments*. These are apartment buildings in which each tenant owns a share of the corporation that owns the building and is known as a cooperative apartment, or co-op. You lease your unit from the corporation and are assessed monthly amounts in proportion to your ownership share. This proportion is based on the amount of space you occupy in the building.

Assessments cover the cost of service, maintenance, taxes and mortgages on the entire building. Notice, though, that they are subject to change depending on the actual building operation costs and corporation's policies. Most policies are determined by the Board of Directors. Since cooperative apartments are not profit-motivated, monthly assessments are likely to be lower than rent on similar accommodations. Also, you, as a cooperative owner, receive tax benefits resulting from property taxes attributable to your proportion of ownership interest.

The second step in selling your home is to know the tax consequences. You can save thousands of dollars if you know the tax rules and work closely with a financial planner or tax accountant. There are three major tax considerations: (1) deferral of gain; (2) exclusion of gain; and (3) reduction of gain.

You can *defer* paying taxes on any gain you realize on the sale of your principal residence as long as you buy (or build) and live in another home within two years. The new home must cost at least as much as the "adjusted" selling price of your old home.

To determine the adjusted selling price, start with the selling price of your home and subtract the expenses associated with selling the home, such as real estate commissions, legal fees and loan origination fees paid by you. Also, subtract any expenses for fixing up the residence for sale, like painting the exterior and fixing leaky pipes. The work must be paid for within 60 days and completed within 90 days of the contract date of the sale. Finally, you subtract the cost of improvements or additions made to your home (see Reduction of Gain). This result is the adjusted selling price.

If you are age 55 or older at the time you sell your home, you are entitled to a once-in-a-lifetime *exclusion* of up to $125,000 in gains from the sale. This can be a wonderful tax savings for many reasons, but there can be pitfalls.

One pitfall is that you must have lived in the house three out of the last five years prior to the sale. Furthermore, you can take this tax exclusion only once. Thus, if your gain is $75,000, for example, then the unused portion of $50,000 is lost forever. Last, this exclusion is allowed only once per marriage and it counts for both spouses. For example, if you and your deceased spouse had already used the $125,000 exclusion, and then you remarry, your new spouse cannot use his or her own exclusion.

Here's an example using the $125,000 Exclusion:

Selling price	$250,000
Less selling costs	–5,000
Amount realized	245,000
Less adjusted basis of current house	–100,000
Realized gain	145,000
Less one-time exclusion	–125,000
Amount of gain not excluded	$20,000

If you are in the 28 percent Federal Tax bracket and a 5 percent state tax bracket, your taxes due are 33 percent of $20,000, or $6,600. If you and your spouse had previously used the $125,000, then the taxes jump to 33 percent of $145,000, or $47,800. This is a crushing $41,200 increase in your taxes ($47,800–$6,600 = $41,200).

If the taxable gain is unavoidable, look for ways to reduce the amount of gain by increasing the amount of "basis" in your own home. Basis is simply the original purchase price plus any expenses directly related to its purchase, such as closing costs. You also can add the cost of any improvements or additions you have made in the house such as remodeling the kitchen or replacing an old roof.

Here's a list of items that can add to the cost basis of your home:

ITEMS THAT COULD ADD TO THE COST BASIS OF YOUR HOME

Note: Receipts, cancelled checks, and other verification of improvements/expenses for a home should be kept for not less than 4 years after a home is sold.

SPECIAL ASSESSMENTS	YEAR	AMOUNT
Sewer and Storm Sewer		
Water		
Streets, Sidewalks and Alleys		
Parks and Lighting		
Other		

OUTSIDE IMPROVEMENTS		
Add'l Acreage/Lots and Surveying		
Additions to Buildings		
Porch, Breezeway and Wings		
Siding and Flashing		
Garage, Workshed and Storage		
Roof Replacement and Repair		
Windows, Screens and Screen Doors		

CHAPTER 11

	YEAR	AMOUNT
Gutters, Leaders and Drains		
Pipes and Dry Wells		
Termite Proofing		
Other		
Other		

LAWN, GARDEN AND GROUNDS

Terraces, Patios and Retaining Wall		
Cement and Asphalt		
Steps, Walks, Driveway		
Bird Bath, Patio, Other		
Fences, Gates and Play Yard		
Kennel		
Water Well, Pump and Sprinklers		
Rototill, Grading, Fill and Topsoil		
Sod, Fertilizers, Seed and Plants		
Trees, Shrubs, Bushes and Vines		
Clothes Dryers and Lines		
Waste Collecting and Burning		
Mail Box and Trellis		
Other		

INSIDE ADDITIONS AND IMPROVEMENTS

Conversions—Attic or Basement into Bedrooms or Recreation		
Inside Walls—Altering and Plastering		
Wood Paneling and Wood Tile		
Room Dividers and Partitions		
Ceilings and Lighting		
Replace or Add Stairs		
Wood Flooring, Tile and Linoleum		
Carpeting		
Cabinets and Cupboards		
Closets and Shelves		
Bookcases and Other Built-ins		
Installed Furniture—Booths		
Bars and Counters		
Fireplace and Equipment		
Radiator Covers and Ventilators		
Windows, Window Seats and Storms		
Other		
Other		

                                                    YEAR   AMOUNT

EQUIPMENT INSTALLED
BATHROOM
Medicine Cabinet and Mirrors
Shower Cabinet and Controls
Tub Racks and Hangers
Sliding Doors and Heater
Other

KITCHEN AND LAUNDRY
Counters, sinks and drainboards
Range, oven, hood and ventilators
Dishwasher and refrigerator
Disposal and Freezer
Washer, Dryer, Mangle and Hotplate
Hamper, Chutes, Table and Racks
Cabinets, Tops and Built-ins
Other

HARDWARE, FIXTURES AND LOCKS
For Cabinets and Closets
For Doors and Windows
For Curtains and Drapes
Lighting Fixtures
Other

MECHANICAL EQUIPMENT
Soft Water System
Hot Water Heater
Furnace and Space Heaters
Fans, Duct Work and Louvers
Air Conditioning and Cooling
Radiators, Valves and Grills
Humidifier and Dehumidifier
Other

ELECTRICITY AND LIGHTING
Fixtures, Switches and Cover Plates
Controls and Fuse and Junction Boxes
Wiring System and Circuit Breakers
Lightening Rods and TV Antenna
Motor
Other

	YEAR	AMOUNT

PLUMBING and SANITATION

Pipes, Tubing, Drains and Traps

Pumps, Septic System and Sump Pumps

Fixtures and Controls

Caulking, Tiling and Waterproofing

Other

COMMUNICATION

Call Bells or Chimes

Intercommunication System

Fire or Burglar Alarms

Other

INSULATION

Ceilings, Floors and Walls

Roof, Attic and Basement

Pipes, Ducts and Weatherstripping

Other

TOTAL OF ALL IMPROVEMENT AMOUNTS $ _____

The costs listed on page 171 will increase your basis, and can reduce the capital gains tax on your house. The smaller the difference between your basis and the adjusted selling price, the smaller the taxable gain.

If you and your spouse owned your house jointly, upon his or her death there is what is called a "stepped up basis" in the house. In other words, for his or her half of the house, the capital gain on it is forgiven by the Internal Revenue Service. Thus, if you sell the property, you only have to count your half of the capital gain. Here's an example to give you a feeling for how this works.

Example of Using Stepped Up Basis and $125,000 Exclusion

Joan and Ted paid $50,000 for their house which was valued at $100,000 at Ted's death. Ted's basis was $25,000 and his half of the gain was $25,000, which was forgiven by IRS at his death. Several years after Ted's death, if the house is now worth $150,000, Joan's new gain is:

Her one-half of gain at Ted's death	$25,000
Her gain since Ted died	$50,000
Total gain now	$75,000

Since the $125,000 exclusion was never used, she could exclude the whole $75,000.

Selling the Family House

Fifteen years ago, when Charles and Betty Warren took early retirement, they sold their home and bought a large townhouse. Charles reasoned there would be less upkeep and yard care with the new townhouse, leaving himself and Betty more time to travel. At the time they sold their first home, they did not use their one-time right to exclude up to $125,000 of capital gain on the sale of a principal residence.

Five years after retirement, Charles became ill and subsequently died of a heart attack. Betty has remained in the townhouse the last ten years, although it is too much home for her. The original price of the townhouse was $50,000. Recently, Betty has been considering selling or renting her home to her only daughter. Her daughter is divorced with two children, and could use the extra room.

Betty would like to move into a smaller apartment in a building where many of her friends already live. The townhouse is worth approximately $150,000 now, but was worth only $100,000 when Charles died.

If Betty rents to her daughter the property looses its residential status and becomes rental property. While Betty will receive rental income along with deductions for depreciation, maintenance and taxes, she will lose the ability to ever use the $125,000 exclusion and/or the stepped up basis in the property at her death. So, if she rents the house, it will have a tax price of $150,000 when she dies, less the adjusted basis in the property (assuming the house is marketed and sold at this price). The depreciation must be recaptured by deducting it from the basis, and will further increase the taxable portion.

If she sells the property to her daughter, Betty can use the $125,000 exclusion to avoid taxes. Also, in this scenario Charles' stepped up basis will additionally reduce the taxable amount. Here are the numbers:

Charles' basis at his death = 1/2 of $100,000 = $ 50,000
Betty's basis of original purchase = 1/2 of $50,000 = 25,000
Total Basis = 75,000
Sales Price = 150,000
Net Gain = $ 75,000

Another option for Betty is to do nothing. In this scenario, at Betty's death all the capital gains are forgiven and there is no tax. Or, if she can afford it, Betty could let her daughter move in without paying rent. Then Betty could rent an apartment and be near her friends. Finally, Betty could set up a life estate as described on page 176.

Keep in mind that the loss on the sale of a personal residence is not deductible and has no affect on the basis of a new residence acquired. For example, let's say you sell your house for $185,000 and you paid $200,000 for it. That $15,000 loss is not deductible and it has no affect on the basis of a new residence acquired.

Tips on Renting or Selling (To Your Children or Anyone)

Renting the Property:

Advantages:

1. Tax deductions for depreciation, maintenance, taxes, insurance and mortgage interest;

2. Rental income.

Disadvantages:

1. Loss of $125,000 exclusion if not already used;

2. Loss of stepped up basis at your death;

3. Becoming a landlord.

Selling the Property:

Advantages:

1. Possible use of $125,000 exclusion;

2. Use of deceased spouse's stepped up basis;

3. Availability of proceeds from sale.

Disadvantages:

1. Loss of stepped up basis at your death.

HAVING YOUR CAKE—AND EATING IT TOO: THE LIFE ESTATE

Many times, surviving spouses are counseled by well-meaning relatives, lawyers, CPAs, or friends to give their house away to a child or children to protect their assets.

However, there is a catch. If you give your home to your children, or anyone, their cost basis for tax purposes is what you originally paid for the house (plus the stepped up basis of your spouses' share at his/her death).

Let's say the house is worth $150,000 on the date you make the gift, but you only paid $50,000 for your house many years ago. Your children would owe taxes on the value that is over $50,000 when they sell the house. If they sell the house for $200,000, they will pay taxes on $150,000.

A better way to go, especially if your total estate is less than $600,000, is called a Life Estate. Using a life estate, you can gift your house to your children (or anyone), live in it for the rest of your life, and provide the recipient with a big tax break. And it costs very little to do.

A life estate lets you continue to live in your home for the rest of your life. How? You set up what is called a lifetime tenancy which expires at your death. At that time the house will belong to your heirs and they will have the tax advantage.

Here's an example: Martha, a 63-year-old widow, has two adult children, Beth and Allan. Martha's $300,000 assets include her $150,000 home and other investments and personal items of $150,000. She wants her children to receive the assets when she dies, but is concerned that the home might have to be sold to pay nursing home costs in the future.

Instead of gifting the house now and creating a future tax problem for Beth and Allan, she can give them the "remainder interest" in her house (they will receive it at her death) while Martha keeps a life estate.

The overall benefits are many:

1. There is no probate of the house at Martha's death.
2. The life estate is easy and fairly inexpensive to set up. An attorney prepares a deed that transfers the remainder interest to the children while Martha retains a life estate.
3. Martha can live in the house the rest of her life, even if her children sell their remainder interest before she dies.
4. Thirty months following the date that Martha makes the life estate, the value of her house is no longer counted as her asset for Medicare purposes.
5. At Martha's death the children's cost basis is stepped up to its value on the date of Martha's death.

Here are the tax ramifications of the life estate:

1. The gift of the house to the children will immediately reduce Martha's $600,000 lifetime estate and gift exclusion by $130,000 (the $150,000 fair market value of the home less the $10,000 annual gift she is permitted to each child).
2. The value of Martha's home at her death will be included in her gross estate for estate tax purposes.

NOTE: Because of the way a life estate is taxed, i.e., the entire value of your house is included in your taxable estate and therefore subject to estate tax, this strategy works best if your estate is less than $600,000.

IF YOU DECIDE TO BUY

Let's reverse gears now and look at what you need to know if, for whatever reason, you're thinking of *buying* a home.

Buying a home usually requires a good deal of time and effort. Learning of the available properties and their prices requires a systematic search and careful property analysis. Most people who shop the housing market rely on real estate agents for information, access to properties and advice. Other sources of information, such as newspaper ads, are also used extensively to identify available properties.

If you need a particular specialized type of property or know exactly what you want, you may wish to advertise your needs and wait for the sellers to contact you. Most buyers rely on real estate agents because of their daily contact with the housing market.

When using an agent, describe your needs explicitly, so he or she can begin a search for the appropriate property. Agents will also help you negotiate with the seller and obtain satisfactory financing. Though not empowered to give legal advice, they may still help your prepare your real estate sales contract.

Most real estate firms belong to a local multiple listing service (MLS). MLS compiles a list of properties for sale from information provided by the member firms in a given community or area. Brief descriptions of each property and its asking price are included. The list is updated weekly. As a rule, it is best to deal with a realtor that works for MLS member firms, otherwise you might lack access to a large part of the market.

You, as a buyer, need to remember that agents are typically employed by sellers. Unless you have agreed to pay a fee to your sales agent, the agent's primary responsibility, by law, is to sell listed properties at the highest possible prices. Also, because agents are paid only if they make a sale, some might pressure you to "sign now or miss the chance of a lifetime deal." Avoid that type of agent!

Select an agent who will work hard to match you with the property you want. Good agents recognize that their best interests are served when all parties to the transaction are satisfied. It needs to be a win-win situation.

Real estate commissions usually range from five to seven percent; however, such commissions are paid by the seller. The buyer usually pays one of the points if there are origination points on the loan.

Obtaining a Mortgage

If you have made the decision to buy a home, then you may need to look at different types of mortgage loans. The fixed-rate mortgage is still the most popular mortgage and accounts for a major chunk of all home mortgages written. With these mortgages, both the rate of interest and the monthly mortgage payment are fixed over the full term of the loan. The most common is the 30-year fixed-rate loan. Yet, because of the lender's assumed risk, it is usually the most expensive form of home financing.

A variation of this standard fixed rate loan rapidly gaining popularity is the **15-year fixed-rate mortgage**. Its chief appeal is that it is paid twice as fast, 15 years versus 30, yet the monthly payments are not significantly larger.

Surprisingly, though, the monthly payment on a 15-year loan is generally only about 10 percent to 20 percent larger than the payment on a 30-year loan. This brings you substantial savings on the mortgage.

Let's assume that you have a $100,000 loan with an 8 percent fixed rate of interest. For the 30-year loan, the regular payment would be $733 per month. The total payments over the life of the loan would be $264,155. With a 15-year fixed-rate loan, the monthly payment is $955, over 15 years, which results in the total payment over the life of the loan of $172,117. This is a savings of $92,137.

ARMs—Another popular form of home loan is the *adjustable rate mortgage*, referred to as an ARM. Unlike the fixed rate mortgage, the rate of interest, and therefore the size of the monthly payment, is adjusted in line with movements of market interest rates. The rate of interest on the mortgage is linked to a specific interest rate index and is adjusted at specific intervals (usually once a year) as the index changes.

When the index moves up, so does the rate of interest on the mortgage and in turn the size of the monthly mortgage payment. The new interest rate and the monthly mortgage payment will then remain fixed until the next adjustment date, when the adjustment process is repeated.

There are many features to consider if you do use an ARM. One is called the adjustment period—the time between one rate payment change and the next. Another feature is the index rate, which is used to measure the movement in interest rates. Many indices use an interest rate that is based on the behavior of one-year U.S. Treasury securities. But there are many other indices. Check which index your particular loan company uses.

Watch the interest rate ceilings (called "caps"). They place a limit on the amount the interest rate can be increased over a given period. Usually two kinds of interest rate caps apply: a periodic cap limits the interest rate from one adjustment period to the next, and an overall cap limits the interest rate increase over the life of the loan. Many ARM's have both the periodic and the overall interest rate cap.

If you do use an ARM, be aware of what is called "negative amortization." This is an increase in the principal balance because the monthly loan payments are lower than the amount of monthly interest being charged. In other words, with this type of loan you can wind up with a larger mortgage balance on the next loan anniversary than the last.

Another form of loan is called the **convertible ARM**. These are loans that allow borrowers to convert from an adjustable rate to a fixed rate loan, usually at some time between the 13th and 60th month. A fee is usually charged to make the conversion to a fixed rate loan.

The Option of Renting

After seriously considering buying or maintaining one's own home, many widowed persons find that they *do not want* the additional responsibilities associated with home ownership. Take Mary Beth as an example. Almost all of her money comes to her from tax-free bonds. Her exemptions provide her with a total of $6,350 in deductions per year, so she pays very little in taxes. A mortgage interest deduction would not help her much, if at all.

She became tired of the responsibilities of ownership and decided to rent in an apartment. Several of her widowed friends live there, or nearby, so renting made sense for her. While she can't control the rent increases, so far they have been reasonable.

Remember that monthly rent payments serve only to pay for the use of the property; they are in no way tax deductible. If you choose to rent, you should be familiar with rental contracts and know how to compare the cost of renting versus purchasing.

Understanding Rental Contracts

When you rent an apartment, a duplex, house, condo or any other similar unit you will normally be required to sign a rental contract, also called a lease agreement.

Because the rental contract binds you (the leasee) you should make certain you fully understand it before signing it. As a rule, the contract specifies the amount of the monthly payment, the payment due date, penalties for late payment, the length of the lease agreement, security deposit requirements, the distributions of expenses, renewal options and any restrictions, which might include children, pets or use of the facilities.

Most leases have a minimum term of either six months or one year, and require payments at the beginning of each month. Most require a deposit or the last month's payment in advance as security against damages and infringement of the lease agreement. In the absence of any serious damage, most of the time the deposit is refunded to the leasee shortly after the lease expires. A portion of the deposit is sometimes retained to cover the cost of cleaning and minor repairs.

Since the landlord has the control over your deposit, you will want to have a written statement describing any damage and evidence prior to your occupancy of the unit. This can help you avoid loosing the entire deposit at the time you leave. You also need to clarify who pays expenses such as utilities, trash collection and other maintenance items. It is a good idea for you to check the various landlord laws in your state or community. This will help you fully understand what your rights may be, as well as your responsibilities.

Can't Decide?

Many people rent because they won't have to submit a down payment or closing costs. Others rent because they'll have more mobility and won't have to worry about maintenance and upkeep.

If you are undecided whether to rent or own, you can at least get a clear financial comparison of the two options by filling in the numbers on the following form:

RENT OR BUY COMPARISON

A. Cost of Renting
    1) Annual rental cost (12 x monthly rent) $ _____
    2) Renters insurance   _____

       Total rental cost   _____

B. Cost of Purchasing
    1) Annual mortgage payments (12 x monthly $)   _____
    2) Property taxes (obtain from real estate agent)   _____
    3) Homeowner's insurance (obtain from P/C agent)   _____
    4) Maintenance (your best estimate—annual)   _____
    5) After tax cost of interest lost on down
       payment and closing costs
       ($_____ x _____% after tax return on funds)   _____
    6) Total costs   _____

Less: (Subtract)
    7) Average principal reduction in loan balance
       (obtain from real estate agent)   _____
    8) Interest portion of mortgage payment $_____ x your
       combined federal and state tax rate of _____% = Tax Savings   _____
    9) Savings due to property tax deduction (Line B2 above x
       combined federal and state tax rate of _____%)   _____
   10) Total value of reductions   _____

Now subtract the total value of deductions (10) from the total costs (6) and compare with the total rental costs in Part A.   _____

Hiring Home Improvement Contractors

To close this chapter, let's focus briefly on something that all widowed homeowners eventually face. Hiring a contractor to do work on your home often involves pitfalls. The most frequently cited complaints are cost overruns, missed deadlines and shoddy workmanship. Worse, there are fly-by-night contractors who take deposits or payments for home improvement and then disappear before finishing or even starting the work. (See Chapter 18).

If you need something done to your home, choose a contractor carefully. Be weary of door-to-door salespeople or telephone solicitors promising "this month only" specials or bargains. Here are some tips on hiring contractors:

1. Use a local well-established contractor. Get some recommendations from a friend or neighbor. Ask the contractor for references and check with those homeowners to find out if the work was done properly, on time and within the contract price.

2. Check with your state or local Consumer Affairs office or the Better Business Bureau.

3. Obtain more than one estimate, especially on larger jobs. Get all promises and plans in writing.

4. Check with your local consumer protection office for specific laws designed to protect you. Some states require licensing, cooling off periods, payment schedules keyed to completion progress and other consumer protections.

5. Study the financing of the job. Be sure that you can comfortably meet the total monthly payment. Also, check with your bank and shop around for the best way to finance your home improvement. Often a home equity loan may be the best answer.

6. Make sure your contractor has liability insurance. Ask to see a copy of his Worker's Compensation policy. You may be liable if a worker is injured on your property during the job. Check with your insurance agent to find out if your homeowner's insurance will cover you and to what extent.

7. Insist that your contractor follow state and local building codes and has obtained the necessary building permits. Find out from your local building inspector what legal obligations are required in regard to building permits.

Here are tipoffs to spot unscrupulous, fly-by-night home improvement outfits:

1. They arrive in an unmarked truck or van.

2. Door to door salespeople claiming to have just done a job nearby. They say they have material left over and can do the job for half price.

3. Promises to use your home as "a demonstration model" at a reduced price.

4. High pressure sales tactics.

5. Refusal to give you a written estimate or contract.

Never pay a contractor the entire cost of a job before he does any work. Usually a down payment of 10 to 20 percent of the total is reasonable with additional payments scheduled when the job is half done. Never release the final payment until the project is completed to your satisfaction and that you have proof that subcontractors and/or employees have been paid. If a completion date is critical, (for example, a swimming pool for summer time use) link the final payment to on-time performance and completion of the job.

Even if you follow all of these guidelines, problems may still arise. Frequently, effective communication between you and the contractor will resolve difficulties. Take time to talk with your contractor, and try to work out any disagreements.

If the problems persist, document your side of the dispute. Put everything that needs to be resolved in writing. Send a copy to the contractor and keep a copy for your file. State and local consumer agencies may help you with home improvement problems. Check your telephone directory for local government listings or call your state consumer affairs office or the Office of the Attorney General.

CHAPTER 11

FUNDING COLLEGE EDUCATION

One of the largest expenses for any parent is paying for a child's higher education. Most people, even those in two-parent families, are simply not prepared for the economic impact college costs will have on four or more years of their lives. If you fit into one of the following groups, this chapter is for you. If not, you may find it interesting, but feel free to move on.

Group 1: You're a young widowed person with small children and some time to prepare for the expense of college.

Group 2: You're a widowed individual in your middle years with children ready for college or already in college.

Group 3: You're an older widowed person with grandchildren whom you'd like to help with future costs.

WHY COLLEGE?

Many people ask, "Is college worth it?" Actually, a college education will give your child an important edge in our competitive world. College graduates are predicted to earn $600,000 or more over that of non-college graduates during forty years of working life.

Your child can probably achieve wealth and happiness without college preparation, but the road may be easier with a B.A. or B.S. In addition, there are many educational opportunities available today to college-age children that open previously-unknown frontiers for learning and future careers. Without a college education, many doors are likely to remain closed.

Over the last ten years, college costs have more than doubled. Some analysts place the annual rate of increase at 8 to 9 percent per year; the

Independent College 500 Index for private colleges cites an escalation of 7.6 percent for 1992; and the National Center for Education Statistics, in its *Digest of Education Statistics*, places the average jump in private college tuition and fees at 9.7 percent over the last 17 years. *The College Costs Book*, available in most libraries, contains the average annual cost of every institution in the United States.

How much you will actually spend on college depends on:

1. Where the college is located;

2. Whether the student attends a community college, state or private university; and

3. Whether the student qualifies for in-state or out-of-state tuition at a state college.

Here's a typical annual forecast of 1992 college costs in the middle United States:

- Community college: $2,353

- State university: $7,650

- Private university: $16,248

Except for community college, these figures include tuition, fees, room and board, books, supplies, and miscellaneous costs such as transportation. Community college costs do not include room and board, because most attendees live at home. At current rates, by 2005 four years of college could reach $68,000 at a public university and $200,000 at a private institution.

Basically, there are only four ways to pay for college: save for it, pay out of current income, cash in assets, or have others pay for it. You may have to look at many aspects of your financial situation to choose the right combination of these.

CAN YOU AFFORD A COLLEGE EDUCATION FOR YOUR CHILDREN?

Many widowed people feel obligated to provide money for college at the expense of their own well-being and financial security. For example, Norma regularly dipped into her $100,000 of savings to fund her son's college education. Not only did she deplete the asset, but she also lost the earning power of that money forever. Afterwards, she realized that there were other sources to help fund a college education, but it was too late.

Particularly if you have young children, the easiest way to give your child the best educational experience you can is to start planning as early as possible. As such, you need to become educated about the following subjects:

1. Financial aid;

2. Saving money;

3. Positioning assets for growth now and income later; and

4. Strategies to minimize the tax impact of your college investment dollars.

If your planning choices are limited because of few assets, *all* your income goes for survival needs. Although there is little chance for a windfall of inherited wealth, there is still hope. Financial aid, student loans, sports scholarships and work-study programs are available, but to get them for your child you must pursue them with vigor.

This worksheet will help you calculate a realistic estimate of how much you will need when your child is ready for college:

WORKSHEET
Estimating College Costs For Your Child

1. Write in the year your child will start college.

2. Use a base number of $2,300 for community college, $6,990 for state university, and $15,310 for private college.

3. Determine the number of years between now and when your child's first year of college will begin, but remember that tuition is due in early August at most colleges.

4. Use the inflation table on page 114, and assume a 6 or 7 percent inflation rate.

5. Multiply the inflation number by the base college costs from step 2, and enter on the appropriate line. Do this for each year for every child.

6. Add the lines across the page for the total cost per year.

7. Add the lines down the page for the total cost for each child.

Laura, a 32-year-old widow has two children, Jody and Sam, ages seven and nine. Her research suggests that college costs will accelerate

CHAPTER 12

at 7 percent annually, and that a state university is all she can handle, financially. She has $65,000 in insurance proceeds and works full-time earning $34,500 a year. Social Security provides another $998 per month.

Actual Yrs. in College	No. Yrs. from Now	Jody	Sam	Totals, Both Children
2000	9	$12,861		$ 12,861
2001	10	13,700		13,700
2002	11	14,679	$14,679	29,358
2003	12	15,727	15,727	31,454
2004	13		16,845	16,845
2005	14		18,034	18,034
2006	15			
Totals		$66,967	$65,285	$122,252

COST FACTOR MULTIPLIER TABLE

No. of Years from Now	at 6%	at 7%
1	1.06	1.07
2	1.12	1.14
3	1.19	1.22
4	1.26	1.31
5	1.34	1.40
6	1.42	1.50
7	1.50	1.60
8	1.59	1.72
9	1.69	1.84
10	1.79	1.96
11	1.90	2.10
12	2.01	2.25
13	2.13	2.41
14	2.26	2.58
15	2.39	2.76
16	2.54	2.95
17	2.69	3.16
18	2.85	3.38

COLLEGE COST WORKSHEET

Actual Years In College	No. of Years From Now	Child 1	Child 2	Child 3	Total Cost Per Year
1993	1				
1994	2				
1995	3				
1996	4				
1997	5				
1998	6				
1999	7				
2000	8				
2001	9				
2002	10				
2003	11				
2004	12				
2005	13				
2006	14				
2007	15				
2008	16				
2009	17				
2010	18				
2011	19				
2012	20	_____	_____	_____	_____
Total Cost/Child		$	$	$	$
Total Cost all Children					$_____

C
H
A
P
T
E
R

12

Using the annual savings chart on page 190, we find that for Jody, $66,967 times .064 equals $4,286 per year. For Sam, $65,225 times .049 equals $3,196 per year. Thus, Laura needs to save $4,286 per year until Jody starts and $3,196 per year until Sam starts to have the lump sums required to fund college costs.

Now, Laura knows what she must do. Her plan may require investing some of the $65,000 she got from her husband's life insurance to cover college expenses, if she can afford to do so. Alternatively, she may want to add the income from a part-time job, help her children become excellent students and qualify for scholarships, or she may decide to limit her expenses by using a community college for the first two years of their education, and state universities for the second two years.

Laura may also want to determine the amount of the lump sum she needs today to fund the $122,252 in future education costs for Jody and Sam. If Laura invests $40,000 after taxes at 8 percent, what will she have when Jody is ready for college in nine years, and Sam is ready in 11 years? Will it last through college or does she need to consider saving more money now?

Annual Savings Chart

The factors below assume a return of eight percent on an investment, and do not account for any taxes due.

Instructions

Take the total estimated future costs for each child from the "Estimating College Costs Worksheet." Using the child's current age, multiply the factor from the table below by the total cost from the worksheet.

Child's Current Age	Factor
1	.025
2	.027
3	.031
4	.034
5	.038
6	.043
7	.049
8	.056
9	.064
10	.074
11	.087
12	.104
13	.126
14	.158
15	.205
16	.285
17	.445
18	.926

Determining the Lump Sum Needed to Fund College Costs

Using the table below, select the yield you believe the investment would generate—for example, 8 percent—and the number of years until the money is needed. For instance, Jody will need $12,861 at the ninth year. The factor for nine years at 8 percent is .50, times Jody's need for $12,861, equals the lump sum of $6,430 that Laura needs to invest today to reach her goal. Repeat this for each year for each child, and then add the results for the total lump sum needed.

MULTIPLIER CHART FOR LUMP SUMS TO FUND COLLEGE

Years Until College Begins	4%	5%	6%	8%	10%
1	.96	.95	.94	.93	.91
2	.92	.91	.89	.85	.82
3	.89	.86	.84	.79	.75
4	.85	.82	.79	.73	.68
5	.82	.78	.74	.68	.62
6	.79	.74	.70	.63	.56
7	.78	.71	.66	.58	.51
8	.73	.67	.63	.54	.46
9	.70	.64	.59	.50	.42
10	.67	.61	.56	.46	.38
11	.65	.58	.53	.43	.35
12	.62	.55	.50	.40	.32
13	.60	.53	.47	.37	.29
14	.58	.50	.44	.34	.26
15	.55	.48	.42	.31	.24
16	.53	.46	.39	.29	.22
17	.51	.43	.37	.27	.20
18	.49	.41	.35	.25	.18

Here are Jody's and Sam's costs, using an 8 percent after-tax return:

	Jody	Sam
	$ 6,430	$ 6,312
	6,302	6,291
	6,312	6,233
	6,291	6,131
Totals	$25,335	$24,967

Thus, the lump sum needed for both would be $50,302. By combining the lump sum method and the annual savings method, Laura should be able to determine what she needs to do to fund the college educations.

COLLEGE PAYMENT STRATEGIES

Knowing how much college costs will be is one thing, meeting them is another. Let's look at some winning strategies.

Aggressive Tactics in Their Younger Years—The younger your child is when you start a college plan, the more aggressive you can be with the investment. For example, use growth-oriented stocks or mutual funds for children who are now under age 14. Then begin moving toward less aggressive, income-oriented investments. By the time your child is 16, the overall goal is to safeguard what you've accumulated by moving to conservative investments, such as money market funds, certificates of deposit, U.S. Treasury bills and income mutual funds.

The "Kiddie Tax"—Take advantage of the "kiddie tax." You will remember from previous chapters that the first $650 of income to your under-age-14 child is tax-free, because it is offset against the child's standard deduction. The next $650 is taxed at the child's rate, which is usually lower than your rate. If your rate and the child's rate are the same, it still makes sense to place enough assets in the child's name to take advantage of the first $650 of unearned income. The table below shows the yield rates and how much you can invest before hitting $650 or $1,300 levels of unearned income for a child.

Yield Rates to Take Advantage of Kiddie Tax: How Much To Invest

Yield Percentage %	Maximum Investment to Earn $650/Yr.	Maximum Investment to Earn $1,300/Yr.
4	$16,250	$32,500
5	13,000	26,000
6	10,833	21,666
7	9,285	18,570
8	8,125	16,250
9	7,222	14,444
10	6,500	13,000
11	5,909	11,818
12	5,416	10,832

Custodial Accounts—Use a custodial account to take advantage of the "kiddie tax" by establishing a plan under the Uniform Gift to Minors Act (UGMA) or the Uniform Transfers to Minors Act (UTMA), as discussed in Chapter 10, Money, Children and You.

Custodial accounts are easy to start and easy to administer. In addition, if your child's earnings from the custodial account are taxed at your child's lower rate, you may be able to accumulate college savings faster.

Other ideas to fund a college education:

1. If you can afford it, buy rental property on the campus where your child will attend college. When your child starts at school, he or she can manage the property while renting it to other college students. Here are the advantages:
   a) You receive an annual tax deduction for mortgage interest, operating expenses and depreciation.
   b) You can pay your child a salary for managing the property, which is also deductible to you as a business expense. Your child can use the wages to offset college expenses.
   c) You receive rental income which, while taxable, will help pay the mortgage costs on the property, and provide funds to pay college costs.

2. Use the $10,000 tax-free gift exclusion, a tactic often used by grandparents. The main purpose is to reduce your estate by

C
H
A
P
T
E
R

12

giving a tax-free gift of $10,000 to each child or grandchild. You can time the gift so it will be used to pay for tuition, books and other expenses.

3. Have your attorney set up a 2503(c) Minority Trust, discussed in detail in Chapter 11. As the trustee, you will have control over the funds until the child is 21, although you can only use the benefits for the minor. Still, your child won't have direct access to funds until he or she is close to, or already finished, with college.

4. Ask your attorney about a "Crummy Trust" with you as trustee. This trust is named after the court case from which it originated, and is similar to the 2503(c) Minority Trust. The important difference is that the recipient of the trust—your child—may withdraw contributions made to the trust for a limited period of time in the year the contributions are made. If the funds are not withdrawn, the contribution is added to the trust principal. The trust can last as long as the trustee decides.

Investing for College

There are many investment choices available to generate funds for college education costs. The basic vehicles are similar to those you might use to invest money for any purpose, including:

- money market funds;

- certificates of deposit;

- Series EE savings bonds;

- municipal bonds;

- corporate or government bonds;

- stock and bond mutual funds;

- unit investment trusts; and

- zero coupon bonds.

In addition, there are several investments that are primarily used for college funding:

1. *Baccalaureate Bonds*. Twenty-two states offer these general obligation municipal bonds, which pay a slightly higher interest rate than other municipal bond issues. They're popular because

they're perceived to be safe, and because of their "non-callable" feature—the bonds cannot be taken away from you until maturity. These bonds are also issued in varying maturities, which makes it easy to match the bond's redemption year to the year you need funds for college.

2. *College-Sure Certificates of Deposit*. This investment vehicle is offered by the College Savings Bank in Princeton, New Jersey. The annual return is tied to an index of full college funding for first-year students at 500 private, four-year colleges and universities. This program offers FDIC insurance, the ability to keep up with college inflation, and the pure safety of an investment in certificates of deposit. It's a popular investment choice for college funding. After an initial deposit of $1,000, you can make additional deposits of as little as $250.

3. *Series EE Bonds*. While you can consider these for funding of college education, there are many restrictions on them that may create a lot of anxiety.

   First, the return on the investment is not inspiring. They pay the higher of 6 percent, or 85 percent of the average return on five-year Treasury Bills. Moreover, that "floating" rate is available only if the bonds are held for five years, so if you are the parent of a 13-year old, you will not find much consolation in EE bonds. In addition, higher income taxpayers are shut out entirely—although the phaseout ranges will be adjusted for inflation—so you may not even qualify to use them for college funding.

   Grandparents who want to retain control over assets earmarked for their grandchildren's education should not invest in EE bonds. The restrictions on them force the grandparents to give the money to the parent, and the parent would have to make the investment in the EE bonds.

   If you do decide to purchase EE bonds to finance your children's college educations, remember that the bonds must be purchased in your name, not in the names of your children. You can get more information about this type of investment by calling 1-800-872-6637 to obtain current rates and additional information on Series EE Bonds.

Using Your IRA to Fund College Education Costs

If you're under age 59-1/2, you have to pay a 10 percent IRS penalty if you cash in an IRA. Between age 59-1/2 and age 70-1/2, you can withdraw any amount of retirement money from your IRA without penalty.

CHAPTER 12

However, if you need money for college education, at any age, you can move your retirement account from its current investment into a life annuity, from which you can take annual payments.

When you start an annuity, you must take roughly equal amounts each year for the next five years, or until you reach age 59-1/2, whichever is later. The amounts you withdraw must be related to your life expectancy and to the amount of interest your remaining funds can earn. If your annuity stops too soon, the 10 percent IRS penalty will become retroactive, and you will have to pay it on the amounts already withdrawn.

For example, if you're fifty years old and you have a $100,000 retirement account, you could pull out of your annuity anywhere from $3,000 to $10,000 per year. The variation in the amount depends on which of several government-authorized methods you use to withdraw the funds. Seek the services of an accountant or a well-schooled financial planner to help design a legitimate withdrawal plan; few people know enough about actuarial science or the intricacies of the Internal Revenue Code to develop a plan by themselves.

Loans

If all else fails, use the following sources of loans:

1. *Life Insurance Policies*. Before borrowing from a policy, check the interest rate on the cash value loan. Older policies usually have the lowest rates. Loans against insurance policies are not subject to demand repayment. In fact, they need not be paid back at all; you simply pay the interest as long as you have the loan. Universal life policies charge you an interest rate that is close to the rate the company pays out on investments, so the net effect is a very low cost to you.

2. *401(k) Plans*. If you have a 401(k) retirement plan through your employer, check to see what loan interest rates will be charged to you if you borrow from the fund. In this case, the higher the rate the better, since you're really paying the money back directly into your account. Each plan has different borrowing rules, so inquire before you make the loan.

3. *Margin Account*. A margin account allows you to borrow against securities you own, and use the interest you pay for the loan as a deduction to lower your taxes on the securities' earnings. Be careful here: if the securities drop in value, you may get a "margin call," and you would have to repay the outstanding loan at that time.

4. *Government Loans*. The two best known government loan programs are the Stafford Student Loan, also known as the Guaranteed Student Loan Program, and the Perkins Loan. You also may wish to investigate the lesser-known Plus Loans and Supplement Loans to Students (SLS). Other loans may be available through federally chartered agencies, such as the Student Loan Marketing Association.

5. *Loans from the College*. The college your child attends may offer loans to parents who do not qualify for financial aid.

6. *Home Equity Loans*. These are loans you negotiate with your bank or other lending institutions, using the equity in your home as collateral. The interest on home equity loans up to $100,000 is fully tax-deductible; the loans are usually available if you qualify to make the additional monthly debt payment.

Financial Aid

Now we will examine all of the previously discussed methods for college funding from a new point of view—financial aid. A critical decision you need to make is whether investments for long-range accumulation of college funds should be in your name at your tax bracket, or in your child's name at the usually-lower child's rate.

The tax bracket for many widowed persons does not exceed 15 percent. If you fall into this category, it may be better to keep assets in your own name: colleges expect 35 percent of any asset in the child's name to go for schooling, which can drastically reduce the possibility of receiving aid. On the other hand, only 5.6 percent of your assets count in this formula.

The basic rule is to save in the child's name if there's no chance your family will qualify for aid, because you'll accumulate money more quickly using the child's lower tax bracket. Then, at college time, spend it all on tuition and other college costs. If there is a possibility of receiving aid, save funds in your name, because your assets are only expected to provide 5.6 percent for your child's education.

Determining your eligibility for financial aid is not easy. The tax laws change continually, and the laws covering student aid confuse laymen and professionals alike. The complete subject is beyond the scope of this book, but you can get a copy of *Don't Miss Out: The Ambitious Student's Guide to Financial Aid*, by Robert and Anna Leider. It's published by Octameron Press in Alexandria, Virginia. Their direct dial phone number is 703-836-5480. Another excellent publication is *The Princeton Review/The Student Access Guide to Paying for College* by Kalman A. Chaney with Geoff Martz, Villiard Books.

CHAPTER 12

Here are other suggestions related to your quest for financial aid:

1. Don't pay a computer service for scholarship searches. Most experts agree that these services are unlikely to be of much help in your quest for financial aid.

2. Apply for financial aid if you feel there is even the slightest chance that your child is eligible. Obtain financial aid forms from your child's high school guidance counselor, or directly from the College Scholarship Service (CSS). Complete the forms and mail them, as soon as possible after January 1 in the year of college applicability, to the College Scholarship Service, P.O. Box 6364, Princeton, NJ 08541. You will need to enclose your tax return for the previous year.

   CSC completes an analysis of your child's eligibility and forwards its findings to the school(s) in which you have expressed interest. The college then determines the level of awards, if any.

3. When your child is in the process of applying for admission, look for colleges that have substantial endowments. These are usually schools that can provide aid, rather than only work-study programs or loans.

4. If you want to receive full consideration for all available programs, you must apply early. Colleges review financial aid applications as they come in, and the institutions often run out of money before they run out of eligible applicants.

5. Reduce your own and your child's income and assets as much as possible. Students receiving financial aid are expected to contribute 70 percent of their after-tax income, and up to 35 percent of their assets, each year to education. You are expected to use as much as 47 percent of your income, and 5.6 percent of your assets annually.

6. Replace all consumer installment loans with home equity loans. One of the criteria for awarding financial aid is based on the net equity in your home; but consumer loans are ignored in figuring your net worth for financial aid purposes.

Other financial aid programs to consider are:

1. *Pell Grants*. While this needs-based program has been cut back in recent years, it is still worthwhile. You can obtain more information about it by calling the Federal Student Financial Information Center, 1-800-433-3243.

2. *Stafford Loans and Plus Loans*. Stafford loans are loans of $2650 to $5500 for your child and are no longer need-based. Plus loans are for parents and under the new rules are limited to the cost of college less financial aid. Even if you have no financial aid you can apply for a Plus Loan.

3. *Supplemental Education Opportunity Grants (SEOG)*. This is a campus-based program for students demonstrating the greatest funding need. Check with the financial officer at the college of your choice.

4. *College Work-Study Programs (CWSP)*. As the name implies, this program is for students who want to earn money for college expenses by working on campus. Inquire about this program at the school's financial aid office.

5. *Federal Perkins Loans*. These five percent loans permit students to borrow up to $3000 a year for undergraduate studies with a maximum of $15,000 over the course of a student's schooling. Graduate study loans are also available. Uncle Sam pays interest on the loans while the student's in school and for a nine-month grace period following graduation.

Planning for your children's college education is one of your biggest challenges. If you allow yourself an appropriate number of years to accumulate assets, you will not feel too much strain when your children are ready to make their way onto campus.

LONG TERM CARE

Long term care refers to the medical and/or personal care services you require if you have a chronic illness or disability. You may require daily medical attention, or need help simply with the basic activities of daily living such as dressing, bathing and walking.

Many long term care services are provided through informal care-giving systems such as your family, friends and relatives. Long term care can also be provided through more formal providers.

In a more recent phenomena, nearly 3 million Americans are now living in retirement communities. Many of these are called Continuing Care or Life Care facilities. Some care communities are operated by non-profit organizations while others are commercial enterprises.

Care communities provide residents, age 65 or older, with an apartment, meals, maid service and entertainment facilities. You must be able to live on your own when entering, but lifetime health care, including long term skilled care, is provided as needed. Senior citizens buying into these life care communities are required to pay fairly large entrance fees before they are admitted, as well as monthly fees thereafter.

An important note is that if your home is sold prior to moving into a life care community, it is generally held that you may not defer the tax on the home sale by claiming that the entrance fee is the equivalent of buying a new home. The IRS has ruled an investment in a retirement community is not the same as buying an actual home. However, if you have been required to move into a nursing care facility because of becoming physically or mentally incapable of self care, then your $125,000 exclusion is still available on the sale of your home.

Formal providers—Formal care providers include home health agencies, senior centers, area agencies on aging, and adult daycare programs, as well as nursing homes and community care homes that provide care in a residential setting.

A typical nursing home stay commonly falls into two types. You can have a short term stay of one to three months, involving skilled nursing care. This type is basically rehabilitative in nature and often follows a hospital confinement. You can also have a lengthy confinement, comprised mainly of maintenance or custodial care. The average duration of these is two-and-one-half years. The latter of the two types should concern you most.

To make an intelligent decision about long term care you need to answer two questions:

1. Do you need it?

2. Can you afford it?

Thereafter, you need to determine which of the many plans available meets your needs.

DO YOU NEED LONG TERM CARE?

It is difficult to predict if you will need long term care. The need can arise gradually as a person needs more assistance with the activities of daily living. Or the need can surface suddenly following, say, a stroke or a heart attack.

The longer you live, the more likely it is that you will need some kind of long term care. Some people who have acute illnesses need nursing home care for only short periods. Others are residents for many months or years, because they require 24-hour care. The care they need may not be available outside a nursing home. However, if you do need nursing care you may be able to receive it in your own home.

According to various sources, such as the Mayo Clinic and the Harvard Medical School, persons age 65 have at least one chance in four of needing an average of two-and-one-half years of long term care. At an average cost of $100 per day, this can translate into over $100,000 for long term care expenses.

NOTE: For most widowed persons, paying extended out-of-pocket expenses can mean financial disaster.

With people living longer than ever before, the demand for health care, including long term care, will significantly increase. The number of persons in nursing homes is expected to increase by over 60% in the next 30 years. Of the people in nursing homes, most—95 percent—receive custodial care, 4.5 percent receive intermediate care and only one half of one percent receive skilled care.

The only Americans not exposed to this risk of nursing home costs are either so wealthy that nursing home costs are inconsequential or so impoverished that they already qualify for Medicaid. For the majority of people caught between these two groups, there is a strong possibility of a costly nursing home stay.

CAN YOU AFFORD LONG TERM CARE?

There are only four sources of funds to pay for long term care:

1. Medicare and Medicare supplements;

2. Medicaid;

3. Long term care insurance;

4. Your savings and assets.

Medicare—Medicare was intended to cover short term needs, primarily hospital and doctor bills, not custodial long term care needs. In addition, Medicare pays only for skilled nursing care. If you're a nursing home patient, you must meet the following criteria to qualify for Medicare:

1. The care must be provided in a skilled nursing facility. Most U.S. nursing homes, about 72 percent, are *not* skilled nursing facilities.

2. The skilled nursing facility must be Medicare approved. Nationwide, only 31 percent of skilled nursing facilities are approved.

3. The care must be provided within 30 days after a prior hospital stay of at least three days.

4. Nursing care must be at a sufficiently skilled level such that it can only be provided by a registered nurse or a licensed practical nurse acting under a doctor's orders.

5. The care must be restorative in nature. That is, it must be designed to make the patient well. Any type of intermediate or custodial care as opposed to skilled nursing care is not covered.

6. The care must be provided continuously 24 hours-a-day. If you need skilled nursing or rehabilitative services only once or twice a week, or do not need to be in a skilled nursing facility to

receive skilled services, Medicare will not pay the charges. Also, even when Medicare's benefit is available, it only pays in full for your first 20 days. From days 21–100, it pays everything except $78.50 per day. After day 100 you pay for everything.

Currently, Medicare covers only 2.2 percent of the nation's nursing home costs. Medicare supplement policies generally do not cover long term care expenses but rather are designed to pay other costs Medicare does not cover such as hospital deductibles or excess physician charges. (See Chapter 9 on Insurance.)

Medicaid—Medicaid is a federal and state finance assistance program for certain needy and low income persons, regardless of age. Nationally, Medicaid today pays for nearly half of all nursing home care. To receive Medicaid assistance you must meet federal poverty guidelines or spend down your assets, usually on health care costs, to meet the eligibility requirements.

Many people who begin paying for nursing home care out of their own pockets spend down their financial resources until they become eligible for Medicaid. Then they turn to Medicaid to pay part or all of their nursing home expenses. One significant characteristic of Medicaid is that it covers intermediate nursing home care, the kind that most institutionalized elderly persons require.

Once your resources for paying for private-pay nursing home care are depleted, the only refuge is Medicaid. Depletion of resources also means that there will be no inheritance for your children or grandchildren.

Eligibility for Medicaid depends on meeting the system's criteria. Some widowed persons make Medicaid plans by structuring their income and transferring assets to fit the criteria. Medicaid planning can be controversial. Some people feel that it is improper, or unethical, to take advantage of what are considered loopholes in the system. Others feel it is unfair to divert resources intended for the poor.

Also Medicaid planning can involve risks. Some widowed persons transfer all their resources to children or grandchildren only to realize that they will not need nursing home care. The result could be the opposite of making the money last and you could have a serious decline in your standard of living. Additionally, Medicaid rules may change, as occurred in 1993, so that all the planning steps will not create the desired result of securing Medicaid eligibility.

Medicaid assistance is based on the amount of your income and capital resources. The more you have, the less likely you are to qualify. Worse, state laws may make you ineligible if, within a specific period of time (usually 36 months), you have transferred more than a certain amount of assets in order to protect those assets and become eligible for aid.

Most states will allow you to have assets up to $2,000, in addition to certain other exempt assets. These vary in nature and amounts from state to state. In general, they include:

1. your home;

2. household goods and personal items up to $2,000;

3. wedding and engagement ring;

4. car of any value, if needed to go to work or receive medical care or you are handicapped. Otherwise your car can be valued only up to $4,500;

5. property of any kind worth up to $6,000, if essential to your support;

6. up to $1,500 in life insurance policy cash values;

7. a burial plot, or up to $1,500 per person for a burial plot.

Transferring Assets to Meet the Resources Test—Medicaid law requires the state to delay your eligibility (the "look back" period) for benefits if you transfer assets within 36 months from the day you apply for Medicaid benefits. Thus, you can be ineligible for up to 36 months.

For transfers made into an irrevocable trust, from which you (the transferor) cannot receive income and cannot take back any part of the trust principal, the "look back" period is 60 months.

Before the Omnibus Budget Reconciliation Act of 1993 (OBRA '93) the look back period was 30 months, regardless of the size of the transfer.

What can be done about this? Remember, if you transfer assets, you are making an irrevocable transfer; you can't change your mind and get these assets back once they are gone. You may also be making what is called a "taxable gift." If you do decide to transfer property to your children, grandchildren, or others, you must make your gift 36 months before you apply for Medicaid.

Each state has a published figure for the cost of private-pay care. This number can effectively raise or lower the 36-month requirement. Assume, for example, that $90,000 is transferred, and your states' cost of care is $3000 per month. The transfer in this example will create a 30-month penalty period for you. If the transfer is $750,000 instead of $90,000 and the cost of care is set at $5000 per month, the transfer will create a 150-month penalty period—a very impractical 12-1/2 years!

If you are already in a nursing home, or are about to go into one, you can keep enough assets to pay for the next 36 months of care and transfer the rest. If you pay your own expenses and apply for Medicaid

36 months after the day you made the last of your asset transfers, you may be eligible.

If you want to leave a large inheritance to your children, or you can't afford lifetime insurance benefits, here is a compromise approach:

> Buy a long term care insurance policy with a three- or five-year benefit period. This policy would give you time to transfer your assets after you enter a nursing facility, 36 months or 60 months later. When the policy runs out, the assets would have been safely transferred for the required 36 months and you will qualify for Medicaid payments on any further nursing home costs.

Also, just as important, you will have entered the nursing home as a private-paying patient. While not officially acknowledged, it seems to be well-known that private-paying patients do seem to receive better care than Medicaid patients.

Once you have a grasp on how Medicaid works, you may be ready to begin what is called Medicaid Planning. *This is a highly complex legal area that requires the help of professionals.* Your local bar association may have a list of attorneys who practice Elder Law who can assist you.

Long Term Care Insurance—This is the most desirable option for many widowed persons and is described in detail starting on page 209.

Your Savings and Assets—If you can pay for your long term health costs out of your own savings and assets, you are among a lucky few . .

How to Successfully Meet Your Needs?

While no one knows for sure how rapidly long term care costs will increase, all the experts agree that they will go up. How do you, as a widowed person, grapple with this cost picture? The following approach requires a number of assumptions on your part. However, using the data available today, they are the only realistic numbers you have to work with.

Assumptions:

1. You will probably need nursing home or home health care at some point in your life;

2. The costs will continue to escalate at 7 percent annually;

3. The average cost today is $25,000 per year;

4. You will need this coverage for a minimum of 2-1/2 years.

Suppose you are now age 60. What will long term care cost based on the above assumptions?

Year	Age	Inflated Cost/Year
1	61	$ 26,750
2	62	28,622
3	63	30,626
4	64	32,769
5	65	35,063
10	70	49,178
15	75	68,975
20	80	96,742
25	85	135,686

Now you need to compare the above numbers with your own financial information. Return to the chapter on Income Planning to determine your current resources. Will those income figures increase in the future? What about expenses? For example, assume you require long term care at the age of 70.

If you go into a nursing home, what will your total costs be? Would you choose to sell your home or continue maintaining it? Most people want to return to their home if at all possible. You could have the cost of long term care in addition to home maintenance, real estate property taxes, utilities and insurance.

Suppose you can stay in your home, but need home health care. All your regular expenses will remain, plus the cost of the care in your home and any special medications, etc. Cheryl, age 67, is an example. Her monthly expenses now run about $2,000 and her monthly income is $2,500, including pension, Social Security and investment income. Her home is paid for and she's currently in good health. Her mother just died at 94 and her father died at 88. Both required long term care in their later years which Cheryl helped pay for. Helping her parents reduced her assets and she has little to fall back on should she require nursing home or home health care. It seems possible that Cheryl too could eventually need long term care.

Cheryl is a candidate for a long term care policy available through various insurance carriers. While she can afford a policy now, as she ages, her health may deteriorate and the cost of coverage will increase substantially each year she puts off buying a policy.

If she needs care at the age of 80, in 13 years, the annual costs could range between $60,000 and $85,000 based on a 7 percent annual increase today. And it's likely she would not qualify to obtain the policy then. A $100 daily policy with a 100-day waiting period and lifetime benefits would cost about $78 monthly.

With Cheryl's monthly surplus of $500, she can afford it, and the benefit would supplement her annual income by $36,000 should she need it. The policy should also contain a home health care rider that would pay for $50 to $100 of daily care in the home. This would add about $21 each month to the premium.

Here's how you can estimate your long term care costs:

1. Call several nursing homes in your area and determine the long term care daily rate. Using an average of these, multiply the rate by 365. (Avg Daily Rate x 365 = $_____ , See Table Below).

Annual Equivalents of Daily Room Rates

Daily Rate	=	Yearly Rate
$ 50		$18,250
70		25,550
80		29,200
90		32,850
100		36,500
120		43,800

2. Then, using this annual cost figure, apply the multiplier factor of 7 percent per year for the year you wish to estimate the cost.

Multiplier Factor for 7% Increase/Year

Year	Factor
5	1.403
10	1.967
15	2.759
20	3.869

For example, the Average Daily Rate of $80 is multiplied times 365 days to derive an annual cost of $29,200. If you are age 65 now, and wish to estimate costs in ten years, multiply 29,200 x 1.967 = $57,436.

What if You are a Younger Widowed Person?—You don't need to be concerned, yet, if you are younger than age 50. However, being aware of all the ramifications of long term care and its costs can provide you with valuable knowledge for later years.

If you're between the ages of 50 and 60, you should examine coverage now available. Here's a comparison of yearly premiums from a cross-section of companies at various ages for $100 in daily benefits with a 100-day elimination period:

Age	Cost	Age	Cost	Age	Cost
50	$405	60	$513	70	$1264
54	441	64	717	74	2004
58	476	68	1034	78	3369

Is it worth it to buy the coverage in earlier years? There's no hard and fast rule. You have to look at your individual situation from a medical and financial point of view. For example, do you have a medical problem now that is likely to worsen as you age? Would it prevent you from acquiring the coverage? Can you presently afford to spend $500 on annual premiums, but probably not $1000 in 10 or 15 years?

BUYING A LONG TERM HEALTH CARE POLICY

There is no single right plan that is perfect for everyone. The right plan for you may be completely different from the right plan for your best friend. Each company and each policy has strengths and weaknesses. To pick the policy that is best for you, you need to understand what types of coverage are available and what these plans entail.

Long term care policies may pay for skilled, intermediate, custodial, home care or adult day care, and each policy may define these terms differently. It is important that you understand these definitions because you receive benefits only if the care you receive is covered in the policy. Some policies make no distinctions among these levels of care. They will pay regardless of the type of care you need.

You also will have a choice in how long the benefits will last. Policy maximums limit the amount the policy will pay in benefits. Some policies state that they will pay benefits for a set number of days, months, or years. For home health coverage, benefit maximums are sometimes expressed as a stated number of visits. Other policies will pay for a certain number of units of care. Still other policies will express their maximum limits in dollars.

Benefits generally vary from $40 per day to as much as $200 per day for each day you need care covered by the policy. These benefits may last for as little as one year or for your lifetime, depending on the policy. (You may have a choice of one year, two years, three years, four years, five years, or lifetime). Some policies pay a smaller benefit for custodial home care or adult day-care.

Over time, the custodial care can be the most costly. Very few people need skilled care for a long period of time, and much of the care in nursing homes is custodial. You should consider a policy that provides coverage for custodial care as well as skilled or intermediate care.

You also have your choice of what are called "elimination periods." These are waiting periods before your policy actually starts paying if you enter a nursing home or receive home health care. A waiting period can be anywhere from 0 days to 100 days. Often 20 days is a popular choice. Some policies offer a 60-day waiting period.

Make certain when you are preparing to buy a policy that it does not require a prior hospital stay before you are eligible for benefits. In addition, you want to make sure that you are not required to spend time in a nursing home before home health care benefits begin.

Your policy should be what is called "guaranteed renewable." This means the policy cannot be canceled by the company as long as you pay the premiums on time. The renewability provision is usually found on the first page of the policy and describes under what conditions the policy may be canceled, or when premiums may be raised. *Note that the company can cancel your policy if you have misrepresented your health status on the application*, and the company relied on these misrepresentations to give you the coverage. Also, look for a policy that covers Alzheimer's Disease.

LONG TERM POLICY ANALYSIS CHECKLIST

A. Benefits

	Company A		Company B		Company C	
1. Daily Benefit	$ _____		$ _____		$ _____	
	Yes	No	Yes	No	Yes	No
Skilled Nursing Care	_____	_____	_____	_____	_____	_____
Intermediate Care	_____	_____	_____	_____	_____	_____
Custodial Care	_____	_____	_____	_____	_____	_____
Home Health Care	_____	_____	_____	_____	_____	_____
Adult Day Care	_____	_____	_____	_____	_____	_____
2. Duration of Benefits	*Days/yr*		*Days/yr*		*Days/yr*	
Skilled Care	_____		_____		_____	
Intermediate Care	_____		_____		_____	
Custodial Care	_____		_____		_____	
Home Health Care	_____		_____		_____	
Adult Day Care	_____		_____		_____	
3. Inflation Benefit Available						
Percent Increase	_____ %		_____ %		_____ %	
Simple or Compound	_____		_____		_____	
Duration of Increases	_____		_____		_____	

4. What does Policy Pay?   *Per day*   *Per day*   *Per day*

    Skilled Nursing Care $ _____ $ _____ $ _____

    Intermediate Care $ _____ $ _____ $ _____

    Custodial Care $ _____ $ _____ $ _____

    Home Health Care $ _____ $ _____ $ _____

    Adult Day Care $ _____ $ _____ $ _____

    Any stay in nursing home $ _____ $ _____ $ _____

Years policy pays benefits   _____ yrs   _____ yrs   _____ yrs

B. *Limits or exclusions*

    Waiting (Elimination Period)

    Nursing Home Care   _____ days   _____ days   _____ days

    Home Health Care   _____ days   _____ days   _____ days

    Adult Day Care   _____ days   _____ days   _____ days

    Time before pre-existing
      conditions are covered   _____ months   _____ months   _____ months

    Alzheimer's Coverage
      (yes or no)   _____   _____   _____

Prior Hospital Stay   Yes   No   Yes   No   Yes   No
   Required for:

    Skilled Nursing Care   ____ ____   ____ ____   ____ ____

    Intermediate Nursing Care   ____ ____   ____ ____   ____ ____

    Custodial Care   ____ ____   ____ ____   ____ ____

    Home Health Care   ____ ____   ____ ____   ____ ____

Prior Skilled Nursing
   Care required for:

    Intermediate Care   ____ ____   ____ ____   ____ ____

    Custodial Care   ____ ____   ____ ____   ____ ____

    Home Health Care   _____

C. *Costs of Policy*

    Monthly/Annual Cost
      w/o riders $ _____ $ _____ $ _____

    Inflation Rider   _____   _____   _____

    Home Health Care Rider   _____   _____   _____

    Waiver of Premium   _____   _____   _____

    Any Discounts   _____   _____   _____

    Total Cost   _____   _____   _____

CHAPTER 13

Companies generally require that a certain period of time pass before the policy pays for care related to a health problem you may have had when you applied for coverage. These types of health problems are called *"pre-existing condition."* This is a condition for which medical advice or treatment was recommended by a physician and/or received by you before you signed the application. Usually, nursing home stays arising from a pre-existing condition will not be covered for six months after the effective date of the policy. Some companies require as long as one year for pre-existing conditions.

There are other features you should have in a policy. One is called *"waiver of premium."* The waiver of premium clause allows you to stop paying premiums during the time you are receiving benefits. Some policies require you to be in a nursing home for a certain number of days, often 90 days, before this clause becomes effective.

Another feature is an *inflation rider*. These riders usually increase the benefits by cost-of-living increases. They may also automatically increase the policy by 3 to 5 percent per year. These benefits may be available at a simple interest basis or a compound interest basis. The inflation benefits may increase every year for the rest of your life, or they may stop after a certain amount of time, 10 or 20 years for example.

The inflation rider will usually add anywhere from 20 to 65 percent to your premium depending on what form of coverage is selected. However, without such an inflation rider, the cost of long term care insurance may be far greater in the future than the benefits you receive when you finally need the care.

A feature that you should consider is called a "non-forfeiture" feature. This is a return of premium feature or return of benefits feature. This feature returns part of what you paid in premiums if you choose to cancel your coverage after a certain period of time, or if your coverage lapses because you have not paid the premium. These benefits will most likely not be paid in cash, but will guarantee some portion of benefits. This feature often requires that you hold the policy for 10 or 20 years.

Finally you should choose a financially stable company. Refer to Chapter 9 on Insurance to choose a company using the rating system outlined in that chapter.

As with most methods for making the money last, the earlier you begin planning for long term care consideration, the fewer surprises and less anxiety you'll experience as you gracefully make your way to old age.

PART IV:

PROSPEROUS TRANSITIONS

GIVING—HOW, WHEN, WHO AND HOW MUCH

Once you have financial security it may be better to give assets and income, moving them out of your estate. However, if your estate is not large and your income needs are substantial, you need to be very cautious in making gifts. Most widowed persons give what they can to friends, relatives and charity.

You may have many reasons to make gifts to others:

1. It makes you feel good;

2. It will often benefit others, especially your close relatives or friends;

3. It can reduce your estate and consequently your federal estate taxes at your death;

4. It can reduce your income taxes now;

5. Your gifts can be used to provide funds to pay for future college educations for children or grandchildren.

You may find it desirable to also make gifts to charitable organizations. Some of these reasons may include:

1. A compassion for those in need;

2. A religious and spiritual commitment on your part;

3. A perpetuation of one's beliefs, values and ideas;

4. Support for art, sciences and education;

5. A desire to share one's good fortune with others.

Before you rush into a giving program, however, you need to determine if you can afford it. While it is natural and understandable that you want to make gifts, giving at the wrong time can create unfortunate results. Money can be given away, but your needs still exist to be met. Your primary objective is to *make the money last*. When you have sufficient amounts of income and financial assets, then it's time to think about gifts.

Review your assets, liabilities and cash flow numbers (refer to Chapter 5 and review the income and cash flow sheets in that chapter). Will you have enough income to continue your well-being and your future standard of living? Also, run the numbers for your future retirement needs (See Chapter 7). Remember, you don't want to be a burden to anyone else at any time in the future. If the numbers show that you can afford to make gifts to children, charity or others, go ahead and do it.

It is important to realize that when you make a gift it is *absolute*. Once you have given the property or money away, you cannot retrieve it. For that reason it is often wise to determine whether you are actually making a gift or a loan. If it is a loan, have a loan agreement signed between you and the person to whom you are loaning the money. (See the chapter on Money and Children for a discussion on this topic.)

As mentioned earlier, giving can reduce your estate taxes, income taxes and probate costs. Giving assets to save estate taxes is especially useful when the asset is likely to appreciate in value, and you would like to have the growth occur in someone else's hands.

Here's an example: Alice has more than enough income and assets to last her lifetime. She has a piece of real estate that is expected to grow in value over the years ahead. By making a gift now, she can remove that asset from her estate, while also removing all the future growth at the same time.

Another advantage of giving is that you know exactly who the person or charity is that you want to benefit from your estate.

MAKING A GIFT IS A SURE THING

Unlike most gifts bestowed after your death, gifts you give during your lifetime—hence, called *lifetime gifts*—can be private. No one but the recipient of the gift has to know any of the details. On the other hand, property that passes under your will must be inventoried, and the list may be filed with the County Register of Wills, at which point it becomes public information. This makes your beneficiaries available to receive sometimes well-intended, but often harmful, advice of those who always "know" how to invest someone else's money. This is not as much of a problem with gifts.

Making a gift while you are alive also gives you the pleasure of seeing the recipients enjoy and use it. For example, you can watch how your son or daughter handles and invests cash. Such observation can help you make decisions about whether or when to make additional gifts either during your lifetime or at your death. Note that while it may provide financial security for those to whom you make the gift, it also insulates that property from claims of your creditors.

Estate taxes are not the only taxes you can save by lifetime gifts. Many gifts are given for the potential income tax savings rather than estate tax savings. For example, Mary's income puts her into the 31 percent income tax bracket. That means that 31 cents of every dollar in her top bracket will be lost to taxes.

By giving a high income mutual fund to her daughter, the income from that mutual fund is no longer taxed to Mary. Instead it is taxed to her daughter in a lower bracket. If her daughter is in a 15 percent tax bracket, the family unit realizes a 16 percent tax savings in the difference.

GIVING IN A NUTSHELL

Giving can be an important estate planning technique, because it can save you estate taxes and probate costs. Giving guarantees that the party to whom you want to give your gift will receive it. It also ensures that the details of the gift will be completely private. Making a lifetime gift gives you the opportunity to enjoy the pleasure of giving to the recipient. It enables you to see how well they handle and manage the gift. And finally, gifts of income-producing property shift the tax onto the income to the recipient and offer an easy way to save income taxes.

WHAT ARE THE COSTS OF GIVING?

It may not cost one cent in taxes even to offer large gifts. The reason? Before any taxes are due, you may qualify for one of the following two gift provisions:

1. An annual $10,000 per donee (i.e., recipient) gift tax exclusion;

2. Use of the unified credit.

Let's see how these two gift tax reducers work.

Annual Gifts—You can give up to $10,000 in cash or other property every year, to as many different people or institutions as you wish with no gift tax liability what-so-ever. This is called the "annual gift tax exclusion." Gifts can be made to individuals, relatives or not, or any other party, such as a charity or a club.

For example, Jane is a 65-year-old widow with three nephews, Bill, Ed and Alex. She gives each nephew $10,000 in cash or other property each year. This means she removes $30,000 each year ($10,000 x 3) from her estate at no federal estate or gift tax cost to her. If Jane remarries, she and her new husband can agree to split the gift and the amount then doubles. Together they can give up to $60,000 ($20,000 to each) to Jane's three nephews.

Since Jane's life expectancy is about twenty more years she can avoid estate taxes on approximately $600,000 (20 x $30,000), if she continues the gift-giving program. The annual exclusion over time can remove massive amounts of property from estates.

Unified Credit—Federal estate tax law provides a single tax credit called the "unified credit." This is a dollar-for-dollar reduction for any gift or estate tax due. The credit is equal to an exemption of $600,000, while the credit is actually $192,800.

Assume Robin makes a $610,000 gift to her son. The computation would be as follows:

Gift	$610,000
Annual Exclusion	10,000
Net Gift	600,000
Tax on Net Gift	192,800
Unified Credit	192,800
Net tax due	–0–

To the extent that you use the unified credit during your lifetime, it will have the effect of reducing any credit available against any estate or gift tax at your death. For estate taxes in Robin's case, there will be no credit left for her estate. She can still make gifts of $10,000 per year to a particular person or entity without incurring taxes but she has used up the total $192,800 unified credit.

Donors must file a gift tax return on or before April 15 following the end of the calendar year in which the gift is made if it exceeds the annual exclusion of $10,000.

WHEN IS THE BEST TIME TO MAKE A GIFT?

The best time to make a gift is *now*, as far as the $10,000 annual gift exclusion is concerned. The exclusion is a non-cumulative opportunity—you either use it or lose it. However, whenever stocks or other assets which can fluctuate widely in value are being considered as gifts, you should give them away when the asset is valued as low as possible. In making any gift decision, carefully consider both your current and long-term financial security.

It is extremely important for you to focus on the circumstances of your financial situation before making a gift. Do not give away any asset if it will reduce your standard of living or financially endanger your comfort level. You should focus on the impact of the gift on your income and your capital needs, as well as your need for liquidity. Again, refer to the chapter on Retirement Planning to determine whether you are in position now, or will be in the future, to make gifts.

WHAT GIFTS TO GIVE

The type of gift or property to give depends on your circumstances and objectives. It may be good to give income-producing property if you are in a higher income tax bracket than the person to whom you are giving the property. Properties which are likely to increase in value substantially, such as life insurance, common stock, antiques, art, or even real estate, are prime candidates.

The future appreciation of these types of properties can be removed from your estate now. The gift should be made when the gift tax value, and therefore the gift tax transfer cost, are the lowest.

Property which has already appreciated can be considered if the sale of such property was contemplated anyway and the recipient is in a lower income tax bracket than you. Property with somewhat low gift tax value and high estate tax value, such as life insurance, makes an excellent gift. It's not a good idea to give away property showing a loss, since the recipient cannot deduct your loss. You should sell the property, take the deduction for the loss yourself, then make a gift of the cash proceeds.

Another type of property which should be considered for giving is property owned by you in a state other than your state of residence. Do this to avoid what is called "ancillary" probate at the time of your death.

Present Interest and Crummey Trusts

Under gift tax laws, you, the donor, must be giving a "present interest" in property or cash in order to qualify for the $10,000 annual exclusion. This means that the recipient must have complete access to the funds which might be very unsettling if you are contemplating making gifts to a minor child. There are, however, a few ways around this concern.

Several years ago the Crummy family (yes, that was their name) wanted to make gifts to their family members and qualify for the an-

CHAPTER 14

nual gift tax exclusion while restricting access to the funds. In order to accomplish this they created trusts. The language in the trust document allowed the beneficiaries to withdraw funds gifted to the trust within a limited period of time. If the funds were not withdrawn, they became trust assets.

This provision became known as a "Crummy Withdrawal Power." The tax court ruled the gifts qualified for the annual gift tax exclusion because the beneficiaries had a present power to withdraw the funds.

Another feature of the Crummy trust is referred to as "5-in-5" powers. They permit withdrawal of $5,000, or 5 percent, of the trust balance, whichever is greater. Your attorney can draft a document which accurately reflects your interest. If you are interested in pursuing this, talk to your attorney about a "Crummy" trust.

Other ways of making gifts to children include the Uniform Gift to Minors Act (UGMA), as well as the Uniform Transfers to Minors Act (UTMA). Both of these options are discussed in detail in the chapter on Money and Children.

Complex giving techniques include Section 2503(b) Trusts and Section 2503(c) Trusts. Setting up these trusts can be fairly complicated, and both require the services of a competent attorney familiar with these trusts.

CHARITABLE GIVING

There are a great many different reasons for making gifts to charitable organizations. You can give cash or checks, securities, a residence, farm or ranch, a family business or personal property like life insurance, works of art, precious stones, precious metals, gold, and silver.

NOTE: You can give almost anything to charity.

While it may not sound very charitable, you need to consider your tax situation when contemplating gifts to charity. Many charitable trust arrangements are attractive based on tax planning and financial grounds alone.

Factors to consider when making Charitable Gifts

Charitable trusts are accepted and enforced in all states. The law provides that there must be a definite charitable purpose in the gift, i.e., religious, educational, etc. The common law of most states will make a gift void, and thus a continuing part of your estate, if the trust does not;

    1. end, and

2. distribute assets within a time period measured by the lives of living beneficiaries, plus 21 years.

Federal income tax law permits you a deduction for gifts made to qualified charities subject to certain limitations. In addition, there are deductions for estate and gift tax purposes for transfers to qualified charities. State income, gift and inheritance tax laws also provide for charitable deductions.

When you make a tax deductible donation, the IRS is interested in the organization that benefits from that donation. You will not be able to reduce your taxable income if the group is not on the list of qualified organizations. You can obtain a copy of this list from the Internal Revenue Service (Publication #78).

Generally, your deduction is safe if you give your property to any of the following: governments (federal, state or local), domestic trust foundations with charitable or similar purposes, and some, but not all, domestic veterans or fraternal organizations. To be sure that your deduction is valid, ask for proof that the organization has been granted tax exempt status. The group should be able to provide you with a copy of a ruling letter from the IRS granting the exempt qualified status.

The IRS also wants to be sure that your gift is made with a charitable intent. Any correspondence with the charitable organization should state your willingness to make the donation to the charity. If there is any hint that the contribution is being made for business purposes, your deduction could be disallowed.

Regulations on charitable contributions can be complex. If you play by the IRS rules, however, there are substantial benefits both for you and for your favorite charity.

Tax Deduction Limitations

Since all gift-giving has tax deduction limitations, let's quickly examine the playing field:

1. Deductions for your contributions of cash or ordinary income property to public charities are limited to 50 percent of adjusted gross income. The deduction is based on the cost of the property or the amount of the cash donated.

2. Deductions for your contributions of appreciated property to public charities are limited to 30 percent of your adjusted gross income. The deduction value of your contribution is based on the fair market value of the property at the date of the gift.

3. Deductions for your contributions of tangible personal property,

unrelated to the charitable purpose of the donor organization, are limited to the cost of the property.

4. Deductions for your contributions of cash or ordinary income to private foundations, war veteran organizations, fraternal lodges and certain other organizations are limited to 30 percent of your adjusted gross income.

5. Deductions for contributions of appreciated property to these organizations listed in item 4 are limited to 20 percent of your adjusted gross income.

Be aware of the alternative minimum tax on gifts of appreciated property. Under the 1986 Tax Reform Act, the untaxed portion of appreciated capital gains property contributed to a charity is treated as a tax preference item. This means that if you are subject to the alternative minimum tax, the charitable contribution deduction is limited to the cost of the property.

There is some relief. Each taxpayer has a substantial exemption from the alternative minimum tax. If you are filing jointly, the exemption is $40,000 per year; for a single taxpayer the exemption is $30,000. The exemption is fully phased out, however, for taxpayers with an alternative minimum taxable income of $300,000 or more on a joint return, or $232,500 for a single taxpayer.

CHARITABLE GIVING THROUGH TRUSTS

Charitable strategies involving trusts are complicated and require an attorney, financial planner or accountant with special expertise in this field. There are several types of trusts, and each has its own special features and rules. These vehicles do, however, offer considerable flexibility in structuring contributions to meet your financial needs. They allow you, in part, to divide an asset into its income and ownership aspects and to give away only one component.

Charitable remainder trusts, of which there are several varieties, allow you to give a future interest in an asset to a charity while keeping an income stream for yourself. These types allow you to transfer assets to a trust with the stipulation that you receive income for a specified period. Property in the trust is transferred to the charity at the end of the trust term.

You can choose one of two options: a charitable remainder annuity trust, which provides a fixed amount of annual income, or a charitable remainder unit trust, which remits a fixed percentage of trust income annually.

The sale of property held by the trust has no immediate tax effect on either you or the trust. Charitable remainder trusts are mainly exempt from federal income tax. Because of this exemption, many people transfer appreciated assets to a charitable remainder trust prior to the sale of the asset. You are liable for taxes only on the payments you receive from the trust.

The trust will not pay taxes on capital gains because the asset is irrevocably dedicated to charity. This can work to your financial benefit. Also, gifts to a charitable remainder trust provide a charitable income tax deduction now. By transferring appreciated assets to such a trust, you can lower your current income taxes, avoid capital gains and estate taxes, and accomplish your charitable goals.

You can even structure a trust to give you a higher level of income than you are currently receiving from your assets:

> Consider Sylvia, a 65-year-old widow with a $350,000 home and $500,000 in other assets. Of this $500,000, she has $300,000 is stock, yielding only 4 percent. If she sells the stock she will incur a sizeable capital gains tax. But, the charitable gift of that stock to a remainder trust could increase her retirement income and her children's inheritance, while also benefiting a charity of her choice.

Here is how it would work: The trust sells Sylvia's stock tax-free and reinvests the securities, generating a greater income. The trust agreement provides for Sylvia to receive an annual income of 5-to-10 percent for the rest of her life. She also receives immediate tax deductions of approximately $95,000 (from IRS tables), and she can use part of her improved cash flow to buy life insurance. At her death, the life insurance would more than replace the value of the gift (see Wealth Replacement Trust below). When Sylvia dies, the charity will get the assets in the trust.

Wealth Replacement Trust

While a charitable remainder trust can help accomplish your current financial objectives, it may not please your heirs. You may be concerned about your surviving family members if they are slighted by your gift to charity. Using the concept of wealth replacement, you no longer must choose between your favorite charity and your family.

This charitable giving strategy offers an attractive annual income, provides you with a current income tax deduction and reduces your estate taxes. Plus, it protects your family's inheritance. You may be able to accomplish all of these objectives by creating a wealth replacement trust in conjunction with a charitable remainder trust.

CHAPTER 14

A wealth replacement trust can be funded with life insurance that pays its proceeds upon the death of the person named in the policy. The premiums for a life insurance policy can often be paid with a the tax savings generated by the current income tax deduction from the charitable contribution. Enough insurance can be purchased to replace the value of the assets left to the charity as part of the remainder trust.

Charitable Lead Trusts

Another trust strategy you can use is called a charitable lead trust. Securities or other assets are placed in a trust that pays all of its income to a charity for a fixed number of years. When that period is up, the trust assets go to a beneficiary you have previously named. The tax impact here is that you get a charitable deduction now for the present value of the monies that the charity will receive over the 10-year period.

The part of the gift that is left to your beneficiary in the future is subject to gift tax, but this tax will usually be low, since the IRS puts a greatly discounted value on such gifts. The benefit here is that you can make a large future gift to your beneficiary with a fairly low gift tax cost.

Suppose you put $100,000 into a charitable lead trust for 10 years, leaving the assets to your children after the charitable interest runs out. Using IRS tables, a 10-year income stream is valued at 61 percent of the value of the trust property. So $61,000 is the amount of your charitable gift and income tax deduction. The gift to your children is valued at only $39,000.

The benefit here is that your children will eventually get the full amount of the gift ($100,000), and the gift tax you pay is still based only on $39,000. Additionally, if the assets increase in value, the gift tax does not increase, but rather it stays the same. Thus, if the $100,000 you donated to the trust grows to a value of $200,000 when your beneficiaries take it, you will still pay a gift tax on only $39,000.

Gifts for an IRA

You might consider making a gift of $2,000 per year to your younger adult children to fund an IRA account. For example, your son is age 21 and now working for a company making $23,000 per year. He is allowed to make the full $2,000 contribution. Since his company doesn't have a pension plan and his income is below $25,000, he can take the full $2,000 deduction.

Let's assume that you continue to make a gift of $2,000 per year until your son is age 27. He then marries, and his and his new wife's combined incomes and company pension plans eliminate their IRA deduction at that time. Here's a look at the benefits of this program:

Annual Deposit $2000
Number of years for deposit 6
Assumed interest rate 8%
Accumulation value after 6 years $14,672

Now allow the lump sum accumulation of $14,672 to continue to grow at 8 percent until your son's age at 59-1/2:

Starting deposit $14,672
Number of years to age 59-1/2 32
Assumed interest rate 8%
Accumulated value at age 59-1/2 . . . . $440,632

All of this was achieved with six years of gifts of only $2,000 each. In addition, your son will be able to take a $2,000 tax deduction in each of those six years.

Making Small Gifts Count

There is another approach to this idea. You may start a savings account for children or grandchildren in order to teach them the value of saving money for the future. If you have a young adult who is really special to you, someone who is just getting started in a marriage or beginning a career, here is another way to help him or her learn the value of investing:

Again, open an IRA account in the young person's name. Make the first contribution and encourage regular investments. Note that he or she must be over 18 and have earned at least as much as the contribution in order to obtain the tax deduction.

Looking back over investment history there is evidence that even a small investment over time can grow to a large value. For example, 40 years ago a $1,000 investment in one of the oldest and largest growth mutual funds in America would be worth $152,000 today with all distributions being reinvested. That is a gift with tremendous leverage. Subsequent investments pay out handsomely, too.

If your young adult added only $500 per year for those 40 years, the fund would have had an additional $495,000. That is a total of $645,000 for a $21,000 investment. Naturally, we are talking about long periods of time. Most younger people would like to have the cash right now, and here is a way they can get some of it.

Your contribution to their IRA is probably tax deductible to them. A gift to them of $1,000 will result in a minimum $150 reduction in federal taxes. That would provide some extra spending money now. If they are in a 28 percent bracket it would provide $280 in extra spending money. Remember that the IRA account must be in their name. You have to give the money to the young adult and they must make the investment.

Done well, giving can yield wonderful tax saving benefits to you and the receiver.

PASSING ALONG YOUR WEALTH—ESTATE PLANNING

You've had to deal not only with the grief of your spouse's death, but also the difficulties associated with settling your partner's estate. Now, you may wish to put your own estate in order. Doing so will ensure that, when you die, your heirs will receive what you want them to have, when you want them to get it, with a minimum of expense, estate taxes and administration.

Estate taxes—which are at a maximum rate of 55 percent—can be the largest tax expense a widowed person will ever face. Your estate is everything you own—all that you've accumulated during your lifetime, including what you've inherited from your spouse.

> **NOTE:** Lack of proper planning could mean loss of over half of what you and your spouse spent a lifetime building.

Estate planning creates a structure by which to manage your property while you're alive, and to provide for its desired distribution upon your death. Without a plan, the estate you wanted to leave may end up being much smaller than you anticipated.

Especially with this chapter, please don't think of it as a replacement for professional advice. It is intended to be a guide, to show you some of the available strategies and provide you with basic concepts. However, estate planning is highly complicated, and the rules change frequently. Before implementing any estate plan strategies, seek the advice of an attorney, accountant or financial planner qualified in estate planning. You can determine whether you already have an adequate estate plan by answering the following questions:

Estate Planning Questionnaire

If you answer "No" to any of the following questions, you are a good candidate for estate planning:

1. Do you have a will?

2. Do you know the value of your estate?

3. Are you comfortable with the executors and trustees you've selected?

4. Have you executed a living will or health care proxy in the event of catastrophic illness or disability?

5. Have you considered a living trust to avoid probate?

6. If you have a living trust, have you retitled the appropriate assets in the name of the trust?

7. Does your will name a guardian for your minor children?

8. Do you have the right amount and type of life insurance?

9. Do you have an irrevocable life insurance trust to exclude insurance proceeds from being taxed as part of your estate?

10. Have you created trusts for family gift giving?

11. If your estate is over $600,000, does your estate plan take advantage of the $600,000 exemption?

12. Are you currently making gifts to take advantage of the $10,000 annual gift exclusion?

13. To maximize future estate tax savings, have you made gifts of assets that are likely to appreciate?

14. Have you considered a charitable trust that could provide both estate and income tax benefits?

15. If you own a business, do you have a management succession plan?

16. Do you have a buy-sell agreement for any interest you hold in a family business?

17. Have you considered a gift program involving your family-owned business?

18. Is your estate plan current, and does it take into account all your personal wishes and all the tax-saving strategies of which you are aware?

ESTATE PLANNING IS DEFINITELY FOR YOU

To handle the distribution of your own estate, you can do nothing; you can prepare and sign a will; and/or you can establish trusts. Here are a few good reasons why estate planning is good for your financial well being:

1. You decide who will receive your assets or portions of assets.

2. You decide in what amounts and when your chosen beneficiaries will receive those assets.

3. You decide, either through will or by trust, who will be the executors and trustees of your assets.

4. You can reduce estate taxes and avoid probate or administration fees.

5. You can select a guardian for minor children.

6. If you own a business, you can plan for its orderly maintenance or its disposal.

If you have no estate plan, state laws determine who gets your assets and when they get them. Without a plan, the court will appoint a guardian for minor children, and an administrator for your estate. To maintain control over these issues, you must act in advance of death.

Five Basic Considerations

The *first* step in estate planning is vital and personal: you need to decide who will receive your assets, and when those individuals or institutions should receive them. You'll have to address the following questions:

1. If you have children, should they share equally, or do any of them have special needs that require more financial help?

2. Do you have grandchildren? If so, how should they enter into the picture?

3. Do you have a life-long friend or other relative whom you would like to include?

4. Do you want any charities to play a role in your inheritance plans?

The *second* step is to consider which assets will go to which parties. For example, if you own a home or other real estate, do you want all the beneficiaries to share equally, or would such an arrangement be too cumbersome? Can all of your beneficiaries appropriately handle a cash bequest? If not, perhaps a trust vehicle would be better than an outright bequest, with a trustee designated to distribute the cash over a period of time.

The *third* step is to decide when the beneficiaries should receive the assets, considering the age of each heir and his or her ability to manage assets. If your beneficiaries are young or immature, perhaps you'd prefer that the assets be distributed over time, as your heirs mature, so they can handle all the assets you intend to pass on to them.

Fourth, consider the drawbacks and the advantages to using trusts in your situation. Perhaps you want a reliable trustee to remain in control of the assets if the size of the inheritance might affect the beneficiaries' work ethic or personality. Or, maybe you should make gifts now to reduce the size of your estate, and to prepare your beneficiaries for asset management.

Fifth, there are several other planning issues that you need to consider. The first is finding the right attorney for you, a process that is covered in detail in Chapter 17. The second is understanding probate and making plans to simplify it; this subject is discussed extensively in Chapter 6. You will want to use as many legal methods as you can to reduce estate taxes.

Why You Need a Will

A will is an essential part of any estate plan, and the primary document by which to transfer your wealth when you die. If you die intestate—that is, without a will—state law will control the distribution of your property.

Before you see your lawyer about drafting a will, you must make some crucial decisions:

1. *Naming an Executor*. The executor is your personal representative after your death. The person(s) or institution(s) you designate is responsible for managing your estate and distributing the assets as you have directed. The executor has to conserve the assets, prepare them for distribution to your beneficiaries, pay taxes and file government documents.

   Choose your executor carefully. You may wish to designate a family member, trusted friend or associate. If your estate is complex, it may be best to name a professional advisor, or an organization such as a bank, as executor or co-executor. Here are some of the advantages and disadvantages of naming personal or institutional executors:

A. *Naming a Financial Institution as Executor.*
   (1) Advantages:
      (a) They are specialists in handling estates and trusts.
      (b) They have no emotional bias.
      (c) They are usually free of any conflict of interest with you or your beneficiaries.
      (d) They remain in the same location and never go on vacation.
      (e) They never get sick or die.
   (2) Disadvantages:
      (a) The staff usually has little familiarity with your family.
      (b) They may have high administrative fees.

B. *Naming an Individual as Executor.*
   (1) Advantages:
      (a) Familiarity with your family situation.
      (b) No—or low—administrative fees.
   (2) Disadvantages:
      (a) Lay people may not be experienced in handling estates and trusts.
      (b) Emotional bias might keep an individual from acting impartially.
      (c) There may be frequent scheduling conflicts.
      (d) An individual may not be able to provide service if he or she is incapacitated or otherwise unavailable.

2. *Creating Trusts.* Your will directs how your estate will be distributed, and can provide instructions for creating trusts to achieve your long-term goals—such as providing funds for an elderly parent, or funding for the education of children or grandchildren. You will have to choose one or more trustees when you create a trust, and you must take even greater care in choosing a trustee than an executor: the trustee's duties may last much longer than the executor's.

3. *Designating Guardians.* To protect your minor children and ensure they will be cared for by people you trust, you will want to name a guardian in your will. You'll want to give careful thought to choosing guardian(s) whose ideas about children and child-rearing are similar to yours. Remember to speak to the person(s) you want to name as guardian(s), and get their consent before designating them in your will.

4. *Waiver of Probate*. You can insert a provision in your will that waives the legal requirement for your executor to be bonded. In the absence of a will, the court will require a fiduciary bond to guarantee replacement of any funds embezzled or diverted by the executor. The cost of the bond must be borne by the estate.

5. *Specific Bequests*. You may use your will to make explicit bequests of jewelry, heirlooms, furniture or cash to specific individuals. In the absence of a will, you cannot be certain that your written or oral instructions will be followed.

6. *Avoiding Additional Expenses*. Sometimes it is necessary to sell assets to pay death taxes and expenses of probate. In such a case, you can avoid additional expenses by stating in your will that your executor may sell assets for such a purpose without having to publish a notice of sale in the newspaper.

7. *The Law of Intestacy*. A will avoids having your assets distributed under your state's intestacy law, which will automatically pass property to certain relatives. Intestacy laws have been drafted to be fair in an average situation, but you may not want your assets to go to some family members, or perhaps not in the amounts the intestacy law mandates. Rather, like most people, you probably want to choose the people who will benefit from your estate.

8. *Peace of Mind*. Although it cannot be measured in dollars, you will benefit from peace of mind when your estate is in order. Eliminating that emotional burden promotes your well-being and that of your family.

Avoiding Probate

Avoiding probate is a high priority in estate planning. Probate, the process to prove your will is genuine and to administer it under the jurisdiction of a court, is a public procedure. This means that anyone who wishes—including creditors, former spouses and sworn enemies—can go to the courthouse, look up a will admitted to probate, and learn what assets are available in the estate.

In addition, probate can be time-consuming and expensive. Thus, avoiding probate should be one of your primary estate planning goals. The basic techniques for avoiding probate are listed in Chapter 6, but another method deserves further discussion here: *the living trust.*

A living trust is a legal document that resembles a will. It can contain all kinds of instructions for managing your assets if you are disabled, as well as directions for distributing your holdings when you die. Once you've set it up, you have to change the legal title to any assets to be placed into the trust to the trust's name.

You still control the assets in a living trust, and you don't need to file a trust tax return or pay taxes out of the trust, providing you declare the trust's income yourself and pay taxes on it as an individual. You are, in other words, the trustee for your own assets. However, when you die, the assets in the trust don't go through probate. Thus, if you've covered all your assets by the techniques outlined in Chapter 6 or by a living trust, your estate will avoid probate.

Consult an attorney about drafting a living trust, and make sure it dovetails with your other estate plans. Also, remember that avoiding probate and avoiding estate taxes are two entirely separate matters.

Estate Tax Reduction Strategies

While federal income tax rates have dropped during the last ten years, estate tax rates have remained high. The top marginal estate tax rate can be as high as 55 percent, and hidden surtaxes can take the rate up to 60 percent. This only applies to federal estate tax; you may also be liable for state and inheritance taxes, as well as administrative costs. The Unified Federal Gift and Estate Tax Table, showing the rates, appears on the following page.

Unified Federal Gift and Estate Tax

Many widowed persons do not have to worry about estate tax because everyone is exempt up to the first $600,000 of lifetime gift and death benefits combined. This means, in effect, that the tax on the first $600,000 of assets in an estate—$192,800—is given to you as a tax credit. Also, without touching your $600,000 lifetime exemption, you can give away up to $10,000 each year to as many people as you like, free of gift tax.

Do you need to worry about estate taxes? Is your net worth over $600,000? Go back to Chapter 5, where you listed your assets and liabilities, and take a look at your net worth. Don't forget to include personal use assets, such as your home, automobile, camper, and your IRA account or pension plans. These items of value are included automatically in your assets for estate planning purposes.

Consider adding to your total net worth any inheritance that you are aware you will receive within the next few years. Also, if you own a life insurance policy on your life, the proceeds will normally be included in your estate at death. Life insurance benefits will not be included if someone else owns the policy—that is, if someone else has the right to choose beneficiaries. Thus, a $250,000 life insurance policy you omitted from your net worth may become a $250,000 asset in your estate when you pass away.

Perhaps your estate is over $600,000, or the current growth of your assets will put you over $600,000 soon. Most widowed individuals are quite surprised at the size of their estate. The form below will help you determine whether your estate will be liable for estate taxes.

Will Your Estate Be Liable For Estate Taxes?

1. What is the net value of your estate? $_____

2. Add life insurance proceeds on your life (if you own
   the policy)   +_____

3. Add inheritance anticipated within two to three years   +_____

Total $_____

4. Less assets that will pass to charity at your death   -_____

Your Net Taxable Estate $_____

If your net taxable estate is $600,000 or less, there will be no federal estate tax at your death. However, if your estate is close to $600,000 or above it, read on. The estate will be subject to a marginal tax rate beginning at 37 percent. You can find your estate tax rate in the table below:

The Estate Tax Table

Taxable Estate	Federal Estate Tax	Marginal Tax Rate (Tax on the Next Dollar)
$ 600,000 or less	–0–	37%
750,000	$ 55,500	39%
1,000,000	153,000	41%
1,250,000	255,500	43%
1,500,000	363,000	45%
2,000,000	588,000	49%
2,500,000	833,000	53%
3,000,000	1,098,000	55%

Strategy No. 1: Set Up an Irrevocable Life Insurance Trust. If you own life insurance policies when you die, the proceeds can be included in your taxable estate. Ownership is determined by who has the right to name or change beneficiaries. You can correct this problem by transferring ownership of the policies to a trust. However, if you should die within three years of the transfer, the proceeds will be cranked back into your estate for estate tax purposes.

This procedure can be used for current life insurance or new purchases of life insurance. In either case, the trust owns the policies and pays the premiums. At your death the proceeds are paid into the trust, are not included in your estate, and are tax-free.

The trust can then provide benefits to your desired beneficiaries, or it can even buy assets from your estate by exchanging cash for estate assets. The estate thus has the cash to pay estate taxes, and the trust has assets which it can pass onto your children. Here's an example:

> Mary Kelly now has an estate of $1.5 million. When her husband died she received most of his pension benefits in a lump sum, but she transferred his IRA to her IRA, thus deferring income taxes on his IRA.
>
> When Mary dies, her estate is facing estate tax of $363,000, plus federal income tax on her IRA account of $27,000, a total of $390,000. Her current income is approximately $105,000 a year.
>
> Mary had her lawyer set up an irrevocable life insurance trust, and transferred some income-producing assets into it. The trust purchased a life insurance policy on Mary's life and pays the premiums. When Mary dies, the $390,000 tax-free proceeds of the life insurance policy flows into the trust, which the trust will exchange for assets in the estate.
>
> These funds will be used by the estate to pay its taxes. The assets in the insurance trust will ultimately go to the named beneficiaries—Mary's children—as they would have through her estate, but now the estate tax can be paid with discounted dollars from the insurance policy.

Strategy 2: Annual Gift Program. You can take advantage of the annual gift tax exclusion to reduce estate taxes, while passing assets onto your family or anyone you choose. Thus, if you have two children, four grandchildren and a favorite charity, and you wish to give each $10,000 a year, you could give away $70,000 this year, reduce your estate by $70,000, and incur no gift taxes. Here's an example:

Ginny has an estate of $2.5 million. If she dies today, the federal estate tax will be approximately $833,000, even with her $600,000 exemption.

Over the next five years, Ginny decides, she will give $10,000 a year to each of her son, daughter, son-in-law, daughter-in-law and four grandchildren, a total of $80,000 a year. Assuming the value of her estate has not changed, in five years its worth will have decreased from $2.5 million to $2.1 million. If Ginny dies then, the estate tax is $588,000, a savings of $245,000.

Moreover, the savings to Ginny's estate are probably greater than $588,000, because the earnings on the money, if it had been left in her estate, would be taxable at her death. Further, if these assets had grown in the estate, Ginny's estate tax problem would have been even higher than originally suggested. Thus, Ginny gave $80,000 of assets a year, and passed on the income from appreciation of those assets.

If you want to qualify for the annual $10,000 exclusion, the law requires that you give a "present interest in the property" to the recipient. This means the person receiving the property must have full and complete use of, and access to, the funds.

Strategy No. 3: Direct Payment of Medical or Tuition Bills. Here's a little known estate tax strategy. If you pay a child's medical and tuition bills directly to the institution entitled to payment, the funds are treated as a gift that is tax-free. This tax-free gift is in addition to the regular $10,000 limit per year.

Thus, Marge, a widow with a large estate, not only gives each grand-child $10,000 a year, but also pays their college tuition of $6,300 a year. This removes $16,300 per grandchild from Marge's estate. If she left the money in her estate, at her 50 percent estate tax bracket, only half of it would go to her heirs after taxes.

Strategy No. 4: The Crummy Trust Provision. This is named after the Crummy family, which wanted to set up trusts that would limit the beneficiary's access to the funds, but still qualify for the annual gift tax exclusion. The trust was written so that the beneficiaries had a limited time to withdraw funds that had been transferred to the trust. If the funds were not withdrawn within the specified time period, they remained as part of the trust.

Because the beneficiaries had the current ability to withdraw the funds, the money qualified for the annual $10,000 gift exclusion. Since the funds were not withdrawn, the original goal of keeping the funds in the trust was accomplished. This became known as the Crummy Trust Provision, or Crummy Withdrawal Power.

Obviously, if you use a Crummy Trust Provision, you risk that the beneficiary could withdraw the funds within the limited time period. However, if you make known your desire that the assets are to remain in the trust, the beneficiary may acquiesce to your wishes.

Strategy No. 5: Giving Assets that Are Appreciating. You can save the most in estate taxes by giving away assets that have, or will have, the highest growth potential. For example, suppose you own a stock valued today at $30,000, that, over the next three years, is expected to grow in value to $70,000. If the projected appreciation actually occurs, you will have moved a $70,000 asset out of your estate. Note that any amount you give away to one person in excess of $10,000/year counts as part of your lifetime gift/estate $600,000 exemption.

Therefore it may make sense to use some of the first $600,000 in your estate to make current gifts. The estate and gift tax system is a combined system, hence the title, Unified Federal Gift and Estate Tax. Thus, the first $600,000 of taxable gift creates no gift tax, just as the first $600,000 of an estate creates no estate tax. However, you are only allowed to claim a total of $600,000—for example, a combination of $300,000 in gifts plus $300,000 in estate values.

You can use the total $600,000 exemption during your lifetime or at death, whichever you desire, but not both. Sometimes it may make sense to use up all or a portion of the $600,000 in gifts during your lifetime.

Suppose you have a property worth $600,000 that is growing at a high appreciation rate. If you give it away now and it's worth $1 million in five years, in effect you've moved $400,000 out of your estate—the $600,000 the property was worth at the time you gave it away, plus the $400,000 that it grew in value. Of course, if you do that, there will be no $600,000 exemption available to your estate when you die.

Strategy No. 6: Charitable Giving. This subject is covered extensively in Chapter 14, but it's worth mentioning again here because it's a valuable estate planning technique.

The premise is simple: direct gifts to charity are fully deductible. Thus, if you share your estate assets with a charity, you will save estate taxes. If you give your entire estate to a charity, there will be no estate taxes at all.

You can also make gifts to charity, and to those close to you personally, by setting up a charitable remainder trust. This trust will pay income to your beneficiaries at your death for a specific period of time, after which the assets pass to the charity.

There are many variations on this theme. For example, you can make a gift to your charitable remainder trust during your lifetime with the provision that income be paid to you until death; then the trust proceeds pass to the charity. Using this device can provide income tax benefits *and* estate tax savings.

You can also set up a charitable income trust. In this situation, income goes to the charity for a period of time, then the remainder passes to your beneficiaries. This kind of trust would also provide estate tax benefits.

Strategy No. 7: Using Generation-Skipping Techniques. If you have a large estate, because of the number of times assets are subject to estate taxes as they are bequeathed from generation to generation, skipping a generation by transferring property to your grandchildren or great-grandchildren is an effective method of avoiding estate tax liability.

If you choose this method, you could be subject to what's called the "Generation-Skipping Transfer Tax" (GSTT), which is designed to eliminate the tax advantages of jumping over several generations, without paying on the generations skipped. However, there is a $1 million exemption available. This is a fairly complex planning strategy and, if you decide to pursue it, you should consult competent counsel.

OTHER ESTATE PLANNING CONSIDERATIONS

If you became so incapacitated that you were unable to make your own health care decisions, whom would you want to decide for you? A *living will* allows you to select, while you're still healthy, the person to whom you want to grant this responsibility.

The living will is a legal document stating your desire that, when death is imminent, loss of mental capacity is substantial, incurable or irreversible, and there is no hope of recovery, extraordinary artificial techniques should not be used to prolong your life. Valid in most states, a living will can help your family, your doctors, hospitals and other caregivers to follow your wishes.

The Supreme Court has decided that no parent, sibling, adult child or friend will be allowed to make life-determining decisions for you unless you have previously provided clear and convincing evidence that their actions carry out your express wishes. Consult with your attorney about proper wording, and about your state's requirements for a living will. Once the document is prepared, make certain you understand each and every term before signing.

Health Care Proxy—Many states have authorized by specific law the use of health care proxies. A health care proxy is broader and more flexible than a living will, because it gives the person you name authority over many types of health care besides those relating to life sustaining techniques. The proxy allows you to appoint someone to make any and all health care decisions on your behalf if you are unable to make your own, unless you limit the authority in the document.

As long as you're able, you can continue to make your own decisions, you can refuse any health care treatment merely by objecting, and you can revoke, orally or in writing, the power of attorney you gave.

Health care proxies are often used in addition to living wills. However, sometimes a proxy is written broadly enough to take the place of a living will.

Anatomical Gifts

The subject of anatomical gifts is an uncomfortable issue for most widowed persons. Nevertheless, whether you are for or against them, you should know how to make such a gift, or protect yourself if you don't want your body used in this way.

The Uniform Anatomical Gift Act (UAGA) provides that persons over age 18 may, at death, donate their entire body, or any one or more of its parts, to any hospital, surgeon, physician, medical, dental school or various organ banks. Organ gifts can be made for educational research, therapy or transplant purposes. However, neither your body nor any of its organs may be donated if you have objected to such a gift in writing.

Durable Power of Attorney

"Durable" is the key word here, because it means that the power you have given your agent—to act in your behalf with respect to financial matters—is not affected by your disability or incapacity. Each state has its own special wording that must be used to make the power durable.

A well-drawn durable power of attorney is often just as important as a will. If you have a durable power, your family won't need to petition a court for appointment of a guardian to handle your assets, in the event you become incapacitated. If you currently are experiencing a physical disability or illness that could lead to permanent or long-term incapacity, you should consider seriously a durable power of attorney.

Springing Power of Attorney

You may have run across the term "Springing Power of Attorney," so named because it takes effect only in the event you become disabled or incapacitated. The definition of disability or incapacity is extremely important in any power of attorney. Some states provide a definition, or you can provide one in the document which specifies that one or more physicians must examine you to certify that you are incapacitated.

The Ethical Will

The so-called "ethical will" is not meant to be a legal document, although many people consider it just as important. An ethical will passes on to your beneficiaries a spiritual legacy.

Ethical wills can take whatever form you wish—a written document, tape recording, videotape or combination of these. They can cover any and all subjects you wish, including instructions, apologies, praise, thanks, love and appreciation, or any other thoughts you have.

Letter of Instructions

This is a private, formal, non-legal document, in which you give specific instructions which cannot or should not be included in your will. Often it will contain:

1. The location of key documents;

2. Funeral and burial instructions, because your will may not be located until after the funeral.

3. How you'd like your obituary to read.

4. Advisors to contact and how to reach them.

5. Friends you'd like notified.

6. Instructions regarding specific care of certain children or parents.

7. Other personal information you feel would be helpful.

You can write a letter of instructions, seal it and place it in an envelope, marked "To Be Opened in the Event of My Serious Illness or Death." Then tell your heirs where you put the envelope. A sample letter is provided below:

Personal Letter to My Family

Dear _____:

I am writing this letter to supplement my estate plan and arrangements. I hope, by explaining my objectives on paper, to help you handle my estate and investment matters, and make other important decisions.

I cannot foresee what will happen between the time I write this and the time you read it. Therefore, my thoughts should not be followed inflexibly, but tempered by consideration of the circumstances existing as I write, and how they may have changed since then.

1. Instructions about My Funeral, Last Rites, Burial Services, Cemetery, etc. _____

_____ .

2. Directions about My Medical and Nursing Home Care, etc.

_____ .

3. My Wishes about Life Support Systems. _____

_____

4. My Wishes about Organ Donor Transplantation _____ .

_____ .

5. People I Would Like My Family to Consult about Medical, Legal and Financial Matters. _____

_____ .

6. My Suggestions about Investment Philosophies for Each of You. _____ .

7. Goals that I Consider Important for Our Family.

_____ .

8. Special Investments or Comments for My Heirs.

_____

9. Other Considerations. _____

_____ .

Date:_____   _____
                                                    Signature

Estate planning is not a "do it once" process. The major elements of wills and trusts can be set into place, but they need to be reviewed periodically to ensure that everything fits your present situation. There are other reasons, also, to review your estate plan:

1. Changes in family situations, such as birth or adoption of children or grandchildren, marriages, divorces and deaths.

2. Changes in financial situation, including drastic increases or decreases in the size of your estate.

3. Changes in the tax law. The estate tax laws are modified constantly. Competent counsel can help you determine whether your estate plans meet new or amended laws.

Last, any other changes in your life may merit a review of your estate plan.

THE FINANCIAL ASPECTS OF REMARRIAGE

Most widowed individuals, thrust into singlehood, miss various aspects of married life. Often, loneliness can lead to ill-timed remarriage, sometimes with negative results. You need to be cautious about remarriage, both emotionally and financially. In this important chapter we will deal with the emotional and financial factors to consider before remarrying.

There are many things for you to assess when contemplating remarriage. Certainly, you should not think about taking a new partner until you feel you've said "goodbye" to your deceased spouse. No one can replace your departed mate, and the other person in a new relationship deserves to be considered as an individual in his or her own right.

One of the most important issues is your children. Most people think only young children feel negatively about a parent's remarriage. However, adult children often find it hard to accept their parent's need for companionship, a sexual relationship and sharing. Because children tend to think of parents as "asexual creatures," your offspring may frown on your remarriage plans.

NOTE: Furthermore, grown children often feel threatened financially by a new spouse, fearing that your funds might be diverted from them in favor of the new partner.

More than likely, your children truly are concerned about you, about your new mate's motives, and about your financial and emotional involvement. However, if you feel your new relationship is worthwhile and you want to marry, ask your children to consider and accept your needs. If you do not receive their approval, you may find yourself in conflict with them. If they cannot accept your situation, your conflict with them may remain unresolved.

There are also other factors for you to consider about remarriage. These include your respective backgrounds, the other relationships that come with you into the marriage, what habits each of you bring, and any differences in financial assets that could become a cause for estrangement.

MONEY TALK

Money can be a major source of tension in a marriage, so you'll need to talk about how you want to spend your money as a couple, whether or not you want joint, separate or combination checking accounts, or any special savings accounts. Decide what important things you will save for and, if you're going to be a two-paycheck couple how to allocate your salaries fairly, especially if one person earns substantially more than the other.

Some newly-remarried couples pay household bills using a ratio based on earnings, which means that each partner contributes to the household in proportion to the income he or she earns. For example, if one partner earns $50,000 a year and the other earns $100,000, the partner earning $50,000 might contribute one-third and the other partner might contribute two-thirds toward household expenses. The funds left over are each person's private money, to spend or save as he or she wishes.

Most remarrying couples are less willing to merge funds completely, not because they lack confidence in their new partners, but because each person has become accustomed to running his or her own finances. No matter how money was handled in your first marriage, you may have to be flexible and do things differently this time around.

Financial Considerations before Remarrying

Here's a quick rundown of the major points that need to be covered before you proceed down the aisle again:

1. Do your respective wills need to be updated or substantially changed?

2. Do you have trusts that need beneficiary changes or new language because of your new relationship?

3. Do you want to change beneficiary designations on life insurance policies?

4. Do you have other kinds of insurance coverage that overlap; for example, if there are two automobiles, can you place both of them with the same carrier, thereby achieving a discount?

5. If you both have health insurance, can one of you go on the other's policy, to reduce overall cost?

6. How will your assets be titled? Will yours remain in your name? Will you own anything jointly?

7. Does your estate plan need to be revised? Note that, when you remarry, you regain the marital deduction. You may wish to consult your attorney about creating a marital deduction trust.

8. How will any pension benefits be affected? Do either of you lose any or all of them upon remarriage?

9. What effect will your remarriage have on Social Security benefits?

10. Do you need a prenuptial agreement? (See next page.)

11. How do each of you view your assets and your current giving programs in relation to your respective sets of children? This is a delicate area; for instance, your spouse-to-be may feel that money is going to your children that should be used for the benefit of the marriage.

12. Review liability insurance policies to reflect the new joint net worth, especially if both of you are bringing substantial assets to the marriage.

13. Does your intended have debts that you would have to assume or share jointly?

Community Property States

There are eight community property states: Arizona, California, Idaho, Louisiana, Nevada, New Mexico, Texas and the State of Washington. If you live in one of these states, property you owned before marriage, or acquired after marriage by gift or inheritance, is considered separate property; it is yours. However, all property acquired by any other means after marriage is considered to be community property, and each spouse may be said to have a one-half interest in all community property, regardless of who is the titled owner.

Before you remarry, you will want to evaluate how each of you will hold your property in a community property state. (In non-community property states property acquired after marriage can be titled individually or jointly).

Prenuptial Agreements

Experts agree that a pre-nuptial agreement is virtually indispensable if you're planning a second marriage. Although second timers swear it won't happen to them, statistics show second marriages run a high risk of failure. Such an agreement is designed to preserve the separate properties of the spouses-to-be for distribution to their respective families, in event of divorce or no matter which of the spouses-to-be dies first. Here's what a pre-nuptial agreement can do:

1. Define your property rights and those of your spouse after the marriage.
2. Avoid having your state's law applied if you or your spouse dies without a will.
3. Set out any rights of your new spouse with respect to the estate of your first spouse.
4. Establish the rights of the spouses-to-be to each other's property in the event they divorce.

Other Advantages:

Such an agreement gives both of you control over what you want, not what various state laws or others decide what you get.

Creditor in a bankruptcy action will go after any asset. Assets can be protected by establishing them as separate in a pre-nuptial agreement.

Usually a surviving spouse can claim part of the deceased spouse's estate ("right of election" law). This claim can be waived or modified. Pre-nuptial agreements supercede both inheritance and right of election laws.

Having your second spouse limit or waive claims on property, gifts or inheritance may be necessary to protect the rights of your children from your previous marriage, not only from unfair property dispositions but also from the stress occurring from litigation.

Most states require that pre-nuptial agreements be fair when made, and not unconscionable at the time of enforcement. Before signing a pre-nuptial agreement, you and your spouse-to-be should each have your own attorney, and each should disclose fully to the other all assets and income.

Some may ignore premarital planning because they don't want to consider the possibility of failure; others may have more practical reasons. For example, wealthy widowed persons may not wish their fiance' to know the full extent of their net worth, which is necessary for a pre-nuptial agreement.

NOTE: You may think it's awkward to discuss a pre-nuptial agreement in the glow before the wedding, but having one may prevent grief later on.

Many widowed individuals don't like to think about the topic, but the discomfort of approaching it before remarriage may be far less than the misery you may experience if you don't approach it at all. In the long run, a pre-nuptial agreement is a great anxiety reducer.

Using the $125,000 Exclusion

An extremely important consideration for you in remarriage is timing the use of the $125,000 exclusion on housing sales to avoid capital gains taxes. This subject is discussed in greater detail in Chapter 11, "You and Your Home."

If you've already used the exclusion, or you and your deceased spouse used it earlier, you can't use it again. Your new spouse can't use it either, once you remarry, whether your new mate ever used it before or not; once you're married, he or she is subject to the same rules to which you are subject. If either of you ever used the $125,000 exclusion, it's not usable once you're married.

There is a strategy, however, that you can use with respect to this exclusion. Let's assume you and the person you want to marry each own a house. You both want to sell and acquire a new home together. If neither of you have used your $125,000 exclusion, you can sell both properties before you remarry. Here's a dollars and cents example:

	Your House	**Fiance's House**
Current Value	$250,000	$300,000
Basis	(150,000)	(200,000)
Gain	(100,000)	100,000
$125,000 Applied	125,000	125,000
Taxed at Sale	–0–	–0–

If you can only use one exclusion because you marry before selling both houses, you will have to pay approximately $33,000 in federal and state taxes ($28,000 federal and $5,000 state) on the $100,000 gain. The only remedy here would be to sell the property that has the $125,000 exclusion available (before marriage), and then live in the remaining property.

Marriage Tax Penalties

It's unfortunate, but a married couple, both age 65 or over, will usually pay more taxes on a joint return than the combined tax they would pay if they were single. The couples who are affected the most by this are the ones with fairly equal but moderate incomes. Often, as single tax-payers they would be in the 15% tax bracket. Because they marry, their joint income moves them into the 28% bracket. One remedy here is to move your investments into tax-deferred or tax-free areas such as variable annuities or tax-free bonds.

Occasionally the opposite can happen. Let's say you earn $28,500/year and your new spouse earns no income. As a couple you will now be in the 15% tax bracket. In this case, the couple with unequal incomes benefits from marriage and filing jointly.

Furthermore, if your income plus one-half of your Social Security benefits exceed certain levels—$25,000 for single people, or $32,000 for a married couple—as much as 85% of the Social Security receipts are taxable. Two singles can receive $50,000 of taxable income before any of their Social Security benefits are taxed. Thus, combining your incomes on a joint return may force you to pay tax on Social Security payments that, if you hadn't remarried, would be completely "Social Security" tax-free.

Another "penalty" for remarriage regards *losses available on rental properties*.

Rental real estate is classified by IRS as a passive activity and falls under the passive gain/loss rules. Basically the rules provide that up to $25,000 of passive losses from rental real estate can be deducted each year against income from non-passive sources such as wages, investments, etc.

However, if the single person's income is above $100,000, the $25,000 is reduced using the following formula:

(Adjusted Gross Income—$100,000) x 50% = Reduction Amount
At $150,000 AGI, the passive loss deduction is completely lost.

Here's an example of how this might affect a remarriage. Jim has an Adjusted Gross Income (AGI) of $120,000. His passive loss is reduced by $120,000–100,000) x 50% = $10,000. Barbara, his fiance, has an AGI of $30,000 and thus does not lose any of the deduction. Once married however their combined AGI is now $150,000, and they lose the entire $25,000 deduction:

(150,000–100,000) x 50% = $25,000

The remedies in this situation are to look for ways to reduce the AGI's, or sell the real estate properties and place the proceeds into other investments with tax-deferred or tax-free features.

Standard Deduction Penalty. For 1994, two single persons have a combined standard deduction of $7,600 versus $6,350 for a married couple filing jointly. If both singles are over age 65 the combined standard deduction is $9,500, compared to $7850 for the married couple.

Other Penalties:

1. IRA phase-out ranges: For two singles the combined range is $50,000–$70,000. For a married couple filing jointly it is $40,000–$50,000.

2. Personal exemption phase-out ranges: Personal exemption in 1994 equals $2450 for each exemption claimed. The exemption(s) are phased out as income increases above certain levels. For two singles, the combined range is $223,600 to $468,600. For a married couple filing jointly it is $167,700 to $290,200.

Estate Planning upon Remarriage

Once you've remarried you may need to review some of the following estate planning concepts with an estate planning attorney.

Use of the Marital Deduction

The marital deduction is a powerful estate planning tool. Any assets passing to a surviving spouse pass estate tax free at the time of the first spouse's death (assuming the surviving spouse is a US citizen). Therefore if you are willing to pass all your assets to your surviving spouse there will be no federal estate tax at that time.

However, this doesn't solve the estate tax problem—it only defers it. If your surviving spouse does not remarry again, he/she will not be able to take advantage of the marital deduction at death. Therefore the assets transferred from the first spouse will be subject to tax in the estate of the second spouse.

One solution to this problem is to set up an irrevocable life insurance trust that holds a second-to-die life insurance policy on the two of you. At the second death, the life policy provides to your named beneficiaries a replacement amount to offset the estate taxes. (See The Irrevocable Life Insurance Trust, described below).

Qualified Terminal Interest Property Trust (QTIP)

The QTIP trust is often used by remarrying couples as a method to ensure that their respective assets will be distributed per their individual wishes at death.

Typically each spouse establishes a QTIP trust as part of his/her will. Both spouses stipulate that when one dies, a predetermined part of the deceased's assets will be held in trust for specified beneficiaries, usually managed by the survivor and a co-trustee. The survivor receives the income from the trust and with the co-trustee's approval, can even tap the principal to uphold his or her standard of living. The beneficiaries of the trust cannot be changed and they receive the full assets of the trust after the second spouse dies. Note that upon the surviving spouse's death, the assets in the trust pass as indicated in the will of the first spouse. Seek expert legal help to set up this type of arrangement.

The Irrevocable Life Insurance Trust

If you own life insurance policies at your death, the proceeds are included in your taxable estate. Ownership is usually determined by who has the right to name the beneficiaries of the proceeds. The way around this problem? Don't own the policies when you die.

Instead, create an irrevocable life insurance trust. The trust owns the policies and pays the premiums. When you die, the proceeds pass into the trust and are not included in your estate. The trust can be structured to provide benefits to your surviving spouse and/or other beneficiaries.

Be sure to get professional advice before setting up one of these trusts. A properly structured trust could save you more than 50% in estate taxes on any insurance proceeds. Thus, a $1 million life insurance policy owned by an irrevocable insurance trust could reduce your estate taxes by over $500,000.

QTIP Charitable Trust

A QTIP charitable trust has proven to be an excellent method to make a deferred gift to a charity and still make the entire estate available for the financial security of your surviving spouse . . . all without any gift or estate taxes. A modification of this plan permits you to benefit your children as well as your spouse and the charity.

For example, you establish a living revocable trust which provides: (1) you would receive all the income for your life; (2) at your death, the trust would continue and all income would be paid to your surviving spouse for life; (3) at the death of the surviving spouse, the trust property would pass to a charitable remainder trust that would pay a 10% annuity to your daughter for her life; and (4) the trust property would pass to a designated charity at the death of the daughter.

When you die, the value of the trust qualifies for an estate tax marital deduction at the election of your executor. And when your spouse dies after you, the then value of the charitable remainder trust is deductible for federal estate tax purposes. Again, this technique requires the expert assistance and draftsmanship of an attorney experienced in estate plans and charitable giving.

Planning with Your New Spouse

While your finances should not control your happiness, the road ahead will be smoother if you discuss and plan your financial life before you enter into remarriage. In finances as in love, it is often what spouses don't tell each other that hurts.

Whether your new marriage should end by death or divorce, you may pay plenty for lack of knowledge. Every estate lawyer has file drawers full of stories about the anguish and expense bequeathed to clients by spouses who died without putting their affairs in order.

Secrecy among mates complicates the chore of settling an estate, yet many newly-remarried couples are reluctant to talk to their new spouses about their assets. Some partners assume that their mates will not understand finances, or are not interested in them; some just don't trust each other when it comes to money.

Partners who may be fearful of divorce often think it necessary to conceal assets and, considering one out of four remarriages fail, the fear is understandable. Nevertheless, it is tough to hide major assets from a sharp divorce lawyer. Furthermore, there is a good chance that the marriage will last, so the most compelling reason to understand your respective financial situations is that 70 percent of wives outlive their husbands.

Perhaps the main reason people don't like to talk about their assets is that they don't like to talk about death. The fact remains that in most successful marriages the partners share with each other information about all their assets. Being knowledgeable also facilitates each spouse's financial strategies, and planning for their respective children and grandchildren.

While you may not share your new partners assets, you certainly should be aware of them. The last thing you need to encounter are financial surprises upon the death of your new partner.

CHOOSING PROFESSIONAL ADVISORS

You can probably do your own planning for many of the topics discussed in this book, but you will need a professional's expertise for other areas. Previously, throughout this book, reference has been made as to the importance of retaining competent experts—an attorney, financial planner, accountant, insurance agent, banker and others. Plan to build on your strengths and don't let your weaknesses frustrate you. Instead, hire competent help by surrounding yourself with other people's knowledge. The basic rule is: Don't try to build on your weaknesses. Build on your strengths and let other people help you in areas in which you are weak.

If you don't already have advisors, let's look in detail at how to choose the right people to work on your behalf.

FINANCIAL PLANNERS

Anyone can call himself or herself a financial planner, and there is no shortage of people who do. Your challenge is to find a qualified planner who understands your problems, whose fees are within the range of your pocketbook, and who demonstrates professional experience and credentials.

First, look for planners who have some or all of the following credentials:

1. *Certified Financial Planner (CFP)*. The Institute of Certified Financial Planners defines a qualified CFP as follows:

> Certified Financial Planner (CFP) is a precise definition of an individual's competence, experience and intelligence in the complex profession of financial planning.

Certification is awarded to those who have passed six comprehensive half-day tests over a two-year period, have three years' experience, offer client references, and provide proof of a college undergraduate degree. CFPs complete a financial planning curriculum that must be registered with, and approved by, the International Board of Standards and Practices of Certified Financial Planners. CFPs also are required to have 15 hours of continuing education per year, and many CFPs belong to their professional organization, the Institute for Certified Financial Planners. CFP's must abide by a professional code of ethics.

The CFP designation is the oldest financial planning credential in the United States, and the one that's best-known by consumers. Advanced programs are available to CFPs for specialties in the financial planning field, leading to a Master's degree.

You can call the Institute of Certified Financial Planners at 303-751-7600 for a list of qualified planners in your area. (Also see the Resources list later in this chapter).

There is also a group of financial planners who belong to the Registry of Financial Planning Practitioners. These planners are required to have practiced financial planning as their main vocation for at least 3 years, earn 30 hours of continuing education credit per year and follow a code of ethics. To obtain a list of these planners call the International Association for Financial Planning at 1-800-945-IAFP.

2. *Chartered Financial Consultant (ChFC)*. This highly regarded certification is issued through the American College located in Bryn Mawr, Pennsylvania. Most planners who carry this certification come from practices heavily involved in insurance.

The comprehensive course of study, which is held in high esteem by professionals within and outside the insurance industry, takes several years to complete and consists of 10 two-hour exams. Several Master's degree programs are also available.

3. *Accredited Personal Financial Specialist (PFS)*. Issued by the American Institute of Certified Public Accountants, this designation is awarded to accountants who are members in good standing of the American Institute of Certified Public Accountants, have valid and unrevoked Certified Public Accountants certificates, complete a one-day exam, and have 750 hours experience in personal financial planning in the 3 years preceding application.

Six references are required, together with a written statement of the Certified Public Accountant's intention to comply with re-accreditation standards: APFS practitioners are required to have 24 hours of continuing professional education annually, that is directly related to personal financial planning.

Other "designations"—Occasionally you may see or hear other designations for financial planners. These are less meaningful in your search for a competent professional, but you should know what they are:

- "LUTC Fellow" means the planner has completed a series of sales courses offered by the Life Underwriter Training Council located in Washington, D.C.

- "Registered Investment Advisor" (RIA) may sound impressive, but most anyone can become one, and the title is no guarantee of competence or skill. The designation means only that people who give investment advice are required to be on file with state and federal agencies, pay a fee and complete many forms.

  Once approved, Registered Investment Advisors must make available a form called the ADV to potential clients. This form discloses detailed information about the advisors, such as how they operate, how they're paid, and what their contracts include.

A good financial planner will have a wide range of knowledge and experience to help you integrate all the financial pieces into a comprehensive plan. Such a professional will be knowledgeable about *all the subjects covered in this book*, and will be able to work with other professionals to make sense out of your situation, coordinate your plans and strategies, and help you move toward to your financial goals.

FINDING A FINANCIAL PLANNER

When you're ready to choose a financial planner, first ask your friends, your attorney and your accountant if they can recommend a trusted advisor. Also, see the Resources list on the next page.

Call some financial planning companies—most are listed in the Yellow Pages under Financial Planners. Ask them to send you information about their firms and a copy of the ADV form. Then interview two or three planners.

Notice if there's any personal chemistry between you, whether the planner is good at "drawing you out" and has a flare for making financial terms understandable. Ask for client and professional references; call the references and ask lots of questions. Remember, you have to trust the planner with a lot of personal information.

Resources: *Associations of Financial Planning-Type Professionals*

American Institute of Certified Public Accountants
1211 Avenue of the Americas
New York, New York 10036-8775
1-800-862-4272

CPAs who have earned the Accredited Personal Financial Specialist (PFS) designation.

American Society of CLU and ChFC
270 Bryn Mawr Avenue
Bryn Mawr, Pennsylvania 19010
1-800-392-6900

Insurance agents and planners who hold the Chartered Life Underwriter and Chartered Financial Consultant designations.

Institute of Certified Financial Planners
7600 E. Eastman Avenue, Suite 301
Denver, Colorado 80231-5965
1-800-282-7526

Financial Planners holding the CFP designation.

International Association for Financial Planning
Two Concourse Parkway, Suite 800
Atlanta, Georgia 30328
1-800-945-4237

Financial Planners who have qualified for the group's "Registry" program.

National Association of Personal Financial Advisors
1130 Lake Cook, Suite 105
Buffalo Grove, Illinois 60089-1974
1-800-366-2732

Fee-only Financial Planners who can provide a useful interview form.

American Association of Retired Persons
601 E Street, N.W.
Washington, D.C. 20049
1-202-434-2277

Provides a 12-page guide, "Facts About Financial Planners."

Here's a series of questions to use when you're interviewing a planner:

1. What's your background, education and experience? How do you keep yourself current with respect to new laws, products and so forth?

2. How do you get paid? Are there conflicts between your interests and mine?

3. My urgent concern is _____; have you handled such problems before. How do you tackle them?

4. What experience do you have working with clients whose income and situation are similar to mine?

5. Are there other people in your office who would be working on my plan? Do you handle all of my concerns yourself? Or, are there other resources you might tap in complex areas such as tax planning, individual stock selection, or insurance policy valuation or estate planning.

6. Can I see a copy, or a sample, of a written financial plan?

7. If you sell insurance and investments, from what companies? Will you tell me your commissions on each product you recommend?

8. If you don't sell financial products, can you recommend specific investments and insurance policies, and can you help to obtain them at a good price?

9. What continuing services will I receive after the initial plan, and what will they cost?

10. Have you ever been reprimanded or disciplined by any regulatory or industry bodies?

Fees and Commissions. Financial planners can be compensated by commissions, fees or a combination of the two.

1. *Commission Only.* These are advisors who receive commissions from life insurance or securities companies for insurance and investment sales.

2. *Fee-Based Only.* This is a common method by which planners are compensated, either hourly or by a set schedule, such as one percent of your assets or net worth.

3. *Fee and Commission*. Here the planner charges a fee, usually less than a fee-only planner, and also receives commissions from those products sold to the client.

NOTE: Choose a planner who is compensated in a way that matches your needs.

If you have a small sum to invest for a grandchild, for example, you don't need a complete financial plan. If you have a complicated estate, need a detailed cash flow analysis, or your requirements for advice are ongoing, you may want a highly qualified planner in your corner.

Once you start working with a planner, how do you tell if he or she is treating you properly? Everyone has heard anecdotes about the life savings of a lonely widow being invested in the Brooklyn Bridge, Florida swampland, pyramid schemes and other swindles.

In fact, most dishonest schemes aimed at widowed persons are more subtle; they make money for some people and dance around the gray areas of the law, to say nothing of decency. For a good financial planner, the term "honesty" suggests more than truth. It includes *fairness, good faith and complete disclosure*. It means looking at the good news as well as the bad. It means knowing all of the important facts and presenting them in an understandable way, not just through twelve pages of small type.

How do you know who is honest and who isn't? Here is a checklist:

1. Is my advisor totally independent of any and all investment products or companies? Was that information offered to me, or did I have to ask for it?

2. Does my advisor focus more on my money than on my concerns and well-being?

3. Does my advisor provide full disclosure of fees, costs and compensation?

4. Does my advisor build long-term client loyalty?

Building a long-term working relationship with a financial advisor who has your complete interests at heart will be invaluable to you. For example, a widow was concerned about one of her investments. The problem was that she'd been receiving what looked like a fantastic yield on shares of a Government National Mortgage Association (Ginny Mae), a pool of mortgages just like the one you have on your home.

She didn't realize, because her advisor hadn't told her, that when she received the monthly payment from the Ginny Mae, she received both principal and income, not just income. Thus, what seemed to be a 14–15 percent return on her investment was really about 6 or 7 percent, plus the erosion of her principal. If she had been told that she'd be receiving principal as well as interest, she could have planned to reinvest the principal rather than deplete it through spending.

Finally, a comprehensive financial planner will sit, figuratively, at the hub of your other advisors, coordinating, explaining and tying up all loose financial ends. Choosing your financial advisor carefully may have a significant impact on your ability to make the money last.

ATTORNEYS

There are attorneys, and there are attorneys. Which one is best for you? Do you need one? Perhaps you already have an attorney, one who was employed by your spouse, or who drafted a will, or helped settle on a house. Do you continue with that attorney, or find someone else?

Unless you are prone to lawsuits, you won't need a lawyer often. Each time you do, your needs can be very different from the time before. Here are a few of the tasks for which you may need an attorney:

1. Drafting your will, a trust, a living will, and a durable power of attorney;

2. Settling an estate;

3. Assisting in the aftermath of an auto accident, or if you have been the victim of a crime;

4. Helping you if you must appear in court as a witness;

5. Defending or prosecuting a civil suit;

6. Dealing with tax issues, real estate transactions and estate planning.

You can see from this abbreviated list that your needs can range from a criminal lawyer to a trial lawyer to an attorney who specializes in estate planning.

How to Find an Attorney.

1. Ask your accountant.

2. Ask your financial planner.

3. Ask your friends who have had a similar problem.

4. Call the local bar association.

5. Ask attorney friends who knew your spouse.

6. Call the legal reference service or legal aid, both of which can be found by calling the information operator in your town.

7. Ask at clubs to which you belong and your religious institution.

8. Consult Sullivan's Lawyers Directory or Martindale Hubbard law directory, both of which can be found at your local library.

When you are soliciting referrals for attorneys, be as specific as you can. You want to use several referral sources. You may rule some out completely, but eventually you will notice that several names are mentioned over and over again. Once you have three to five names, you can investigate each one.

Talk to the lawyer on the phone or in person. Ask right away what the charges are for an initial visit or a phone conversation. Remember, you're hiring someone to do a particular job for you, and the person you retain will be working for you as well as with you. Here's a list of questions to help you get started when interviewing an attorney.

Fees and billing:

1. How much do you charge?

2. Do you require a retainer; if so, how much?

3. Do you charge for phone calls?

4. On what do you base your fee?

5. How often will I be billed?

6. Will I be charged if I talk to your secretary?

7. Are there any other fees or charges?

Practice specifics:

8. Will you be working with me exclusively, or will other members of your firm be involved?

9. Do you practice in the local courts?

10. Do you specialize? If so, what is your specialty?

11. What other kinds of work do you do?

12. In what states are you admitted to the bar?

13. How large is your firm and how many people work for you?

14. How did you become interested in law or in your particular specialty of law?

Specialized services:

15. Do you do your own financial analysis for your clients?

16. Does your firm provide accounting as well as legal services?

17. Have you worked with widowed persons; if so, how many and under what circumstances?

It's a good idea to meet with all the lawyers you will interview within several days of each other. That way, your impression of every individual will be fresh in your mind. Once you've interviewed at least two lawyers, compare your notes and opinions of them; you may find you have additional questions that you want to ask over the phone.

Be ready to make a decision once you feel you have enough information. If you let it drag out over a long period of time, the impressions you got from your painstaking work will become hazy, and you'll just have to start all over again.

ACCOUNTANTS

The answers to the following questions will let you know whether you need an accountant:

1. Is your estate large?

2. Do you have many liabilities?

3. Do you own or operate a business?

4. Are there many tax consequences in your financial situation?

5. Do you believe your financial situation is complex?

6. Do you own stocks and bonds or tax shelters?

7. Do you need help in filing tax forms, preparing estimated taxes, etc.?

If you answered yes to any of these questions, if your financial situation is complex, or if your attorney is weak in tax and financial knowledge, you may want to hire an accountant. The individual you retain should work for you and report to you. Then, if you decide to change lawyers or financial planners later on, you will not have to change accountants as well.

Smaller accounting firms generally charge about 30 percent less on an hourly basis than large ones, and some people feel they get better and more reasonable service from a smaller firm. Others think their interests are best served by one of the larger, better-known firms. The well-known, "big six" accounting firms are listed below in alphabetical order:

Arthur Andersen & Company
Coopers & Lybrand
Ernst & Young
Deloit & Touche
Peat, Marwick
Price Waterhouse & Company

You want an accountant who can help you rethink your tax situation in light of any new tax laws, who can guide you through financial transactions, and who can tell you which tried-and-true tax-savings strategies are good, and which aren't. You also want your accountant to tell you about new tax-savings opportunities that won't put you at risk, and to alert you to tax traps in financial dealings in which you're already involved.

How to Find an Accountant. You can use the following checklist to conduct a methodical search for an accountant.

1. Ask for recommendations from friends, neighbors, members of clubs you belong to, or other advisors. Word-of-mouth is by far the best way to find the right accountant.

   Give additional weight to recommendations from those whose financial situations are similar to yours.

2. Ask your banker or attorney for recommendations; they are financial professionals who probably know some of the best tax accountants in the area.

Once you've received recommendations, select three or four possible candidates and telephone for interviews, as you did with attorneys. Ask about fees and all the other matters relative to your situation. A competent tax professional will want to see copies of the income tax returns you filed over the past few years, as well as any other important papers involved in your financial situation.

Once you've narrowed down the candidates, you can make your final decision. Professional qualifications and fees being equal, the final choice is a personal one: select an accountant with whom you feel comfortable.

INSURANCE PROFESSIONALS

There are approximately 350,000 life insurance agents eager to receive your business. The problem is finding one that is well trained, represents a variety of financially strong companies, has personal and business integrity, and is interested in your long term well-being.

Ask your other professional service providers who they use. Attorneys, accountants, trust officers, and financial planners generally employ quality insurance professionals—Chartered Life Underwriters—whose educational credentials in the insurance field are on par with their own.

Chartered Life Underwriters receive this designation from the American College in Bryn Mawr, Pennsylvania, and have completed 10 semester courses and 10 examinations over 5 years.

If the agent whom you are interviewing has passed the 10 advanced courses, it indicates two things: 1) the individual is committed and capable of taking and passing such exams, and 2) the agent is committed to learning more in order to serve you better. The agent has, in effect, worked to become qualified to serve as your insurance consultant.

Further, if the prospective agent is a member of the National Association of Life Underwriters (1922 F Street, Washington, DC 20006) it indicates a willingness to help promote and strengthen the insurance industry as well as abide by standards set by the best agents in the world.

A key question to ask prospective insurance consultants is "Are you a member of your local life underwriters association, and if so, have you held offices there?" An affirmative answer indicates the individual's dedication to the life insurance profession.

Here's a quick checklist for evaluating insurance agents:

- What is their educational background?

- Do they represent one company or many?

- How long have they been in the business?

- Can they provide references?

- Are they obligated to complete continuing education requirements?

- Are they licensed to sell securities?

- Do they owe money to any insurance company?

- Have they ever been terminated by an insurance company for reasons other than not making quota?

- Have they attended or taught life underwriting training courses?

- Do they have a particular expertise in the insurance industry?

- Do they have experts they can call upon for advice in those areas outside their specialties?

- Are they comfortable for you to work with?

Once you've collected answers to these questions, the well-qualified agent will become readily apparent, and choice of agents will be easy.

PROPERTY AND CASUALTY INSURANCE AGENTS

This professional is often overlooked whenever financial advisors are chosen. However, a good P & C agent can provide valuable services to you when it comes to protecting your home and automobile.

Those who have demonstrated comprehensive professional knowledge through course study and testing in addition to that required for state certification can use the designation CPCU after their names— Chartered Property Casualty Underwriter.

The P & C Agent's primary role is to protect your assets from sudden, devastating loss due to a natural disaster, lawsuit, fire, or other misfortune.

The American Institute for Property and Liability Underwriters can provide a list of agents in your area if you are unhappy with your current agent.

BANK TRUST OFFICER

A Bank Trust Officer, through the bank's trust department, is often useful to surviving spouses seeking confidential, honest assistance for their financial plans. Since the bank will not die or become incapacitated, it can be relied upon to provide competent, professional services for as many years as you and your heirs might need its services.

You may need the services of a trust officer in the following situations:

1. Your spouse's will named a bank trust department to oversee your assets, left under their care; or,

2. You may want the services of a bank trust department to be trustee of a trust you have, be executor of your will, or provide management services related to paying for health costs should you be incapacitated.

   In some situations the bank trust department acts solely as custodian of the trust assets. The bank holds the assets, but someone else outside the bank manages them. In these cases, the bank will charge a custodial fee, but not a fee to manage the assets.

If the trust department is managing assets in a trust for you, you will receive monthly or quarterly statements detailing all the relevant financial data. Trust departments have historically provided rather low returns on investments due to their pronounced conservatism. As mentioned above you can have the bank provide custodial and accounting services, while the investments can be handled by outside professional money managers.

If you are considering a trust department, investigate the fees you will pay and who your trust officer will be. Developing a relationship of mutual trust and interest can be highly valuable.

Ask a lot of questions about all the services the trust department can provide, how the services are implemented, ongoing costs, and how the bank can inter-relate with other members of your financial team.

One final note: Ask to see the investment results of their typical portfolio and any mutual funds offered through the trust department. Some trust departments do a very creditable job, while others do not.

Too many surviving spouses trust to luck or the yellow pages to lead them to competent financial advisors. The only one method of rating professionals is to *ask questions*. A technique used successfully is to make the financial planner the quarterback of your financial team—you're the coach. Now it's the planner's role to find all the other advisors for you—with you having the final word on them joining the team.

Finding and building long-term relationships with financial advisors is an important step in your quest to making the money last.

FRAUDS AND SCAMS: PROTECTING YOURSELF

Do not take lightly any warnings you hear about swindles that are perpetrated on widowed persons, especially if you are newly widowed. There are far too many instances in which the unsuspecting have been burned financially. You may feel that you are aware and alert, but you may have many other things on your mind at this stage. If you find yourself listening to someone who supposedly was "a good friend of your spouse" whom you "never met," and who has a "terrific investment for you," beware.

TYPES OF CON GAMES AND SCAMS

There are many variations of the con games that follow. Once you understand the basics, it should be fairly easy to spot similar actions.

Granny Fraud. Widows and elderly women are usually the prey in this "bank examiner's" con game. Here's one version:

1. Phony 'bank examiner' or 'bank official' telephones potential victim at home to ask her help in catching a dishonest teller who is looting her account.

2. As instructed, she calls 'police' at a certain number (sometimes 911). 'Police official' asks her to withdraw funds from her bank and meet him at a designated spot (often a parking lot near bank).

3. She withdraws large sum of money from bank, keeping the reason a secret as instructed.

4. She meets 'police official' who shows her his badge and gives

her a receipt in return for her money. He tells her he will call with further information.

5. Hours later, victim may be told all is going well, but a further withdrawal is needed. She does so, turns money over again and never hears from the 'police' or the 'bank examiner' again.

The "Pigeon Drop" Scam. In this age-old con, one person mentions to you that someone has found a lot of money. Within minutes another person joins in saying they are the one with the money and don't know what to do with it. Soon, you are promised a piece of the action if you'll drive to your bank and withdraw your funds so that a so-called expert friend of one of the group could compare bills to see if the found money is counterfeit. Most victims never see their money again.

Phantom Banks. One of the newest scams going on right now is that of "Phantom Banks." These scams target the wealthy and elderly with ads for Prime Bank Notes promising returns far beyond current market rates. Using official-sounding names and upscale addresses, these banks are not really banks but fake companies existing only on paper. For example, a bank in Rochester, N.Y., supposedly affiliated with a bank in the former Soviet Union, sold millions of dollars of phony CD's. The number of these "Phantom Banks" is on the rise according to regulators.

Diamonds. Diamond scams come back into vogue every few years. These hustlers sell stones by mail, over the phone, or via road-show "investment seminars".

A typical operation will promise huge profits. In reality the diamond peddlers are the only ones to make money. You, the customer, ordinarily will pay more than retail price, although you are lead to believe you're paying much less. When it comes time to sell, you will probably receive only a fraction of what you originally paid. Note that appraisals that accompany these stones are often not reliable since the appraiser is in on the con.

Ponzi Schemes and Pyramid Games. The pyramid pitch tends to be made person-to-person or via chain letter, with the scammers and scammees constantly changing as people buy in, cash out or go bust. Other types of swindles are more straightforward: crooked people prey on credulous ones. Such schemes are often national in scope and involve the use of "800" numbers and mass mailings.

Airplane is a big-money variation on the pyramid game—which should be familiar to anyone who has received a chain letter with a request for $1 and the promise of many dollars to come later on. It also goes by the alias "Friends Helping Friends".

A "captain" is at the apex of a four-tier pyramid. Below the captain are two "co-captains". Below them are four more players, and below them, at the base, are eight empty squares. New-comers pay the captain $1500 each to buy one of the eight squares. In theory, each captain collects $12,000 from eight new passengers—eight times his or her own initial investment of $1500. Everybody in the pyramid is responsible for bringing in new players.

After all of the eight bottom squares are sold, a captain cashes out and flies away. The pyramid then splits in two, with the two co-captains now on top of their own pyramids. Once again at the bottom of each are eight new empty seats to be sold at $1500 per square. In theory, entrants eventually move up to a captain's chair and collect, too.

For a pyramid scheme to work, the number of players has to keep doubling and redoubling. And that is impossible.

In a Ponzi scheme a relatively small number of influential persons in a community are approached and offered an opportunity to invest—with a high guaranteed return. The schemes today are often high-tech and sophisticated sounding. Soon, other investors are approached and sold into the scheme, often through referrals obtained from the initial investors. A portion of the money received from the second set of investors is used to pay large profits to the original groups. As word spreads about the high paybacks, even more investors put up even larger sums of money. Some of this money is then used to recycle the fake profit payments and as word spreads, more and more investors are pulled into the circle. At some point in this process the operators quietly pack up and leave town—with all the money.

The Perfect Forecaster. It works like this. You receive a phone call from a person who says he is an investment forecaster. He doesn't want you to invest a cent. However, he will demonstrate his skill in picking stocks (or most anything) and gives you the name of a stock that he feels will have a significant price increase. And sure enough, the price went up.

A second phone call followed the pattern of the first. He simply wants to share his expertise with you and prove that a certain stock will go down (or up). His pitch is that his forecasts, or his firm's, will help you decide whether his outfit is the kind of firm you might some-day want to invest with. Sure enough, the stock again follows his prediction.

At the third call you're pretty much a believer and the perfect forecaster looks good. You not only want to invest but you want to invest enough (at his subtle urging) to make up for what you missed out on the first two recommendations.

What you would not know is that the perfect forecaster started with a list of 400 people. In the first call he told 200 that the price would go up, and the other 200 were told that the price would go down. When it went up, he made the call to the first 200 who had been given the "correct" forecast. Of these 200, he again split the group, with 100 forecasted up, and 100 down.

At the third phone call he had 100 eager investors—who all lost their money.

Other Con Games. A con artist may call, telling you that your spouse ordered a product or a service—maybe even a gift for you—and ask when he or she can deliver it (or do the service) and pick up your payment. They usually ask for cash.

Or a person may call directly at your home with a C.O.D. package containing an inexpensive item (often a Bible). Sometimes they will want to start performing some service and then demand payment.

Also a con artist may pretend to be a city inspector who claims there is something seriously wrong with your home, such as plumbing, wiring, furnace, etc. He then will tell you that some vital area of your house must be shut down until repaired, but he has a friend who can fix it quickly and cheaply.

GUIDELINES TO PROTECT YOURSELF

Investigate anyone who wants to make house repairs at bargain prices, offers to sell you anything or invest your money. Don't give out information about yourself over the telephone. Ask callers for their names, their companies' names and phone numbers, and say you will call back. Check the numbers in the telephone directory to ensure that they're working numbers for the companies the callers said they represent.

Listed below are some general guidelines you can use to protect yourself from being "taken."

1. Learn to say, "No," especially in the face of a pressured "hard sell."

2. Deal with reliable local dealers, service providers and merchants.

3. Never buy on a sales representative's first visit to your home.

4. Don't be afraid to ask questions because you fear the other person will consider your inquiries "dumb."

5. Avoid buying anything "sight unseen."

6. Read and understand contracts before signing.

7. Check with someone who knows a product before you buy it.

8. Stay within your income; do not be oversold.

9. Suspect a phony if any of the following apply:
    a) You're asked to sign your name right now;
    b) The prices are too good to be true;
    c) The salesperson discredits others who sell similar products;
    d) A cash payment is necessary, or the contract has vague or tricky wording.

The National Futures Association (1-800-621-3570) provides an excellent booklet titled *Investment Swindles: How they Work and How to Avoid Them*. It is free to the investing public.

The traditional advice—to check on a company through a Better Business Bureau or consumer-protection agency, or with consumer groups located where the company is headquartered—is much more unreliable. There is often a lag between the time people start getting scammed and the point at which consumer protection agencies get the word and start putting out warnings. A dirty company can look clean when you call consumer authorities to check on it.

Also, don't be sure you'll short-circuit a scam by requiring the names of previous satisfied customers. Sometimes scammers give fast, prompt service to the first dozen or so "customers" and then supply their names to anyone who asks for references. Everyone gets scammed from then on.

If you think you've been cheated, don't be silent. Complaining may help you, and others as well; if you don't take action, the shady practices will be allowed to continue. Check out a company with consumer groups and ask for references before buying. At the very least, this slows the process down and gives consumers time to think. Scammers tend not to keep bothering people who say they'll do some checking.

Call the National Fraud Information Center's hotline at 800-876-7060 (Monday through Friday, 10 AM to 4 PM, EST) if you think you're being scammed. The service will give you advice on reporting a scam and the process for recouping your loss. They will give you advice on evaluating a mail or phone deal before you lose any money. You will also hear warnings about the newest scams taking place nationwide. Free education materials will be sent to you upon request.

C
H
A
P
T
E
R

18

PUTTING IT ALL TOGETHER—YOU AND YOUR NEW FINANCIAL WORLD

This chapter provides a checklist of the most critical and important steps you can take to make the money last. If you have done all of the items appropriate for you, you can feel comfortable in that your financial world is well on its way to being anxiety-free. You will have the self-confidence and peace of mind that comes from being in control, being well-organized, and knowing you are taking all the necessary steps to be financially self-sufficient.

CHAPTER 1:
THE FINANCIAL ASPECTS OF WIDOWHOOD

Here's a roster of the basic questions you should now have answers for:

1. Do I have enough money for immediate needs?

2. Will there be enough money to last, even if I need long-term health care at some point?

3. Will the rising cost of living adversely effect me?

4. Will I have enough for retirement years?

5. What about medical insurance coverage?

6. How should I invest life insurance proceeds?

7. What should I do with 401(k), IRA and company pension funds?

8. Should I sell our home in favor of a smaller, less expensive home?

9. Should I use the one-time $125,000 capital gains tax exclusion now?

10. Will I have to file quarterly estimates for income taxes?

11. Can I afford to help my children or grandchildren with college expenses?

12. Should my will be changed?

13. Should I have a living will?

14. Will I have enough income to live on without working?

15. (If there are young children) how will I finance day care if I return to work?

16. Have claims been filed for everything that's coming to me?

17. When can I expect the Social Security check to arrive?

18. Should I and how do I choose a financial advisor?

19. What should I do right now?

20. What should I do first?

Most importantly you have made the decision to take responsibility for your financial life by:

1. Collecting the information you need;

2. Assembling and organizing this information; and

3. Using the information to make correct or corrective decisions.

CHAPTER 2:
FIRST THINGS FIRST: IMMEDIATE CONCERNS

1. Put off making long-term money decisions until you are able to face them unemotionally.

2. Keep your money in a safe place.

3. Have adequate medical and disability insurance.

4. Be careful of impulse spending.

5. Recognize that you are in mourning.

AND:

1. **DON'T** make any major money decisions now that can be deferred to a later time.

2. **DON'T** remodel your house or buy a new car.

3. **DON'T** buy life insurance.

4. **DON'T** invest with well-meaning friends or relatives.

5. **DON'T** put your funds where you can't get at them quickly and at little or no cost.

6. **DON'T** borrow money.

7. **DON'T** make major money decisions "for the good of the kids," unless that decision is good for you, also. Give it a little time.

8. **DON'T** give away money, even to friends or relatives, until you've had time to determine how far your money will take you.

WHAT TO DO RIGHT AWAY:

1. Set up child care, if needed.

2. Keep accurate records.

3. Maintain a phone log.

4. Categorize incoming mail.

5. Photocopy all outgoing mail and file copies.

6. Examine checking and savings accounts.

7. Determine immediate cash resources.

8. Determine immediate cash requirements.

9. Find spouse's will and important papers.

10. List outstanding debts.

11. Check with spouse's employer for benefits.

12. Contact insurance companies for life, accidental death, credit and mortgage life.

13. Review health, homeowners, automobile policies.

14. Review contents of safe deposit box.

15. Review CD's, IRA's, and other investments.

16. Apply for Social Security and other government benefits.

17. Change beneficiary designations on your IRA's, insurance policies, etc.

18. Change titles on cars, homes, etc.

19. Review your will.

20. Reject outside pressure to make changes until you are comfortable doing so.

21. Protect yourself from frauds and scams.

CHAPTER 3:
CLAIMING EVERYTHING THAT'S YOURS—PRIVATE SOURCES

1. Locate all life insurance policies and annuities.

2. Apply for benefits in lump sum or annuity forms.

3. Determine and apply for all pension survivor benefits.

4. Review IRA's and make necessary changes for your situation.

CHAPTER 4:
CLAIMING EVERYTHING THAT'S YOURS FROM GOVERNMENT SOURCES

1. Contact the local Social Security Office and determine if you qualify for any of the following survivor benefits:
   a) Survivor insurance benefits,
   b) Disability insurance benefits,
   c) Supplemental income benefits,
   d) Medicare and Medicaid benefits.

2. Apply for Federal Employee Survivorship benefits if your spouse worked for federal government:
   a) Life insurance,
   b) Retirement.

3. Apply for Veterans Administration benefits if you qualify as a beneficiary for:
   a) Life insurance proceeds,
   b) Educational assistance for dependent.

CHAPTER 5:
GETTING ORGANIZED—BRINGING ORDER TO YOUR FINANCIAL HOUSE

1. Prepare a Net Worth Statement.

2. Prepare a Cash Flow Statement including all expenses and all income for one year.

3. Determine what an adequate cash reserve is for you.

4. Analyze your net worth and cash flow statements.

5. Develop your own plan to control cash flow.

6. Place appropriate items in your safe deposit box.

7. Consider a power of attorney agreement.

CHAPTER 6:
SETTLING YOUR SPOUSE'S ESTATE

1. Locate and Organize all important documents.

2. Select professional advisors, especially legal assistance.

3. Determine what assets, if any, are part of the probate estate.

4. Act as executor, if named by the will, or be appointed personal representative.

5. Provide estate management.

6. Determine claims and debts against the estate.

7. Pay claims.

8. File and pay taxes.

9. Distribute assets to beneficiaries.

10. Close the estate.

CHAPTER 7:
RETIREMENT PLANNING—MAKING THE MONEY LAST

1. You are aware and can gauge the effect of the following on your income/retirement planning:
   a) Inflation,
   b) Social Security and pensions,
   c) Long term care.

2. Determine your current living costs and their future value using the table in Chapter 7.

3. Determine your current income and your future projected income.

4. Determine the steps needed to protect yourself from inflation, provide safety, income and liquidity.

5. Take steps to investigate and understand your retirement options.

6. If you're a young widow(er) with children determine the impact of college education cost and investigate procedures and products to provide the necessary funding.

CHAPTER 8:
THE SURVIVING SPOUSE'S GUIDE TO TAXES

1. Determine filing status as qualifying widow(er), head of household, or single.

2. Determine if you need to file estimated taxes; if so, determine how much you're required to pay.

3. Determine if you can claim dependents, using all five tests required to qualify.

4. Determine tax treatment if you take IRA withdrawals.

5. Determine tax treatment on lump sum distributions on pensions or rollovers to IRA accounts.

6. Determine if any part of Social Security benefit will be taxed. Review methods to avoid the tax.

CHAPTER 9:
INSURANCE—UNDERSTANDING THE GREAT MYSTERY

1. Determine if you need life insurance, how much and what type.

2. You're able to chose a life insurance company based on the company's experience and reputation, independent rating reviews, and investment portfolio and investment philosophy.

3. Determine whether you need disability income, if you qualify, and how much coverage you can obtain.

4. Review your health insurance.

5. Review your automobile insurance.

6. Review your homeowners insurance.

7. Review or purchase liability insurance.

8. Understand the "kiddie" tax.

9. Develop custodial accounts for children, if appropriate.

CHAPTER 10:
MONEY, CHILDREN AND YOU

1. Review your financial situation with your children if you feel it is appropriate.

2. Help (grand)children learn the habit of saving.

3. Help (grand)children learn how money is spent—a child's budget plan.

4. Help (grand)children begin an investment program.

5. Explain credit cards to children.

6. If giving money, determine if you can afford it.

7. If giving money, determine whether it should be a loan or gift.

CHAPTER 19

CHAPTER 11:
YOU AND YOUR HOME

1. You understand the tax advantage of home ownership:
   a) Interest mortgage deduction,
   b) Deferral of gain on increased value of home.

2. Refinancing depends on:
   a) Upfront costs,
   b) How long you will remain in your home,
   c) Amount refinanced,
   d) Difference in interest rate between existing mortgage and new mortgage.

3. Determined how to choose a mortgage broker.

4. Understand reverse mortgages and how they operate.

5. Before selling your home you've:
   a) Decided what and where your next house will be,
   b) Analyzed the tax ramifications, especially basis, and the $125,000 exclusion.

6. Before buying another home:
   a) You've chosen a real estate agent that knows and will look for what you want,
   b) You understand mortgages; types and terms,
   c) You've considered the option of renting,
   d) Understand a life estate and whether it is appropriate for your situation.

7. You understand the areas of concern when hiring home improvement contractors.

CHAPTER 12:
FUNDING COLLEGE EDUCATION

1. You understand why a college education is important for children today.

2. You are aware of the need to learn about:
   a) Financial Aid,
   b) Saving and investing money for college,

      c) Positioning assets for growth in the early years and income for the college years,

      d) Strategies to minimize the tax impact of your college investment dollars.

3. You have determined a realistic estimate of the cost of college education.

4. You have determined the savings/investment totals required to fund college costs.

5. You have a complete list of all sources of funding available to you and steps you can take to access these sources.

CHAPTER 13:
LONG TERM CARE

1. You determine if you expect to need long term care.

2. You examine the only four sources of funds to pay for long term care:
    a) Medicare and Medicare supplements,
    b) Medicaid,
    c) Long term care insurance,
    d) Your savings, assets and income.

3. You determine if you can afford long term care, or will need supplemental insurance coverage.

4. If buying a long term care policy you examine the following carefully:
    a) Coverage for skilled, intermediate, and custodial care,
    b) How long benefit payments last,
    c) The amount of benefit payments,
    d) Elimination (i.e., waiting) period,
    e) Guaranteed renewability of the policy,
    f) Inflation and waiver of premium riders,
    g) Limitations and exclusions,
    h) The cost.

CHAPTER 19

CHAPTER 14:
GIVING—HOW, WHEN, WHO AND HOW MUCH

1. You are aware of the many reasons for making gifts and whether any of these reasons match your own objectives.

2. You are comfortable with your personal reasons for making gifts.

3. You understand the annual gift exclusion of $10,000 per year.

4. You understand the value and nature of the Unified Credit of up to $600,000.

5. You understand the concept of charitable giving and are aware of the various charitable trusts available.

CHAPTER 15:
PASSING ALONG YOUR WEALTH: ESTATE PLANNING

1. You understand the need for expert competent advisors.

2. Your will is current and expresses your wishes, including the executor of your choice.

3. You are aware of the various types of trusts and the benefits they can provide.

4. You understand how to avoid probate.

5. You understand the concept of a living trust and have yours drafted to meet your needs.

6. You have reviewed estate reduction strategies, determined if your estate is large enough to have an estate tax, and considered some or all of the following strategies:
   a) Irrevocable Life insurance trust,
   b) Annual gift program,
   c) Direct payment of medical and/or college tuition bills for (grand)children,
   d) Use of the Crummy Trust provision,
   e) Giving appreciated assets,
   f) Charitable giving techniques,
   g) Use of generation-skipping techniques.

7. You have a durable power of attorney.

8. You have a letter of instruction written and filed with your survivors.

9. You have set up a schedule to review all your estate plans once a year.

CHAPTER 16:
THE FINANCIAL ASPECTS OF REMARRIAGE

1. Wills updated or substantially changed?

2. Review trusts for beneficiary changes or new language because of your new relationship?

3. Change beneficiary designations on life insurance policies?

4. Review all insurance coverage, especially health coverage, to reduce overall cost?

5. Review how your assets will be titled: individual or joint.

6. Review your estate plan for revisions, especially use of the marital deduction and various trusts.

7. Review if any pension benefits will be affected?

8. What effect will your remarriage have on Social Security benefits?

9. Do you need a prenuptial agreement?

10. Review how each of you view your assets and your current giving programs in relation to your respective sets of children?

11. You have jointly examined the use of the $125,000 exclusion pertaining to house sales.

12. You are aware of the following marriage tax "penalties":
    a) Higher taxes paid on joint incomes,
    b) Changes in losses available on rental properties,
    c) Standard deduction penalty,
    d) IRA phase-out ranges,
    e) Personal exemption phase-out ranges.

CHAPTER 17:
CHOOSING PROFESSIONAL ADVISORS

1. You understand the designations of CFP, ChFC, and APES for financial planners.

2. You have a procedure for choosing a financial planner and a series of qualifying questions.

3. You realize the various specialities for attorneys and can pick the one for your needs.

4. You have a system to use to find and hire an attorney.

5. You have a system to use to find and hire an accountant.

6. You are aware of the designation CLU for life insurance agents and have a procedure for choosing a life agent.

CHAPTER 18:
FRAUDS AND SCAMS: PROTECTING YOURSELF

1. You are familiar with various con games and scams.

2. You know the guidelines to protect yourself.

3. If it sounds too good to be true, it is.

INDEX

A

AARP, 168, 294
ADV, 255
Accidental Death, 13, 28, 31, 53, 275
Accountant, 16, 78, 115, 196, 227, 253,
  254, 256, 261, 262, 284, 291
Accredited Personal Financial Specialist
  (PFS), 254, 256
Accurate Records, 9, 275
Adjustable Rate Mortgage (ARM), 179,
  180, 291
Administrator, 81, 85
Adult Day Care, 209, 210, 211
Advisors:
  Accountant, 261
  Attorney, 259
  Financial Planner, 255
  Insurance Agent, 263
  Trust Officer, 264
Aesop's Fable, 95
Alternate Valuation Date, 91
American Council of Life Insurance, 77,
  139
The American Institute of Certified
  Public Accountants, 254, 256
The American Psychiatric Association,
  291
American Legion, 15
American Society of CLU and ChFC, 256
Anatomical Gifts, 239
Annual Gift Exclusion, 156, 218, 228,
  282

Annuities:
  Claims, 35
  Types, 35
  Variable, 35
  Fixed, 35
  Options, 34
Appointment as Personal Representative,
  84
Assets, 62, 63, 65, 66, 79, 81, 95
Attorneys, 16, 17, 75, 78, 84, 87, 194,
  227, 259, 260, 261, 262, 263, 284
Automobile Insurance, 16, 29, 143, 144,
  279
Average Rate of Return, 98, 99
Average Rate of Return Worksheet, 100
Avoiding Probate, 232, 233

B

Baccalaureate Bonds, 194
Balance Sheet, 62
Banks, 8, 14, 15, 16, 18, 19, 20, 61, 73,
  76, 116, 152, 160, 264, 265, 267, 268
Beneficiary:
  Arrangements, 229
  Changes, 16
Bibliography, 293
Bills, paying, 10, 12, 13, 17, 18, 68, 87,
  236, 244
Bonds, 63, 64, 65, 70, 159, 194, 195
Budget:
  Cash Flow Statement, 67
  Cash Flow Control Plan, 68

I N D E X

C

Calendar, monthly expenses, 106
Calendar, monthly income, 106
Capital Needs Analysis Worksheet, 132
Cash Flow:
  Analysis, 68
  Statement, 67
  Control Plan, 68
  Simplified Planning Sheet, 69
  Detailed Planning Sheet, 70
Cash Requirements, Immediate, 10, 12, 275
Cash Reserve, 63, 65, 66, 67, 132, 277
Certificate of Deposit, 8, 11, 14, 61, 65, 70, 72, 74, 104, 160, 194, 195
Certified Financial Planner (CFP), 253, 254, 256, 284, 294
Certified Public Accountant (CPA), 16, 115, 176, 254, 256
Charitable Giving:
  Factors to Consider, 220
  Tax Limitations, 221, 237
  Through Trusts, 222
Charitable Remainder Trust, 222, 223, 237, 250
Chartered Financial Consultant, 254, 256
Chartered Life Underwriter, 256, 263
Checking Accounts, 11, 16, 63, 64, 66, 68, 69, 74, 86, 87, 244
Child Care, 9, 69, 71, 275
Children:
  College Costs, 186
  Credit Cards, 153
  Custodial Accounts, 159
  Investments, 156
  Kiddie Tax, 159
  Loans, 154
  Loan Agreements, 155
  Money, 151, 152
  Social Security Benefits, 45
  Taxes, 158
Civil Service Retirement System (CSRS), 54

Claims:
  Annuities, 35
  CSRS, 54
  FERS, 54
  Government Benefits, 45, 53
  Individual Retirement Accounts, 37
  Life Insurance, 27
  Pensions, 37
  Social Security, 45
COBRA, 13
Codicil, 81
College Education:
  Annual Savings Required, 190
  Cost of, 186, 191
  Cost Estimate Worksheet, 187, 189
  Loans, 196
  Payment Strategies, 192
  Using Your IRA, 195
  Value of, 185
  Work Study Programs, 199
College-Sure Certificates, 195
Collision Insurance, 144
Community Property States, 245
Compound Interest Table, 114
Comprehensive Insurance, 144
Con Games, 267, 284
Condo, Buying, 169
Contestable Period, 31
Cost Basis, 171, 176, 177
Cost of Living Adjustment (COLA), 107, 109
Counselors, Professional, 78
Credit and Mortgage Insurance, 14, 28
Credit Cards, 19, 20, 25, 64, 65, 74, 77, 87, 116, 132, 153, 154, 279
Creditors, 13, 17, 18, 19, 79, 85, 86, 87, 90, 232, 246
Crummy Trust, 194, 220, 236, 237, 282
Custodial Accounts, 159, 160, 193, 279

D

Death Certificate, 13, 14, 15, 16, 30, 31, 48, 54, 57, 61, 72, 76, 77, 88
Debts, 13, 17, 18, 28, 63, 80, 84, 85, 87,

88, 89, 130, 131, 132, 136, 155, 156, 167, 245, 275, 277
Decisions, Financial, 3, 4, 5, 78, 151, 154
Deferred Annuities, 35, 63, 65
Demands for Cash, 17
Dependents, 56, 120, 121, 126, 158, 278
Diamond Scams, 268
Disability Insurance, 8, 45, 50, 72, 140, 141, 274, 276
Distributions:
  Lump Sum, 33
  IRA's, 38
  Taxes, 39, 88
Dividends, 11, 69, 70, 73, 103, 104, 105, 106, 158, 159
Divorce, 20, 37, 45, 46, 49, 57, 61, 72, 76, 241, 246, 251
Durable Power of Attorney, 239

E
Early Distributions Penalty, 38
Early Retirement, Social Security, 59
Education *(See College)*
EE Bonds, 63, 195
Employer:
  Benefits Tracking Form, 43
  Claims Process, 36
  Notification of Death, 36
Epilogue, 297
Estate Planning:
  Basic Considerations, 229
  Claims and Debts, 87
  Distributions, 75, 79, 89
  Documentation, 76, 80
  Election Against the Will, 91
  Income and Expense Record Book, 73
  Glossary of Terms, 81
  Management, 86
  Planning Questionnaire, 228
  Settlement, 75
  Taxes, 233, 234
  Tax Return, 88
  Tax Reduction Strategies, 233
Estimated Taxes, 119, 120, 128, 261, 278

Estimated Tax Tracking Form, 128
Ethical Will, 240
Excess Personal Liability Policy, 146
Exclusion, House Sale, $125,000, 170, 171, 174, 175, 176, 201, 247, 280, 283
Executor/trix, 75, 77, 82, 84, 85, 86, 87, 90, 228, 231, 277, 282
Exempt Property Award, 91
Expenses, 12, 62, 66, 67, 68, 69, 70, 71, 73, 87, 99, 100, 101, 107, 108, 116, 232, 277
Expenses in Retirement, 101

F
Family Settlement Agreement, 91
Federal Employees Retirement System (FERS), 54
Fee-Only Commission Financial Planners, 257
Files:
  Headings, 61
  Setting Up, 61
Filing Status, Taxes, 117, 278
Financial Advisors, 77, 253, 256, 274, 292
Financial Considerations of Remarriage, 244
Financial Planner, 77, 78, 107, 170, 196, 222, 227, 253, 254, 255, 256, 257, 258, 259, 263, 284, 291
Financial Planning, 253, 254, 255, 256, 291, 294
Five-year Averaging, 41, 123
Fixed Annuities, 35
Foreign Death Certificates, 15
Formal Care Providers, 201
Forward Averaging, 41, 123
Fraternal Organizations, 15, 221
Frauds and Scams, 267, 276, 284

G
Gifts for an IRA, 224
Giving:
  Absolute Nature, 216

Annual Exclusion, 217
Best Time to Make, 218
Cost of, 217
Glossary of Estate Terminology, 81
Government:
    Claims, 47, 53
    Survivor Benefits, 46
Granny Fraud, 267
Guardian, 82, 137, 228, 229, 231

H

Health Care Insurance, 51, 141
Health Care Proxy, 228, 238, 239
Home Equity Loans, 164, 197, 198
Home Improvement Contractors, 182
Home Loans, 179
Home Ownership, Benefits of, 163
Homeowner's Insurance, 145
Homestead Allowance, 90

I

IAFP, 254
Immediate Concerns, 1, 4, 7, 274
Important People/Organizations List, 22
Income:
    Estate, 73
    Retirement, 95
    Sources, 101, 103
    Planning, 95, 98
    Projections, 67, 107
    Sample Form, 110
Income Taxes, 5, 14, 38, 62, 71, 88, 115,
    119, 121, 122, 124, 126, 128, 158, 159,
    160, 215, 216, 217, 221, 223, 224, 235,
    262, 274
Inflation, 58, 66, 95, 96, 97, 98, 99, 102,
    107, 108, 109, 140, 187, 210, 211, 212,
    278, 281
Inheritance Tax, 16, 78, 86, 89, 221
Installment Refund, 34
Insurance:
    Auto, 143

Claims Tracking Forms:
    Claims, 42
    Company, 43
Disability, 140
Homeowners, 145
Hospital, 141
Liability, 143, 146
Life, 130, 134
Long Term Care, 209
Major Medical, 142
Medical, 141
Notification of Death, 30
Insurance Claims, 17, 27, 29, 33, 42, 292
Interest, 11, 25, 30, 33, 66, 69, 70, 103,
    104, 105, 106, 107, 128, 152, 154, 155,
    156, 158, 164, 165, 166, 167, 179, 196,
    197, 198, 199
Intestate, 16, 82, 84
Investment Advisor (RIA), 255
Investment Assets, 64, 65, 66, 97
IRA:
    for College, 195
    Rollover, 38, 41, 122, 123, 124
    Tax Treatment, 38
    Transfer, 38
Irrevocable Life Insurance Trust, 228,
    235, 250, 282

K

Kiddie Tax, 158, 159, 161, 162
Kiddie Tax Worksheet, 162

L

Labor Unions, 16
Lawyers *(See Attorneys)*
Letters, Sample:
    Insurance Claim, 30
    to Employer, 36, 55
    to Family, 240
Level Term Insurance, 133
Liabilities, 62, 63, 64, 65, 66, 67, 82, 261
Liability Insurance, 144, 146, 182, 245

Life Estate, 175, 176, 177, 280
Life Expectancy Table, 113
Life Insurance:
    Amount of, 130
    Beneficiary Changes, 16, 137
    Claims, 27, 30, 47, 57
    on Children, 137
    Companies, 138
    CSRS, 54
    Letter to Company, 30, 36
    FERS Claims, 54
    Ownership, 136
    Policy Search, 28
    Proceeds, 35
    Types, 131, 134
    Veterans, 55
Living Trust, 16, 79, 228, 232, 233
Living Will, 5, 228, 238, 239, 259, 274
Loans, 64, 65, 68, 87, 132, 154, 155, 165,
    166, 167, 179, 180, 196, 197, 198, 199
Location of Important Documents,
    Checklist, 20
Long Range Retirement Planning
    Worksheet, 111
Long Term Care:
    Cost of, 203
    Need for, 202
    Insurance, 209
    Policy Analysis Checklist, 210
Lump Sums, distributions:
    Life Insurance, 33
    Retirement Plans, 37, 89
LUTC Fellow, 255

M

Mail:
    Incoming, 10
    Outgoing, 10
Margin Account, 196
Marginal Tax Brackets, 119
Marital Deduction, 82, 89, 245, 249, 283
Marriage Penalties, 247
Medicaid, 52, 98, 164, 203, 204, 205,
    206, 276, 281

Medical Insurance, 4, 43, 52, 141, 142,
    143, 273
Medicare, 11, 45, 51, 52, 53, 59, 97, 143,
    177, 203, 204, 276, 281
Medigap Policy, 143
Minority Trust (2503(c)), 160, 161
Money and Children, 151
Money Market Fund, 18, 68, 87
Money Talk, 244
Mortgages, 63, 64, 65, 73, 74, 76, 87,
    116, 130, 131, 132, 133, 163, 164, 165,
    166, 167, 168, 179, 180, 181, 193, 280,
    291
Mortgage Broker, Choosing a, 166
Mortgage Insurance, 133
Mortgage Interest; Rules for Deducting,
    116, 165
Mortgage Refinance Analysis, 166
Motor Vehicle Department, 19
Mourning, 7, 8, 9, 151, 274

N

National Association of Life
    Underwriters, 139, 263
National Association of Security Dealers,
    292
National Fraud Information Center, 271
Net Worth:
    Analysis, 66
    Calculations of, 66
    Statement, detailed, 65
    Statement, simple, 64
Non-probate Property, 79
Normal Retirement Age, 58
Notification of Death, 15, 16, 29

O

Office of Inheritance Tax, 78
Organization:
    Files, 61
    Finances, 61

P

Pell Grants, 198
Penalties, Marriage, 247
Period Certain Payments, Annuity, 34
Perkins Loans, Federal, 199
Personal Financial Specialist (PFS), 254, 256
Personal Liability Policy, 146
Personal Representative, 75, 77, 84, 86, 87, 277
Personal Use Assets, 63, 65, 66
Phantom Banks, 268
Photo Copy Rules, 10
Pigeon Drop Scheme, 268
Ponzi Schemes, 268, 269
Post Mortem Estate Planning, 90
Power of Attorney, 239, 259, 277, 283
Premarital Agreement (Prenuptial), 20, 76, 245, 246, 247, 283
Premium, Waiver of, 140, 211
Probate, 3, 77, 78, 79, 81, 82, 84, 85, 177, 219, 228, 229, 232, 233, 277, 282
Property and Casualty Insurance Agents, 264
Protection Against Con Artists, 270
Pyramid Schemes, 268, 269

Q

QTIP Charitable Trust, 250
QTIP Trust, 249
Qualified Disclaimer, 81, 90

R

Reading the Will, 76
Real Estate, 18, 61, 62, 74, 88, 103, 116, 160, 163, 167, 169, 170, 178, 280
Real Estate Agent, 178
Records, 9, 61, 72, 73, 74, 275
Refinancing, 164, 165, 166, 280
Registered Investment Advisor (RIA), 255
Registry of Financial Planning Practitioners, 254

Remarriage, 49, 243, 283
Rent or Buy Comparison, 181
Rental Contracts, 180
Renting, 175, 176, 180, 181, 193, 280
Resources Directory, 291
Retirement:
    Expenses, 100
    Income Needs, 99
    Income Projections, 107
    Income Sources, 103
    Planning, 95
    Worksheet, 100, 102, 103, 105, 106, 110, 111
Reverse Mortgage, 167, 168, 280
Right Away Activities, 9
Rollover, IRA, 38, 41, 122, 123

S

Safe Deposit Box, 14, 62, 72, 77, 78, 275, 277
Savings Accounts, 8, 10, 11, 64, 65, 74, 99, 152, 275
Scams, 267, 268, 271, 276, 284
Securities and Exchange Commission (SEC), 292
Self-employment, 20, 27, 70, 76, 103, 106
Selling Your Home, 168, 280
Series EE Bonds, 63, 195
Servicemen's Group Life Insurance, 56
Settling with the IRS, 128
Shopping for Term Insurance, 133
Single Premium Deferred Annuity (SPDA), 35
Social Security:
    Benefits, 45
    Death Benefits, 47
    Delayed Benefits, 59
    Early Retirement, 59
    Notification of Death, 49
    Retirement, 58
    Sample Letter, 49
    Survivors Benefits, 45
    Taxation of, 126

Taxation Worksheet, 127
When, How to Apply, 47
Working after Retirement, 60
Special Averaging Tax Methods, (5-year
    and 10-year), 40, 123
Springing Power of Attorney, 239
Stafford Loans, 199
Stepped-up Basis, 83, 174
Supplemental Security Income (SSI), 50
Survivor Benefits, 27, 37, 38, 45, 54, 95,
    276

T

Taking Charge, 5
Taxes:
    Estimated, 119
    Estate, 88, 233
    Filing Returns, 124
    Filing Status, 117
    Income, 115
    Life Insurance, 126
    on IRA's and Qualified Plans, 121
    on Social Security, 126
    Planning, 115
Telephone Log, 21
Ten-Year Averaging, 123, 124
Term Insurance, 131, 133, 134
Transfers:
    Qualified Plans, 123
Trust Officers, 264, 265
Trusts:
    Charitable Lead, 224
    Charitable Remainder, 222

Minor Children, 225
QTIP, 249
Wealth Replacement, 223

U

Umbrella Liability Policy, 144
Unified Federal Gift and Estate Tax, 233
Uniform Gifts to Minors Act (UGMA),
    137, 160, 193, 220
Uniform Transfers to Minors Act
    (UTMA), 137, 160, 193, 220
Universal Life Insurance, 135

V

Valuable Documents, 72
Variable Annuities, 35
Variable Life Insurance, 135
Veterans Administration Claims, 57
Veterans Benefits, 55
Veterans Group Life Insurance, 56

W

W-2 Form, 15, 48, 76, 124
Waiver of Premium, 140, 211, 212, 281
Wealth Replacement Trust, 223, 224
Whole Life Insurance, 134
Wills:
    Contest, 91
    Living, 238
    Purpose, 230
    Reading of, 76
Worthless Securities, 125

TELEPHONE NUMBER RESOURCE DIRECTORY

American Association of Retired Persons   202/434-2277

American Psychiatric Association   202/682-6000

American Society of Certified Public Accountants   800/862-4272

American Society of Appraisers (ASA)   800/ASA-VALU

Best Fares   800/880-1234
(for up-to-date travel deals)

Discount Brokerage Firms
- Jack White   800/233-3411
- Kennedy Cabot   800/252-0090
- Quick & Reilly   800/221-5220
- Charles Schwab   800/435-4000
- Waterhouse   800/934-4410

Car Buying Services
- Autoadvisor   800/326-1976
- Automobile Consumer Services   800/223-4882
- Carbargains   800/475-7283

Car Pricing Services
- Car Price Network Consumer Reports   800/227-3295
- Auto Price Service   800/933-5555

Checks at a Discount
- Checks in the Mail   800/733-4443
- Current Inc.   800/733-3973
- Image Checks   800/562-8768

Consumer Credit Counseling Service   800/388-CCCS

Consumer Loan Advocates   708/615-0024
(to check the accuracy of your adjustable rate mortgage)

Credit Bureaus
- Equifax   800/685-1111
- Trans Union   216/779-7200
- TRW   214/390-9191

FDIC   800/934-3342

Federal Reserve Bank of Washington   202/874-4000
(Treasury Direct)

Institute of Certified Financial Planners   800/282-7526

Internal Revenue Service
- Blank forms   800/TAX-FORM
- Problems & Resolutions   800/829-1040
- Refund Hotline   800/829-4477

International Association of Financial Planning   800/945-4237

Medicare & Medigap Telephone Hotline 800/638-6833

National Association of Claims Assistance Professionals 708/963-3500
(they will help with your insurance claims)

National Assoc. of Personal Financial Advisors 800/366-2732

National Association of Securities Dealers 800/289-9999
(to check out your broker)

National Association for Self-Employed 800-232-NASE

National Center for Retirement Benefits 800/666-1000
(to be sure your lump sum payout is correct)

National Council of Senior Citizens 202/347-8800

National Fraud Hotline 800/876-7060

National Insurance Consumer Helpline 800/942-4242
(they can answer your insurance questions)

Older Women's League 202/713-6086

Pension Rights Center 202/296-3776

Rating Services
- A.M. Best (Insurance) 908/439-2200
- Moody's 212/553-0377
- Standard & Poor's 212/208-8000
- Weiss Research 800/289-9222
  (for insurance ratings)

Securities and Exchange Commission 800/732-0330

Small Business Administration 800/827-5722

Social Security Administration 800/772-1213

Stock Search International 800/537-4523
(to find out what your old stock certificates are worth)

Veribanc 800/44-BANKS
(bank safety ratings)

Veteran's Administration 800/827-1000

BIBLIOGRAPHY

OTHER PUBLICATIONS AND REFERENCE BOOKS

Armstrong, Alexandra and Donahue, Mary R. *On Your Own.* Dearborn Financial Publishing, 1993.

Brothers, Dr. Joyce. *Widowed.* New York: Ballantine Books, 1992.

Brown, Judith N., LLB, and Christina Baldwin. *A Second Start: A Widow's Guide to Financial Survival at a Time of Emotional Crisis.* New York: Simon & Schuster, 1986.

Caine, Lynn. *Widow.* New York: Bantam Books, 1974.

Colgrove, Melba, PhD. and Peter McWilliams. *How to Survive the Loss of a Love.* New York: Prelude Press, 1991.

DAWN—*Divorced and Widowed Women's News.* Founder: Sharon Grinage, Suite G., 455 DeVargas Center, Santa Fe, NM 87501.

Foehner, Charlotte, and Carol Cozart. *The Widow's Handbook: A Guide for Living.* Golden, Colo.: Fulcrum, 1988.

Gates, Philomene. *Suddenly Alone.* New York: Harper Collins, 1990.

✓Ginsburg, Genevieve Davis. *To Live Again: Rebuilding Your Life After You've Become a Widow.* New York: Bantam Books, 1989.

✓Grollman, Earl A. *Living When a Loved One Has Died.* Boston: Beacon Press, 1987.

Jackson, Edgar N. *When Someone Dies.* Philadelphia: Fortress Press, 1971.

Jones-Lee, Anita. *Women and Money.* Haippauge, N.Y.: Barron's Educational Series, 1991.

Klott, Gary L. *The Complete Financial Guide to the 1990s.* New York: Times Books, 1990.

Krause, Lawrence A. *Sleep Tight Money.* New York: Simon & Schuster, 1987.

Kubler-Ross, Elizabeth. *On Death and Dying.* New York: Macmillan, 1969.

Kushner, Harold S. *When Bad Things Happen to Good People.* New York: Avon, 1981. *On Being Alone,* AARP Fulfillment, 601 E Street, NW, Washington, D.C. 20049.

Loewinsohn, Ruth Jean. *Survival Book for Widows.* Washington, D.C.: AARP; Glenview, ILL.: Scott, Foresman, 1984.

Magee, David S. *Everything Your Heirs Need to Know: Your Assets, Family History and Final Wishes.* Chicago: Dearborn Financial Publishing, 1991.

Martin, Don and Renee. *Survival Kit for Wives.* New York: Villard Books, 1986.

Neeld, Elizabeth Harper, PhD. *Seven Choices.* New York: Clarkson N. Potter, Inc., 1990.

Nudel, Adele Rice. *Starting Over: Help for Young Widows and Widowers.* New York: Dodd, Mead, 1986.

Parkes, Colin Murray, and Robert S. Weiss. *Recovery from Bereavement.* New York: Basic Books, 1983.

Rando, Theresa A. *Grieving: How to Go on Living When Someone You Love Dies.* Lexington, Mass.: D.C. Health & Co., 1988.

Schiff, Harriett Sarnoff. *Living Through Mourning: Finding Comfort and Hope When a Loved One Has Died.* New York: Viking, 1986.

Shane, Dorlene V., and The United Seniors Health Cooperative. *Finances After 50: Financial Planning for the Rest of Your Life.* New York: 1989.

Sinclair, Carol. *When Women Retire.* New York: Crown, 1992.

Temes, Roberta. *Living with an Empty Chair.* New York: Irvington, 1980.

Truman, Jill. *Letter to My Husband: Notes about Mourning and Recovery.* New York: Viking Penguin, 1987.

Ungar, Alan B., CFP. *Financial Self-Confidence, A Woman's Guide for the Suddenly Single.* Lowell House, 1989–1991.

U.S. Government Printing Office. *A Summary of Veterans Administration Benefits.* VA Pamphlet 27-82-2. Washington D.C.: 1984.

Viorst, Judith. *Necessary Losses.* New York: Fawcett Gold Medal, 1986.

Westberg, Grander E. *Good Grief.* Philadelphia: Fortress, 1962.

Worden, J. William. *Grief Counseling and Grief Therapy.* New York: Springer, 1982.

EPILOGUE

THE WIDOWED PERSON'S FINANCIAL PLANNING SERVICE

During my years of work with widowed individuals, I have come to recognize the array of potential financial disasters that can beset them. To deal with these issues, I have developed a comprehensive personal and financial advisory service to assist new or veteran widowed persons.

The Widowed Person's Financial Planning Service is a personal money management service providing service in all financial aspects for widows and widowers. Our service can help you in the areas of taxation, money management, financial planning, estate planning, claims processing, personal planning, and elder care planning.

Like physicians, who concentrate on maintaining the patient's physical and mental health, we focus on helping you to achieve your desired level of financial health and well-being. We can assist you in coordinating investment strategies, and finding the best solutions to your financial problems.

We maintain an extensive list of professional references whom you can contact, and we welcome your inquiry into our professional background. If you're interested in receiving additional information about this program, please contact us at:

> The Widowed Person's Financial Planning Service
> Bennett Financial Advisors
> P.O. Box 244
> Fairfax, Virginia 22030
> (703) 691-9200